# Budgets, Bonds, and Ballots

*Lexington Books Politics of Education Series*
Frederick M. Wirt, Editor

Michael W. Kirst, Ed., *State, School, and Politics: Research Directions*

Joel S. Berke, Michael W. Kirst, *Federal Aid to Education: Who Benefits? Who Governs?*

Al J. Smith, Anthony Downs, M. Leanne Lachman, *Achieving Effective Desegretation*

Kern Alexander, K. Forbis Jordan, *Constitutional Reform of School Finance*

George R. LaNoue, Bruce L.R. Smith, *The Politics of School Decentralization*

David J. Kirby, T. Robert Harris, Robert L. Crain, Christine H. Rossell, *Political Strategies in Northern School Desegregation*

Philip K. Piele, John Stuart Hall, *Budgets, Bonds, and Ballots: Voting Behavior in School Financial Elections*

# Budgets, Bonds, and Ballots

Voting Behavior in School
Financial Elections

Philip K. Piele
University of Oregon

and

John Stuart Hall
Arizona State University

Lexington Books
D.C. Heath and Company
Lexington, Massachusetts
Toronto          London

**Library of Congress Cataloging in Publication Data**

Piele, Philip K
   Budgets, bonds, and ballots.

   Bibliography: p. 171.
   1. Education—United States—Finance. 2. Voting—United States. 3. Community and school—United States.
I. Hall, John S., joint author. II. Title.
LB2825.P48     379'.121     73-12481
ISBN 0-669-90621-2

*Copyright © 1973 by D. C. Heath and Company*

All rights reserved. No part of this publication may be reproduced or transmitted in any form or by any means, electronic or mechanical, including photocopy, recording, or any information storage or retrieval system, without permission in writing from the publisher.

Published simultaneously in Canada.

Printed in the United States of America.

International Standard Book Number: 0-669-90621-2.

Library of Congress Catalog Card Number: 73-12481

To Sandi and Connie

# Contents

| | | |
|---|---|---|
| | **List of Figures** | ix |
| | **List of Tables** | xi |
| | **Foreword,** by Harmon Zeigler | xiii |
| | **Preface** | xv |
| **Chapter 1** | **Voters and the Schools: The Problem of Declining Support** | 1 |
| | School Financial Elections Past and Present | 1 |
| | General Explanations | 2 |
| | The Geometric Accumulation of Research Findings: A Pleasant Problem | 5 |
| **Chapter 2** | **Determining What We Know: A Methodological Problem** | 9 |
| | Retrieval | 9 |
| | Theory Building | 11 |
| | Propositional Inventories | 18 |
| | Adapting Principles of the Evaluative Inventory to a Research Case: The Format We Followed | 25 |
| **Chapter 3** | **Voters and Nonvoters: Who and Why** | 31 |
| | Participation in National and Local Elections | 32 |
| | Approaches to the Study of Voter Participation | 34 |
| | Research Findings | 41 |
| | Summary and Conclusions | 51 |
| **Chapter 4** | **Variations in Voter Turnout: Causes and Effects** | 55 |
| | "Normal" Turnout | 55 |
| | Explanations of Turnout Variations | 56 |
| | Voter Turnout as a Symtom of System Health | 60 |
| | The Relationship between Voter Turnout and Outcome of School Financial Elections: Research Findings | 63 |
| | Individual Participation and Aggregate Turnout: Synthesis and Implications | 69 |

| | | |
|---|---|---|
| Chapter 5 | **Environmental Determinants** | 73 |
| | School District Characteristics | 74 |
| | Community Conflict | 78 |
| | Communication, Information Flow, and Campaign Techniques | 83 |
| | Election Characteristics | 91 |
| | Miscellaneous Findings | 96 |
| | Summary and Synthesis | 97 |
| Chapter 6 | **Socioeconomic Determinants** | 99 |
| | Economic Determinants | 99 |
| | Social Determinants | 109 |
| | Socioeconomic Determinants: A Synthesis | 121 |
| Chapter 7 | **Psychological Determinants** | 123 |
| | Partisan and Nonpartisan Attitudes | 124 |
| | Attitudes toward Taxes | 127 |
| | Attitudes toward Community | 127 |
| | Attitudes toward Governments and Governors: Schools and School Officials | 130 |
| | Attitude Conflict | 134 |
| | Synthesis | 137 |
| Chapter 8 | **Theory, Practice, and Future Research** | 139 |
| | Differences in Focus | 139 |
| | Emerging Partial Theories | 141 |
| | Theory of the Normal Vote: Promise and Problems | 152 |
| | Linking Research to Theory and Practice | 156 |
| | Appendix. Synthesis of Empirical Research on Voting in School Financial Elections: Correlates to "Yes Voting" and Election Success. | 159 |
| | **Bibliography** | 171 |
| | Part I. Basic Empirical Research | 171 |
| | Part II. Theory | 191 |
| | Part III. Observations | 201 |
| | Part IV. Methodology | 205 |
| | **Index** | 209 |
| | **About the Authors** | 217 |

## List of Figures

| Figure | | |
|---|---|---|
| 2-1 | The Research-Theory Relationship: A Time Sequence Model | 17 |
| 2-2 | Dimensions for Classifying Propositions | 20 |
| 2-3 | Illustration of Evaluation Dilemma | 24 |
| 2-4 | Sample Format for Statement of Propositions | 28 |
| 3-1 | Alternative Explanatory Paths between Selected Information and Interest Variables and an Individual's Decision to Vote in a School Financial Election | 43 |
| 3-2 | Alternative Explanatory Paths among Selected Variables Related to an Individual's Decision to Vote in a School Financial Election | 46 |
| 3-3 | Alternative Explanatory Paths among Variables That Appear Strongly Related to Participation in School Financial Elections | 52 |
| 4-1 | Hypothetical Turnout Rates for Different Types of Elections–Community X | 55 |
| 4-2 | Probable Participants in "Normal" School Financial Elections | 71 |
| 7-1 | The "Funnel of Causality" Leading to Voting Decisions | 124 |
| 7-2 | Examples of Cross Pressures in Voting in Local School and National Partisan Elections | 135 |
| 8-1 | A Typology of Research Approaches to the Study of Voting Behavior in School Financial Elections | 140 |
| 8-2 | One Causal Map of the Relationship between Community Conflict, Voter Turnout, and Outcome in School Financial Elections | 150 |
| 8-3 | The Causal Relationship between Turnout Stimulants, Turnout, and Outcome in School Financial Elections. | 150 |

## List of Tables

| Table | | |
|---|---|---|
| 1-1 | Nationwide Approval Records for School Bond Issues: 1962-1972 | 3 |
| 3-1 | Social/Psychological Characteristics Frequently Correlated with Voter Turnout | 36 |
| 3-2 | A Typology of Potential Voters According to Two Factors That May Affect Citizen Interest in the Outcome of School Financial Elections | 38 |
| 4-1 | Comparison of Research Approaches and Settings in the Literature Investigating the Relationship between Voter Turnout and Success or Failure in School Financial Elections: 1960-1971 | 68 |
| 5-1 | Multivariate Models of Voting in School Financial Elections: Percent of Variance in Direction of Vote and Percent of Success in Discriminating between Winning and Losing Districts Accounted for by Selected Financial Variables | 95 |
| 6-1 | A Typology of Voters in School Financial Elections According to Two Factors That May Affect Direction of the Vote | 99 |
| 6-2 | Proportion of Adults That Should Vote Yes on Issues to Increase Taxes for School Purposes: 1969-1972 | 102 |
| 6-3 | Characteristics of Voters Most Likely to Favor or Oppose School Financial Issues | 122 |
| 8-1 | A List of Partial Theories Used to Explain Electoral Behavior in School Financial Elections | 142 |
| 8-2 | Characteristics of Individuals Most Likely to Participate in and Vote in Favor of School Financial Elections | 151 |
| 8-3 | Actual and Intended Voting Behavior for a School Financial Election: 1969 | 152 |
| 8-4 | Response of National Sample to Gallup Poll of Public Attitudes toward Education: 1969-1972 | 153 |
| 8-5 | Percentage of Adults That Would Vote against School Tax Increases by Selected Background Characteristics: Gallup Surveys of 1969 and 1972 | 155 |

# Foreword

My involvement with this book began in 1969, when John Hall was enrolled in my course in State and Local Government. Hall expressed an interest in what was then the beginning of the taxpayer revolt and asked for an "Incomplete" so that he might more thoroughly survey the literature. Since that time, Piele and Hall have performed what I regard as an extraordinarily exhaustive search of the literature. Needless to say, the "Incomplete" was removed.

However, this book is more than the usual bibliographical essay. Topical as the taxpayer revolt may be, those students who wish some understanding of the dynamics and stability of voting behavior will find much to intrigue them. While all chapters are of merit, I think Chapter Four will strike most readers as especially rewarding. Much controversy has surrounded the central finding of this chapter: the larger the turnout, the smaller the percentage of favorable votes cast in a school financial election. Yet, the preponderance of the evidence clearly supports Piele and Hall's conclusion.

There is no escaping the fact that the main thrust of Piele and Hall's book is not a pleasant one for those who place their hopes for an expanding and innovative educational system in an enlightened local electorate. Perhaps we ought to engage in a serious reassessment of the social mythology of local control of education.

**Harmon Zeigler**

# Preface

This book summarizes and analyzes more than a decade of empirical research on voting in school financial elections. We have spent a large portion of the last four years extracting and synthesizing this research, all of which was conducted since 1960. The material we have reviewed consists of more than 100 research reports from several academic disciplines and employs a wide variety of techniques and methods; the research is geographically representative of the United States.

We intend this book to accomplish two things that are at least partially contradictory. In the first place, we systematically and objectively catalogue the findings from a significant body of literature. Secondly, we evaluate the findings and relate them to each other. The reason that these two objectives often come into conflict is that even the most modest attempt at evaluation inevitably results in the drawing of conclusions, which in turn stimulate the search for additional evidence directly related to those conclusions. This dilemma and related ones are discussed at length in Chapter 2. For now, let us simply emphasize that for the five substantive chapters (3-7) of the book we have tried not to deviate from the mean of objectivity. In these chapters, we have studiously limited our analysis to the research as it is and to factors involved in the production of that research that may have affected its results.

At the same time, the attempt to provide some sort of coherent vehicle for the presentation of research findings and propositions has resulted in a chapter framework, which, like any other taxonomy, specifies order and hence implies evaluation. In other words, this propositional inventory, like most others, has been subject to the natural human tendency to classify, catalogue, and evaluate during its construction. However, we believe that it survives as an objective baseline statement of what is known about voting in school financial elections and that at the same time amplifies some areas of theory about voting behavior that will serve to promote further inquiry.

Though not so divided formally in the text, the chapters nonetheless fall into four major parts. The first part introduces the problem of declining support for school financial issues (Chapter 1) and prescribes a methodological means for helping researchers and administrators in their efforts to understand and solve this problem (Chapter 2). The second part focuses on participation in school financial elections: Chapter 3 describes the participants and assesses several explanations for their participation. Chapter 4 examines some of the causes and effects of turnout fluctuations in these elections, particularly the relationship between turnout size and election outcome. In the third part we direct our attention to the determinants of voter behavior and election outcome. Chapter 5 focuses on environmental determinants, Chapter 6 on socioeconomic determinants, and Chapter 7 on psychological determinants. Finally, the fourth part (Chapter 8) links major propositions to suggest credible partial theories and future research needs.

We were fortunate to have had invaluable individual support during the writing of this book. At the earliest stages, both authors benefited from the specific suggestions and insights of others. In particular, LeRoy Peterson's observations concerning the need for a systematic model of school election determinants led directly to Piele's interest in applying the techniques of propositional inventory to this literature. Hall's interest in voter behavior in these elections was greatly stimulated by Harmon Zeigler's insights and hypotheses.

Preparation of the basic bibliography and extraction of the major findings from the literature were originally done for a research analysis paper published by the ERIC Clearinghouse on Educational Management at the University of Oregon.

Several individuals provided essential feedback by reading and reacting critically to parts of the manuscript at different phases of the writing. After reading various parts of the manuscript, Raymond McCulloch, Lawrence Pierce, Mike Robinson, David George, and John Orbell all made comments that have been incorporated into its final form. Richard O. Carlson's short but penetrating critique of Chapter 2 led to key revisions of that chapter.

Finally, we are most deeply indebted to those researchers who are cited throughout the text. Without their original investigations there obviously could have been no inventory of research. Hopefully, we are able to reciprocate by relating their findings to similar studies and passing the results on to a wide and interested audience.

Budgets, Bonds, and Ballots

# 1

# Voters and the Schools: The Problem of Declining Support

The status quo in American life has undergone significant and widespread attacks in recent years. Although there is a noticeable lack of agreement concerning the desirable direction and speed of social change, it is clear to anyone who reads a newspaper or watches the nightly news on television that an increasing number of groups and individuals seek change. It is equally apparent that the most important cliche in the change rhetoric, "reordering priorities," is not limited to debates on national policy. Virtually all institutions are considered part of the status quo, or "establishment," and consequently are targets of criticism.

Although the word "revolt," when applied to contemporary activities in the United States, usually engenders images of campus violence, racial war, and so forth, it has also evolved as part of another cliche that describes the increasing propensity of voters to reject local financial referendums. In school districts throughout the nation, voter approval of school financial issues (school bond, budget, and tax issues) has declined steadily since the middle 1960s.

## School Financial Elections Past and Present

The school official's problem is apparent in the trend indicated in Table 1-1. This table establishes an increasing voter opposition to school bond elections reflected in the percentages of both elections and monies approved.

Although comparable nationwide data on voting in other types of school financial issues—that is, budget and special tax levies—are not available, other evidence suggests that these issues have fared no better. A survey of the nation's 342 largest school systems (those with pupil enrollments exceeding 12,000) found that 52.1 percent of their budget and tax referendums were approved during the 1970 school year.[1] This survey found that the approval rate for bond elections is slightly higher, 53.2 percent, the same figure reported by the study of all school systems as shown in Table 1-1. Studies of particular geographical areas confirm that the trend in budget defeats closely parallels increases in bond issue rejections.[2]

---

[1] *ERS Information Aid* 10 (August 1971), (Washington, D.C.: Educational Research Service, 1971), p. 4.

[2] For example, one study of sixteen Oregon school districts, covering the decade 1960 to 1970, found that while all the districts were able to pass their budgets on the first attempt

Clearly, the change in voting patterns is perplexing to the school administrator. Most school districts rely heavily on local property tax revenues. Any request by a district to increase its share of these revenues normally requires voter approval, regardless of the form of the request. The data from Table 1-1 confirm a fact that would provide many school officials with pleasant reminiscences: in the early 1960s voter approval was frequently viewed as a formality. Today, however, voter approval is often the most significant hurdle facing school officials attempting to meet specific educational demands and needs. The school practitioner needs to know the answers to at least two questions: What has caused the change in voting patterns for school elections? And what can be done to reverse the trend?

## General Explanations

The shift in approval rates has been attributed to a number of forces somewhat independent of the educational system. Some of the predominant general explanations become quickly apparent by conversing with informed observers or perusing newspaper articles and editorials.

Although the phrase "taxpayers' revolt" has been used as verbal shorthand to describe the change in voter approval rates, it also can be used to describe a popular explanation for the change. According to this view, the change in voting patterns is attributed to a general revolt of taxpaying voters against ever-increasing taxes for all forms of governmental services. School financial elections receive the brunt of this dissatisfaction, say the proponents of this theory, simply because they represent one of the few opportunities the voter has to oppose a tax increase.

A logical corollary to the taxpayers' revolt explanation is frequently offered to explain why the change occurred during the late 1960s. According to this view, the economic recession during that period served to color many voters' perceptions of dollar values and tax bills. Because of the recession, the personal incomes of many citizens were restricted or stabilized even though taxes and other costs of living continued to increase. The logical result, according to this "state-of-the-economy" interpretation, was an increase in voter opposition against new taxes.

Other popular explanations can be combined with the taxpayers' revolt theory to explain the apparent continuation of the trend developed in Table 1-1.

---

in 1959-60, the same number of districts required thirty-five elections to pass their budgets in 1970-71. See Bureau of Governmental Research and Service, "Record of Vote on Proposed School District Special Tax Levies to Exceed the Six Per Cent Constitutional Limitation," University of Oregon, BGRS, 1971, unpublished. During the period 1965-70, New York voters increased their proportion of budget rejections each year, moving from a 1.7 percent rejection rate in 1965 to 20 percent in 1970, according to Robert J. Goettel in "Voter Behavior and School Budget Election," *APSS Know How* 23 (September 1971): 1-5.

**Table 1-1**
**Nationwide Approval Records for School Bond Issues: 1962-1972**

| Fiscal Year Ending | Number of Elections | | | Value of Issues in Millions | | |
|---|---|---|---|---|---|---|
| | Total | Approved | Percentage Approved | Total | Approved | Percentage Approved |
| 1962 | 1,432 | 1,034 | 72.2 | 1,849 | 1,273 | 68.9 |
| 1963 | 2,048 | 1,482 | 72.4 | 2,659 | 1,851 | 69.6 |
| 1964 | 2,071 | 1,501 | 72.5 | 2,672 | 1,900 | 71.1 |
| 1965 | 2,041 | 1,525 | 74.7 | 3,129 | 2,485 | 79.4 |
| 1966 | 1,745 | 1,265 | 72.5 | 3,560 | 2,652 | 74.5 |
| 1967 | 1,625 | 1,082 | 66.6 | 3,063 | 2,119 | 69.2 |
| 1968 | 1,750 | 1,183 | 67.6 | 3,740 | 2,338 | 62.5 |
| 1969 | 1,341 | 762 | 56.8 | 3,913 | 1,707 | 43.6 |
| 1970 | 1,216 | 647 | 53.2 | 3,285 | 1,627 | 49.5 |
| 1971 | 1,086 | 507 | 46.7 | 3,337 | 1,381 | 41.4 |
| 1972 | 1,153 | 542 | 47.0 | 3,102 | 1,365 | 44.0 |

Source: Irene A. King, *Bond Sales for Public School Purposes 1971-1972*, Washington, D.C.: U.S. Department of Health, Education and Welfare, Office of Education, Government Printing Office, 1973.

In practice the rejection of a bond or budget issue has usually meant that the issue was resubmitted to voters after being amended to carry a lower tax price. Thus, the greater number of ballot rejections has required a greater total number of elections. Coupled with an increasing number of issues offered by other government agencies, the total number of trips to the polls has greatly increased for the average voter in local elections. As a result, some observers have suggested that many voters are so saturated with issues that they devalue the importance of any single issue.

In addition, the multiple choice nature of many school financial elections (particularly budget elections) suggests that many voters and administrators are now perceiving school financial issues as forums for bargaining. According to this view, the first proposal will purposely be higher than necessary to allow school officials to go through the motions of reducing the amount of money requested in the second proposal (and, if necessary, third or fourth proposal). Both the voter saturation and voter bargaining models suggest a cyclical pattern portending increased frustration for public officials in years to come.

The explanations above we have termed "general" because they normally imply a random effect. That is, "taxpayer-voters" and "voters" are used interchangeably without differentiation as the recipients of the forces stressed in these explanations. Of course, explanations like these raise additional questions. Not all school financial elections fail, nor do all voters cast negative ballots. Thus, the key questions are: What factors determine the direction of voter choice and what factors determine the outcome of school financial elections?

A potential source of answers to these questions is the literature on voting behavior in school elections. Unfortunately, this body of literature, which has grown with the increase in no votes, can be frustrating to analyze because sometimes the answers are contradictory. The contradictions are fairly easy to understand in the case of one segment of the relevant literature—the "how-to-win a bond issue" articles that frequently appear in education journals. One reviewer assesses this type of literature as follows:

For the most part, these articles are written by school administrators whose districts have just successfully passed a school bond issue, often after several defeats. In view of this recent success they offer advice on the proper techniques to use, or the techniques to avoid, in order to pass a school bond issue. The advice . . . is often conflicting and usually based upon a single case.[3]

The problem with advice of this type is that it is difficult to determine the validity of cause and effect assertions when no controls were used to assess the effect of unconsidered variables.

A component of the literature that could be expected to provide more

---

[3] George M. Beal et al., *Iowa School Bond Issues Data Book* (Ames, Iowa: Department of Sociology and Anthropology, Iowa State University, 1966), p. 5.

reliable answers is "empirical research."[4] Political scientists, educational researchers, sociologists, social psychologists, and economists have used varying approaches to systematically gather and assess data for explaining the determinants of voting patterns in school and other types of local financial elections. Empirical research, as opposed to the anecdotal case study, provides a more solid base for generalization.

Ironically, however, the steady accumulation of reports of empirical research concerned with voting in school financial elections has been of only scant use to the most interested observer of the "taxpayers' revolt"—the practicing school administrator. As in most other substantive areas of social science inquiry, practitioners and theorists alike are unable to use the results of previous research effectively and efficiently. The following section describes this ironic situation.

## The Geometric Accumulation of Research Findings: A Pleasant Problem

Proponents of empirical inquiry have good reason to be pleased with the general pace and direction of basic research in the social sciences during the past decade. The field of voting research provides an excellent illustration of the geometric accumulation of information in the social sciences. Technological advancement in the form of third generation computers and programmable calculators has played the major role in greatly increasing our capacity to accumulate various types of data (election, census, survey, etc.) that are requisite for understanding and explaining the voting act.

More importantly, the new technology has greatly enhanced the researcher's capacity to analyze these data. Multivariate analysis is now a practical technique for most researchers. The major justification for the use of the term "science" in describing contemporary social research—the ability to control, at least partly, for the effects of extraneous forces prior to the assertion of an explanation of some social phenomenon—has been greatly enhanced by the increased use of this one technique. In other words, there has been qualitative as well as quantitative improvement in our *capacity* for analysis and explanation in the social sciences.[5]

---

[4]The bibliography for this volume contains over 100 citations of such literature made available during the last decade.

[5]For an analysis of sixty-two major advances in the social sciences since 1900, see Karl W. Deutsch, John Platt, and Dieter Senghaas, "Analysis of 62 Advances Since 1900 Shows that Most Come from a Few Centers and Have Rapid Effects," *Science* 171 (February 5, 1971): 450-59. Among the sixty-two contributions, these authors list factor analysis, large-scale sampling in social research, attitude survey and opinion polling, linear programming, and multivariate analysis linked to social theory. They conclude that these contributions are directly related to a qualitative growth in knowledge; "statements such as 'we know no more about human psychology and politics than Aristotle did' mainly express the ignorance

Although these new methods of analyzing data have been used in recent studies of school financial elections, very little has been done to relate the findings of one research project to the findings of another.[6] Most individual reports of empirical research on voting in school financial elections exist in the form of professional journal articles or Ph.D. dissertations. Although these reports often include "reviews of research," they are of little aid in analyzing and comparing different findings. Such sections contain interpretations of prior research that vary remarkably in selectivity and quality. The nature of these interpretations is not surprising given their source. Individuals engaged in basic research (who write the interpretations) are frequently concerned with the advancement of knowledge on one small front, assuming that their island of research will be linked to others at some time in the future.

This limited concern, accompanied by the technological innovations mentioned above, may serve to stimulate necessary basic research activity. But basic research and reports of it are in themselves insufficient for true progress in any area of inquiry. In fact, reports of such research will have no impact at all if they cannot be retrieved—a danger that grows proportionately with the geometric expansion of research efforts.

It is not only the school official who is confused by or unaware of the meaning of various research findings. Because of the increase in the number of studies—particularly of the unpublished variety—it is becoming increasingly difficult for those conducting basic research to be aware of all relevant findings, much less their interrelationship and theoretical importance. One social theorist writes: "This flow of research findings, in fact, has become so great that it is now a losing game to try to keep abreast of all the findings. Monographs, journal articles, research proposals, mimeographed reports overtake man."[7]

---

of those who utter them" (p. 455). See also Kenneth Janda, *Data Processing: Applications to Political Research* (Evanston, Illinois: Northwestern University Press, 1965), p. 183. Following his convincing discussion and illustration of the need for applying the most powerful statistical tools warranted by a given data set, the author notes: "The complex procedures and countless calculations involved in multivariate methods ... are done routinely with available computer programs. Familiarity with computer methods of data processing enables the researcher to analyze quantitative data *more adequately*" (emphasis added).

[6]There is a noticeable lack of literature in any form that summarizes relevant research on determinants of voting in school financial elections. Exceptions are Frederick M. Wirt and Michael W. Kirst, *The Political Web of American Schools* (Boston: Little, Brown and Co., 1972), Chapter 6, pp. 96-110; Wayne Overbeck, "Junior College Bond Elections: Why Do They Fail (Or Pass)?" unpublished seminar paper; Beal et al., op. cit., Chapter I; and Dewey H. Stollar et al., *Analysis and Interpretation of Research for School Board Members. Final Report*. (Knoxville: Department of Educational Administration and Supervision, Tennessee University, 1969). An excellent critical review of research on local voting behavior is presented in the first chapter of Alvin Boskoff and Harmon Zeigler, *Voting Patterns in a Local Election* (Philadelphia: J.B. Lippincott Co., 1964), pp. 15-29.

[7]Hans L. Zetterberg, *On Theory and Verification in Sociology: A Much Revised Edition* (Totowa, New Jersey: The Bedminster Press, 1963), p. 3.

The immediate danger that arises when a body of literature becomes unmanageable is that of inefficiencies. The problem becomes quite clear when viewed in light of the scarce research resources available to contemporary social science:

Because we fall behind in comprehending or even reading the relevant literature, we introduce great inefficiencies in our research efforts. There is an increasing probability that important relevant materials will be overlooked. By falling behind in our reading we may collect data that have already been collected or conduct a study that has already been done. By falling behind in theory construction, we undertake research projects without an effective strategy for assigning research priorities.[8]

Clearly, it is important that social scientists increase their concern with, and improve their technology for, precisely determining the state of inquiry. As we have emphasized above, the need is urgent not only for the translation of research into action,[9] but also for improved communication linkages among researchers.

The literature addressed to the study of voting behavior in school financial elections provides one, albeit small, example of the problems and promises associated with contemporary social science research. The next chapter analyzes this contemporary research situation in greater detail and describes some of the prescriptions that have been advanced to deal more effectively with existing knowledge. We think that these "methodological" considerations should be made explicit since they provide the basis for this and similar studies.

Some readers, however, may want to move directly to Chapter 3. That

---

[8] Kenneth Janda, *Information Retrieval: Applications to Political Science* (Indianapolis: The Bobbs-Merril Co., 1968), p. 16.

[9] It is commonplace to pay lip service to the need for improvement of communication between social researchers and those responsible for social policy. Excellent specific statements of the need that include guidelines for improving the linkage are provided in: Edward A. Suchman, *Evaluative Research: Principles and Practice in Public Service and Social Action Programs* (New York: Russell Sage Foundation, 1967); and Leslie T. Wilkins, *Social Deviance: Social Policy, Action, and Research* (Englewood Cliffs, New Jersey: Prentice-Hall, 1965).

Of course this is not to argue that social science is currently capable of solving all of mankind's social problems. As Robert K. Merton has noted in *Social Theory and Social Structure; Revised and Enlarged Edition* (Glencoe, Illinois: The Free Press, 1957), p. 8, it is an incorrect view of the stage of development of social science to say that it must immediately provide answers to the highly visible and pressing problems "plaguing men in modern society." According to Merton it would be equally fallacious to assume that the inability of seventeenth century medicine to cure or prevent such critical illnesses as coronary thrombosis meant that medical science at the time had no promise for future development. But given this caveat—that social science is changing and developing in a changing and developing society—we may still assume that knowledge related to certain contemporary social problems is available and should be used: "necessity is only the mother of invention; socially accumulated knowledge is its father. Unless the two are brought together, necessity remains infertile."

chapter begins the substantive analysis of determinants of voting in school financial elections, the subject perhaps of greatest interest to policymakers, administrators, and interested citizens. In addition, researchers and other scholars who are aware of the research linkage and theory construction concerns stressed by Robert Merton, Hans Zetterberg, and others may find little that is new in the first half of Chapter 2.

# 2

## Determining What We Know: A Methodological Problem

The preceding chapter describes the two principal problems accompanying the rapid growth in the number of research reports: retrieval and theory building. Problems of retrieval are mainly technical. The increased volume of information surrounding most research subjects makes it difficult to locate all the relevant material for solving a particular problem or to proceed with important and needed research.

The second problem, theory building, is complicated more than caused by the increase in empirical research. But the fact that the problem of rigorous theory construction persists and is compounded during the accumulation of new research increases our concern regarding the allocation and direction of scarce research resources.

### Retrieval

As noted earlier, our technological capacity for retrieving social science information has increased and shows great promise, given future innovations in computer and microform technology.[1] Scholars in the Northwestern University political science department have moved beyond the discussion stage and have tested political science information retrieval systems that represent the frontiers of social sciences retrieval techniques. Among their most promising developments is a computer program called TRIAL (Technique to Retrieve Information from Abstracts of Literature). The program can retrieve, on a key-word basis, information on the relationships among any combination of variables as well as information summarizing research reports that have been abstracted and input to the system.[2] Although this system is highly advanced compared to other

---

[1] Much of this discussion of information problems and prospects is based on the excellent work by Kenneth Janda, *Information Retrieval: Applications to Political Science* (Indianapolis: The Bobbs-Merrill Co., 1968). For general discussions see Stein Rokkan (ed.), *Data Archives for the Social Sciences* (Paris: Mouton & Co., 1966); Ted Gurr and Hans Panofsky (eds.), *American Behavioral Scientists* (June 1964, entire edition); and Paul W. Hamelman and Edward M. Mazze, "Toward a Cost/Utility Model for Social Science Periodicals," *Socio-Economic Planning Sciences* 6 (October 1972): 465-76. Full-scale computerized retrieval systems based on modern abstracting and indexing techniques that have been developed for education and anthropology respectively are the Educational Resources Information Center (ERIC) and Human Relations Area Files systems.

[2] Janda, op. cit., pp. 18-31 et seq. An alternative system, similarly capable of retrieving specific findings, was tested in an analysis of the literature surrounding comparative political

information retrieval systems in the social sciences and although the system shows great potential, new research technology will be required to keep pace with the growing quantities of information available. Kenneth Janda has underscored the scope of the future task:

> The title (TRIAL) is not only descriptive of the method, but it also reflects the exploratory nature of the effort. Some day automated information retrieval systems will be commonplace aids to scholars, but many exploratory steps must be taken first. New developments will doubtless improve on the system described here, and technological breakthroughs may make the TRIAL approach altogether obsolete. In the meantime, the system should be able to provide some valuable experiences in the methodology of information retrieval while giving some assistance to scholars in *managing their literature*.[3]

Janda contends that the retrieval problems posed by the geometric accumulation of literature will not be solved by either increased specialization or traditional methods of note-taking, citation gathering, etc. In the first case, specialists must keep abreast of general developments in related disciplines in order to make their specialty meaningful. In fact, as Carl Landauer has noted, "There is a dialectic in the development of scholarly endeavor as there is in many other human activities: the more we increase specialization, the more we are in need of synthesizing efforts."[4] A laissez faire application of traditional methods of note-taking, etc., appears equally unlikely to solve problems associated with volumes of literature because these techniques represent the personal, idiosyncratic responses of individual scholars to problems and thus "do not lend themselves to coordination, cumulation, and collective use."[5]

Janda's principal concern is that organization be imposed on the process of inquiry to obviate "some of the currently wasteful duplication of effort."[6] He recognizes that such organization will require more than technological improvement—perhaps a coordinated abstracting effort coupled with an automated information storage, search, and retrieval system.

---

parties. Developed by Eastman Kodak, this system (MICRACODE) retrieves directly from microfilm copies of original documents. As the author notes, the pervasive influence of computing technology tends to obscure the potential of alternative retrieval systems such as this one, which when applied to large volumes of literature may prove more economical by avoiding keypunching costs. At least until optical scanners of printed texts become reliable and economical, systems such as MICRACODE deserve the consideration of scholars (see pp. 32-44).

[3] Ibid., p. 18, emphasis added.

[4] Carl Landauer, "Toward a Unified Social Science," *Political Science Quarterly* 86 (December 1971): 564.

[5] Janda, op. cit., p. 16.

[6] Ibid., p. 17.

**Theory Building**

Closely related to the basic problem of retrieval is the more taxing one of assessing the significance of retrieved findings. To thoroughly understand the meaning of a given research finding requires, as a first condition, awareness of the results of related research. When building inductive theory one must systematically evaluate findings in light of all relevant corroborating and contradicting findings. Perhaps the most important contribution new retrieval systems can offer theory building is their potential for improving the two-way relationship between theory and empirical research.

Those who share the view that it is important for modern social science to proceed inductively frequently advocate developing "systems of information packed descriptions of what we know" in relatively specific topics of inquiry.[7] Such descriptions may then be collected and reformulated for use by the systematic theorist who attempts to "explain particular kinds of phenomena with sufficient clarity and concreteness to imply a set of interrelated hypotheses that can be applied to several apparently diverse phenomena."[8] Explanation at this level of abstraction is normally referred to as "middle-range" theory.[9] Most social scientists who hold this view see empirical research and theory construction as dynamic and reciprocal activities. Seen in this perspective, research plays a role much larger than the limited and one-way role of verifying and testing theory often assigned to it in essays on scientific methods. As Robert Merton notes, modern social research "plays an active role ... it does more than confirm or refute hypotheses ... it performs at least four major functions which help shape the development of theory. It *initiates,* it *reformulates,* it *deflects* and it *clarifies* theory."[10]

Given the general state-of-the-art of inquiry in the social sciences, it is less important to solve the "chicken and egg" dilemma regarding the primacy of theory or research than it is to develop viable, practical linkage mechanisms between the processes of (1) coding and synthesizing the array of empirical generalizations (findings) to develop sets (systems) of interrelated propositions called theories and (2) testing theory through research that is consecutive, cumulative, and formally derived.[11]

---

[7]Hans L. Zetterberg, *On Theory and Verification in Sociology: A Much Revised Edition* (Totowa, New Jersey: The Bedminster Press, 1963), p. 1.

[8]Hubert M. Blalock, Jr., *An Introduction to Social Research* (Englewood Cliffs, New Jersey: Prentice-Hall, 1970), p. 79.

[9]Ibid.

[10]Robert K. Merton, *Social Theory and Social Structure; Revised and Enlarged Edition* (Glencoe, Illinois: The Free Press, 1957), p. 103, author's emphasis.

[11]For the best treatment on the need to link theory and research see Ibid., Chapters 2 and

Although most social scientists would agree that these twin needs are urgent, neither has received the attention philosophers of science have said it deserves. For the most part, theory and research activities in the social sciences remain poles apart, resulting "in marked *discontinuities* of empirical research on the one hand, and systematic theorizing unsustained by empirical test, on the other."[12] Indeed, it is difficult to find examples of conscious efforts toward improving the connection between empirical research and theory. Rather, the state-of-the-art (or science) of inquiry is still accurately summarized by Merton's description published in 1957:

There are conspicuously few instances of consecutive research which have cumulatively investigated a succession of hypotheses derived from a given theory. Rather, there tends to be a marked dispersion of empirical inquiries, oriented toward a concrete field of human behavior, but lacking a central theoretic orientation. The *plethora of discrete empirical generalizations* and of *post factum* interpretations reflect this pattern of research. The large bulk of general orientations and conceptual analyses, as distinct from sets of interrelated hypotheses, in turn reflect the tendency to *separate* theoretic activity from empirical research.[13]

*Replication*

Indications of the viability of a link between theory and empirical research may be found in examples that refine, retest, and replicate existing theories in the research literature. The scientific method is based on continual replication and refinement:

... the propositions which a science puts forward for study are either confirmed in all possible experiments or modified in accordance with the evidence. It is this self-corrective nature which allows us to challenge any proposition but which also assures us that the theories which science accepts are more probable than any alternative theories. By not claiming more certainty than the evidence warrants, the scientific method succeeds in obtaining more logical certainty than any other method yet devised.[14]

Although this type of statement is found almost universally in descriptions of the scientific method, the absence of usable replication in social research is frustratingly apparent from the most cursory examination of operational definitions of the key concepts. Examples of this lack abound. Two that stand

---

3, pp. 85-115. Codification and Formal Derivation (1 and 2 above) are offered as working models of the logical procedures of induction and deduction, respectively, pp. 99-101.

[12] Ibid., p. 99, author's emphasis.

[13] Ibid., p. 100, first and third emphases added.

[14] Morris Cohen and Ernest Nagel, *An Introduction to Logic and Scientific Method* (New York: Harcourt, Brace, and World, Inc., 1934), pp. 395-96.

out are the treatments in the research literature of the concepts of alienation and social class status. Documentation of the proliferation of meanings associated with these terms will appear in our treatment of their relationship to voting contained in subsequent chapters.

The research literature does contain exceptions to the lack of replication. There are areas in which research has systematically retested existing findings and propositions. These exceptions serve to underscore the requirement of replication to avoid static and sometimes misleading theories. An excellent example is the replication of Kenneth and Mamie Clark's classic 1940 study of ego development and self-awareness in black children.[15] The finding of this famous study was that a majority of black children preferred white to brown dolls. In the social-psychological literature, it is one of the most frequently cited studies on self-esteem, intergroup tension, prejudice, and racial identification. Yet a recent replication of the study (1969) found that black children preferred the doll of their own skin color.[16] The systematic nature of this replication greatly increases our confidence in its finding, which, in turn, adds a new dimension to several theories.

This case clearly illustrates the danger inherent in relying on evidence—no matter how persuasive—obtained by one study, in one setting, at one point in time. The replication requirement present in any theory building endeavor is neatly summarized by two researchers whose research in community politics follows their own prescription for repeated testing over time:

As with experimental research in the physical sciences, a single experiment, no matter how crucial, must be followed by other experiments. One cannot construct a valid theory, whether of nuclear physics or of community educational politics, based on the kind of instant knowledge derived from a single piece of experimental research.[17]

Although the need for research that replicates and clarifies existing knowledge is clear, there is a more pressing problem involving the research-theory link.

---

[15] See the following condensed version of the original unpublished study: Kenneth B. Clark and Mamie P. Clark, "Racial Identification and Preference in Negro Children," in Eleanor E. Maccoby, Theodore M. Newcomb, and Eugene L. Hartley (eds.), *Readings in Social Psychology: Third Edition* (New York: Holt, Rinehart and Winston, 1958), pp. 602-611.

[16] Earl Ogletree, "Skin Color Preference of the Negro Child," *Journal of Social Psychology* 79 (October 1969): 143-44.

[17] Robert E. Agger and Marshall N. Goldstein, *Who Will Rule the Schools: A Cultural Class Crisis* (Belmont, California: Wadsworth Publishing Co., 1971), p. 36. Few researchers have paid as much attention to obtaining comparable measures of social phenomena over time as Robert Agger and his associates—hence few are able to speak as authoritatively about such basic concepts as cause and effect and attitude change in assessing community politics. See Robert E. Agger, Daniel Goldrich, and Bert E. Swanson, *The Rulers and the Ruled: Political Power and Impotence in American Communities* (New York: John Wiley & Sons, 1964).

*The Research-Theory Relationship*

Since much of existing social science research is not "formally derived" and often stems from unreconciled theories, we are frequently faced with a literature that lacks uniformity and presents innumerable obstacles to comparison and generalization. Nevertheless, recent social science research literature, including virtually any substantive subset of that literature, contains "a plethora of empirical generalizations."[18] Variously referred to as propositions or findings, these generalizations summarize "observed uniformities or relationships between two or more variables"[19] on the basis of a systematic examination of cases. Such generalizations represent both the immediate return on a large total investment and the potential raw material for the creation of empirically based theory—that is, systems of logically interrelated propositions that allow us to predict and explain other empirical generalizations that would, prior to the construction of theory, appear disparate.[20] Thus, theory may emerge from the coordination of *"many methodologically imperfect findings into a rather trustworthy whole,* in the form of a small number of information-packed sentences or equations."[21]

---

[18] Merton, op. cit., p. 95.

[19] Ibid.

[20] Ibid., p. 96. Throughout our discussion we assume that the powerful theories provide both explanation and prediction. But the imperfect state of our knowledge in the social sciences generally dictates *partial* explanation that may be insufficient for prediction. Philosopher of science Abraham Kaplan provides the following example: "An automobile accident is said to be due to defective brakes or excessive speed or to a drunken driver; none of these things allow us to predict the accident, but in particular cases they may have considerable explanatory force"; see his *The Conduct of Inquiry: Methodology for Behavioral Science* (San Francisco: Chandler Publishing Company, 1964), p. 348. Kurt Lewin also contends that under certain conditions, theories that simply explain known facts are of value "particularly if the theory combines into one logical system known facts which previously had to be treated by separate theories; it would have a definite advantage as an organizational device." See Kurt Lewin, *Field Theory in Social Science: Selected Theoretical Papers* (London: Tavistock Publications Ltd., 1952), p. 20. From a practical viewpoint, Kaplan is probably correct in noting that "it is not much help in the conduct of inquiry, especially inquiry in behavioral science, to hold up the ideal of explanations having the predictive power of celestial mechanics. Why should behavioral science make demands on itself that are so seldom imposed by physics or biology?" (p. 349). Yet the danger, noted by Lewin (p. 20), in being satisfied with this level of theory is that empirical data in social science are frequently amenable to a number of different interpretations. Thus arises the problem described by Merton as *post factum* explanation—explanation applied only to data already collected: "The method of *post factum* explanation does not lend itself to nullifiability, if only because it is so completely flexible" (p. 94).

Of course in almost all areas of inquiry, ranging from astronomy to medicine, to voting behavior, we find examples of well-established empirical generalizations that predict but do not explain. As useful as some of these generalizations are, they do not constitute theory. See Kaplan's discussion, pp. 349-51.

[21] Zetterberg, op. cit., foreword, author's emphasis.

At this point the analytical distinction between the two principal types of relationships connecting empirical research to theory should be made clear so that the actual process and needs of theory building will become equally clear. Figure 2-1 presents a dynamic model of theory building that shows empirically derived research findings being ordered (codified) by partial theory that in turn requires additional corroboration or contradiction. Whether the original theory is supported or contradicted, the modification provides input to new and perhaps broader theory. The process can then be repeated to further strengthen the theory.

The model applies to theory building at any level. The array of small circles and squares found in the time 1 funnel represents an informally derived conglomeration of research and theory. The time 1 funnel represents a codification process that attempts to synthesize and lend order to a previously less organized mass.

From this codification, we derive tentative generalizations and some of their logical interrelationships, thus creating partial theory at time 2. This partial theory provides the impetus for directed research—symbolized by the larger, orderly circles in the time 3 verification funnel—designed to test the findings of time 1 research and to explore important questions unanswered by the tentative time 2 theory. These new research findings require a modification of the initial theory and, coupled with other partial theories,[22] provide the basis for a revised, more comprehensive theory at time 4. The process continues through time 7 with theory and research becoming more efficient. Closer communication reduces the time lag between the questions raised by theory and the answers provided by research.

The model's temporal dimension should not be allowed to obscure the reciprocal nature of theory and research in the ideal state. A more accurate picture of that ideal would show haphazard connecting arrows between the bits and pieces of research and theory portrayed in time 1. Similar connections would be required among pieces of research and between research and theory throughout the process to denote communication and feedback. We omit lines such as these because they would only create confusion in the model.

In the diagram, gradually larger symbols are presented in a gradually more symmetrical manner to indicate greater efficiency in the research-theory relationship. Efficiency is essential for the achievement of "middle-range" theory as defined by Merton:

> ... theories intermediate to the minor working hypotheses evolved in abundance during the day-by-day routines of research and the all-inclusive speculations

---

[22] Only two other similar processes are indicated by straight time sequence lines, but that is because of space limitations. Depending on the substantive area and level of theory, the number of similarly derived partial (and overlapping) theories is infinite. In fact, we must ask the reader to imagine that each square (theory) in the model, no matter how small, is simultaneously the cause and effect of processes similar to the one diagrammed here.

comprising a master conceptual scheme from which it is hoped to derive a very large number of empirical uniformities of social behavior.[23]

Our model portrays a continuous filtering of evidence from multiple outcroppings, a constant testing and retesting of partial theories, that eventually leads to cumulative theories of the middle-range (time 5+). Such a prescription would not be needed if we were unconcerned about the pace of progress in inquiry or if we had unlimited research resources. Even without this emphasis on efficiency in research, important middle-range theories would eventually be produced informally by individuals and teams using traditional methods of scholarship. As long as men pursue scientific inquiry, "dramatic breakthroughs" and occurrences of "serendipity"[24] will play important roles in the creation of theory. But resource limitations and concern for pressing social problems require that the accumulated islands of research and theory shown in the time 1 area of Figure 2-1 be linked wherever possible to form stronger bonds of knowledge that will facilitate progress in scholarship.

In most fields of social science the relationship between theory and research is obscure at best, and theories of the middle range are almost nonexistent. Many individual research findings and hypotheses exist, and a few grand theories are offered. We agree with Hans Zetterberg, who notes that the next step for sociology (the reader may substitute any branch of the social sciences) is "to sum up its knowledge in the form of theory and to use this theory to gain control over its research efforts."[25]

In summary, we believe that some amount of codification is possible for almost every substantive area of inquiry in the social sciences and is necessary for efficient and productive theory building. We share Ted Robert Gurr's assumption

... that *social science theory ought to build on what is already known* about the subject being theorized about and that it ought to be consistent with or at least not directly contradictory to what is more generally known about the nature and processes of individual and aggregate human behavior. This is not to say that hypotheses must be consistent with what Levy calls "going common sense" but rather that it is nonsensical and inefficient to invest research effort in testing hypotheses that contradict what is precisely known unless there are compelling, logical or empirical grounds for questioning what is assumed to be "precisely known."[26]

---

[23] Merton, op. cit., p. 5.

[24] Ibid., see pp. 103-108 for his discussion of the relationship of serendipity pattern to theory and pp. 103-104 for the etymology of the term.

[25] Zetterberg, op. cit., p. 84.

[26] Ted Robert Gurr, *Why Men Rebel* (Princeton, New Jersey: Princeton University Press, 1970), p. 17. This study of political violence is superb testimony in the argument for rigorous synthesis and retrieval of available knowledge. For this effort Gurr was awarded the 1970 Woodrow Wilson Foundation award for the best book in the area of government, politics, or international affairs.

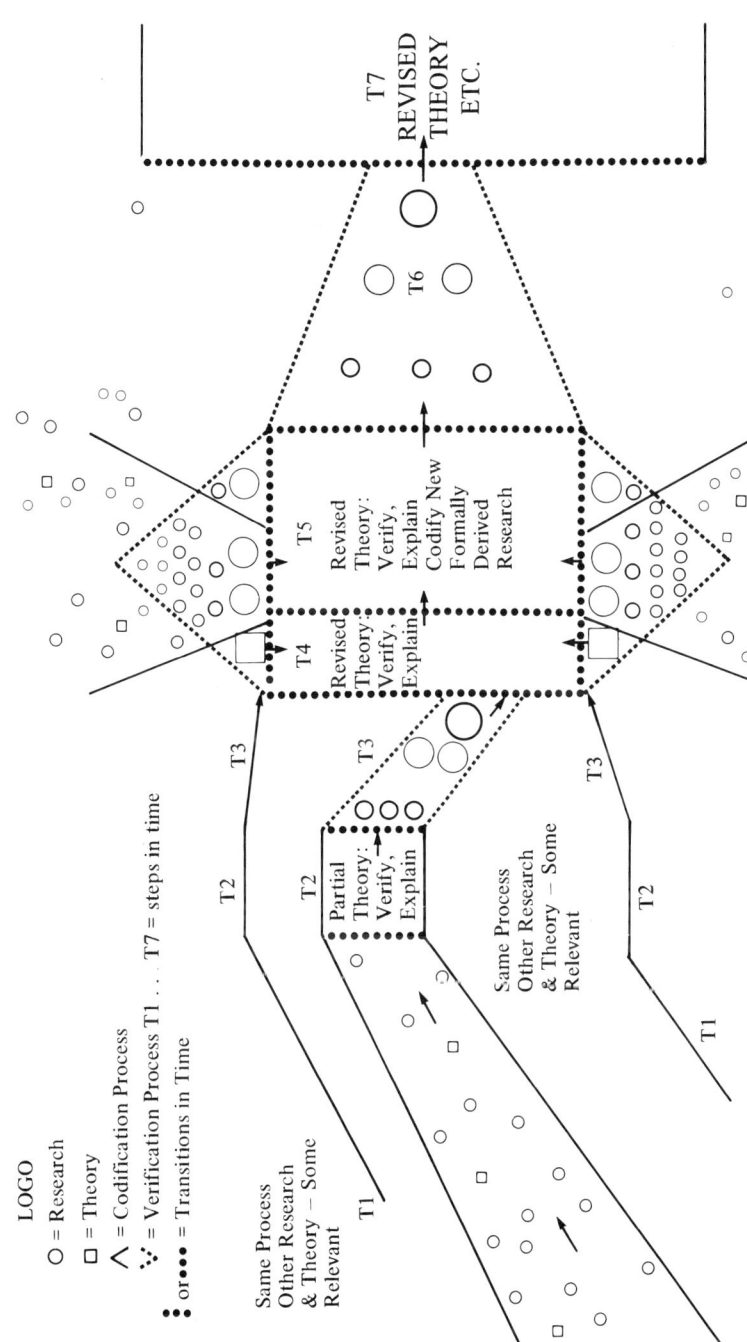

**Figure 2-1.** The Research-Theory Relationship: A Time Sequence Model

Note: Size of the symbol reflects relative efficiency or power of the research or theory symbolized.

It is important to note that Gurr prescribes a building process for social science theory. The dynamic or evolutionary nature of the theory construction process is often overlooked by those contending that more information and research are needed before theorizing can begin. The position taken above is that theory building—regardless of its tentative or partial nature at the outset—requires the ongoing attention of scholars. This position is based on the more liberal view of theory that we have attempted to stress throughout: "A theory . . . is a sword that cuts two ways. On the one hand, it is a system of information packed descriptions of *what we know*; on the other hand it is a system of general explanations."[27]

In the social sciences we can expect that the results of efforts to determine what is known will vary greatly. At the outset, codification efforts in many substantive areas are likely to result in greater confusion than clarity. Confusion may be an accurate reflection of the state-of-the-knowledge to be codified, a result of the quality and accuracy of the codification effort, or both. In the first case, the effort would remain worthwhile only if the areas of confusion are highlighted, not hidden. By specifying what we *do not* know, we suggest needed theoretic links and guide future research.

Inaccurate or misleading attempts at synthesis are worse than no attempts at all. Hopefully, the quality of codification will improve with increased experience in synthesis and retrieval. Presently the list of quality efforts in this form of scholarship is small and represents substantial variation in technique and subject matter. Yet important steps have been taken by a few social scientists who have produced systematic inventories of the findings and propositions from significant bodies of literature. A few admirable examples provide the basis for the following discussion of the propositional inventory.

**Propositional Inventories**

In the preceding sections we have emphasized problems and promises that have accompanied growth in basic research in the social sciences. By now it should be clear that the problems are less likely to be solved and the promises less efficiently fulfilled if progress must depend on the informal efforts of scattered researchers and theorists. Yet, to date, little formal effort has accompanied the almost universal belief among social scientists that a better link between empirical research and theory is desirable. Robert Merton points out that this position is trivial so long as it remains simply a position: "If it is to be more than another announcement of conventional faith, this interest in consolidation must be *specific* and must be *concretely* exemplified."[28]

---

[27] Zetterberg, op. cit., foreword, emphasis added.

[28] Merton, op. cit., p. 4, author's emphasis.

As a practical matter, most contemporary social scientists are specialists in basic research, teaching, or some combination of the two. Hans Zetterberg sees the need for two new types of specialists to advance theory in sociology (social science): "the man who develops new partial theories out of his own or other people's basic research, and the man who takes a number of partial theories developed by others and integrates them into a more inclusive theory."[29]

Although limited in size, a volume of important literature that reflects the concerns of Merton and Zetterberg and that provides concrete examples of attempts at "consolidation" is available. Generally, we may refer to these studies as "propositional inventories." Before looking at similarities and differences in some salient examples of inventories, we will take time to make explicit our use of several concepts at the heart of this literature.

*Definition of Terms*

In logic, a proposition is defined as "an expression in which the predicate affirms or denies something about the subject."[30] Philosophers of science have distinguished two different types of propositions: hypotheses lack evidence of their validity, whereas *invariances* possess sufficient evidence and are considered valid.[31] Invariances may be classified further: At one end of a continuum of informative value is the "ordinary invariance," commonly referred to as a finding or empirical generalization and formally referred to as a generic or existential proposition.[32] At the other end is the "theoretical invariance"[33] or law, which is a statement of the highest informative value.

In the contemporary social science literature, there are few laws but many ordinary propositions suggested by individual pieces of research. It is difficult to assess the exact location of a given finding in the continuum portrayed in Figure 2-2. There is really no way to distinguish between a high level hypothesis and a low level ordinary invariance. Even if a method for determining precisely when enough evidence has been accumulated to move a proposition from the hypothetical to the theoretical realm could be found, it would be hard to apply because of the difficulty in establishing exactly how much empirical support does exist for a given proposition.

---

[29] Zetterberg, op. cit., pp. 2-3.

[30] *Webster's New World Dictionary of the American Language: College Edition* (Cleveland: The World Publishing Company, 1960), p. 1168. A slightly more exclusive—albeit slightly more esoteric—definition is provided by Zetterberg, op. cit., p. 12: "Propositions relate *variates* to each other . . . we need, at the very minimum, two variates to have one proposition."

[31] Zetterberg, op. cit., p. 35.

[32] Kaplan, op. cit., pp. 93-94.

[33] Zetterberg, loc. cit.

| HYPOTHESES | THEORY | LAW |
|---|---|---|

**PROPOSITIONS**

| No Evidence | Some Evidence | Substantial Evidence | Universal Evidence |
|---|---|---|---|

**Figure 2-2.** Dimensions for Classifying Propositions

*Examples*

Propositional inventories can summarize any type of proposition. Most existing inventories begin by summarizing available low informational propositions. Usually the object of this effort is to create propositions of a higher level (further removed from the hypothetical end of the continuum). These "inventories of determinants"[34] can be particularly useful as first efforts at systematic codification in a specific field. Zetterberg provides the most succinct justification for their use: "Researchers need them for their research designs, and practitioners need them as bases for concrete advice to clients."[35]

The most notable examples of propositional inventories proceed by retrieving and synthesizing the evidence from individual studies regarding the relationships between one dependent and several independent variables. By means of this somewhat systematic and objective examination of an entire body of literature, certain relationships are corroborated more often than others, and certain findings are found to logically precede or follow others. The propositions can thus be restated at a higher informational level as better hypotheses or partial theory, depending on their location on the continuum in Figure 2-2.

Most existing propositional inventories roughly follow Zetterberg's blueprint for an "inventory of determinants." The means they use is to translate a number of discrete findings into a set of more general propositions "specifying the determinants of some phenomenon."[36] Among the phenomena (dependent variables) that have been inventoried in such a manner are the following, which exemplify a wide range of topics and methodologies: human behavior,[37]

---

[34]Ibid., p. 72.

[35]Ibid., p. 21.

[36]James L. Price, *Organizational Effectiveness: An Inventory of Propositions* (Homewood, Illinois: Richard D. Irwin, 1968), p. 1.

[37]Bernard Berelson and Gary A. Steiner, *Human Behavior: An Inventory of Scientific Findings* (New York: Harcourt, Brace, and World, Inc., 1964). This work represents an admirable attempt at synthesis and integration, but the vast scope of their subject matter led to severe problems of manageability. See David Cort's critique in the *New York Times Book Review*, April 5, 1964, p. 230, which criticized the tautological nature of several of the book's 1,045 conclusions.

political violence,[38] political participation,[39] organizational effectiveness,[40] and executive succession.[41] These examples are cited because they represent rigorous, book-length inventories that most closely resemble the propositional inventory model described above. Other excellent synthesis and retrieval efforts, available in more traditional forms, are highly relevant to our substantive concern[42] (voting in school financial elections).

The studies cited in footnotes 37 through 42 have been welcomed by social scientists concerned about the lack of attention to synthesis and continuity noted earlier. Lane and Milbrath (footnotes 42 and 39 respectively) identify and summarize important generalizations concerning the correlates of political participation. Taken collectively, their work has substantially advanced our

---

[38] Gurr, op. cit. This is perhaps the best illustration of the benefits that can accrue from systematic retrieval and codification in the social sciences. The author synthesizes the findings from an important body of literature and restates the consequent generalizations in the form of testable, general, and interrelated hypotheses. The resulting rigorous partial theory concerning the sources, magnitude, and forms of political violence provides a solid base for future theory and research in the field.

[39] Lester W. Milbrath, *Political Participation: How and Why Do People Get Involved in Politics?* (Chicago: Rand McNally & Co., 1965). This is an excellent summary of important research findings translated into broader testable propositions. The substantive concern of the inventory—political participation—overlaps our substantive treatment.

[40] Price, op. cit. This inventory follows most closely the prescriptions of Zetterberg and Merton concerning the formal construction of an "inventory of determinants." The author imposes rigid criteria on the literature to be inventoried, which makes his task of assessing the determinants of organizational effectiveness more manageable. The fifty studies included for review provide a list of testable, general propositions. The first chapter contains an excellent discussion of the propositional inventory technique.

[41] Francis Clement Thiemann, *A Partial Theory of Executive Succession,* Ph.D. dissertation, College of Education, University of Oregon, 1968. This is an excellent, highly suggestive piece of scholarship. The author uses computerized keyword indexing, the propositional inventory technique, and principles of formal symbolic logic to construct a partial theory of executive succession. The result is a rigorous partial theory admittedly "miniature in scope but broad enough to illustrate the interrelation between the units and concrete enough to serve as a basis for further study" (p. 67).

[42] Inventories of a grander scope than those cited above are less useful in the direct construction of testable partial theory but often provide needed clarification, useful definitions, and provocative frameworks for future inquiry. In political science two excellent examples are Harold D. Lasswell and Abraham Kaplan, *Power and Society: A Framework for Political Inquiry* (New Haven: Yale University Press, 1950); and Andrew M. Scott, *The Functioning of the International Political System* (New York: The Macmillan Co., 1967). No discussion of synthesis and retrieval in political science is complete without acknowledging the classic—albeit dated, as most footnotes to it now advise—summary, in traditional form, of the discipline's knowledge concerning political participation provided by Robert E. Lane in *Political Life: Why and How People Get Involved in Politics* (New York: The Free Press, 1959). Derivatives of the propositional inventory technique that are useful as systematic summaries of propositions concerning voting in partisan elections may be found in the appendix to Bernard R. Berelson, Paul F. Lazarsfeld, and William N. McPhee, *Voting: A Study of Opinion Formation in a Presidential Campaign* (Chicago: University of Chicago Press, 1954), pp. 327-47; and in the concluding chapter of Anthony Downs, *An Economic Theory of Democracy* (New York: Harper and Row, 1957), pp. 295-300.

knowledge about why people participate in political activities. Perhaps more importantly, the constant reference to these two sources in recent literature on political participation is testimony to their heuristic value. One recent study is typical: following introductory remarks concerning the proliferation of research directed at "socio-demographic correlates of voter participation," McCleskey and Nimmo note that many gaps in our knowledge remain and that these gaps "emerge most clearly from the efforts by Lane and Milbrath to summarize what is known about the social and economic correlates of voter participation,"[43] McCleskey and Nimmo then use these gaps—quite legitimately—as justification for further research.

Each of the propositional inventories cited in footnotes 37 through 42 leaves gaps in specification of relations among variables while pursuing its inquiry. Indeed these gaps are inevitable in initial codifications normally aimed only at lending some order to existing knowledge or, at best, creating partial theory. But it is here that the propositional inventory presents its grand potential, by summarizing and stating explicitly what we know, we often specify what we do not know. The systematic inventory device greatly increases the intensity of the spotlight on the gaps in our knowledge.

*Evaluation*

A damaging criticism of propositional inventories involves their lack of attention to techniques for ranking and evaluating the findings and propositions they retrieve.

One review, in most respects complimentary, of Milbrath's political participation inventory is correctly critical in noting that this and similar efforts have not been able to "weight various factors *relative to each other* in their explanatory or predictive powers. A whole host of factors have been found to be related to political participation but there is little ranking or weighting possible among them."[44] The reviewer suggests that some form of evaluation is necessary to

---

[43] Clifton McCleskey and Dan Nimmo, "Differences between Potential, Registered and Actual Voters: The Houston Metropolitan Area in 1964," *Social Science Quarterly* 49 (June 1968): 103.

[44] From the review of Milbrath, op. cit., by Jack Dennis, *The American Political Science Review* 59 (December 1965): 1027, emphasis added. A partial exception to this criticism, among the examples cited earlier, is Gurr, op. cit., who weights findings on the basis of an arbitrarily assigned minimum correlation value. For example (see pp. 18-19), he requires that a relationship based on measurement of interval data exhibit a product-moment correlation coefficient of .30 or better for acceptance in his inventory. The author leaves unanswered the obvious question raised by such a procedure: How does one assess correlation coefficients based on other scales of measurement and other statistics? Even under ideal conditions for comparison—when all coefficients are product moment from interval level data—this procedure can be misleading. The number of cases examined in a given piece of research can greatly affect the magnitude of reported correlation coefficients. In other

order accurately the "almost exclusively bivariate" relationships and to account for potential change in these relationships over time and/or according to place or "level of analysis."[45]

The factors of time and place compose the research setting while the level of analysis is an important component of the research approach. Any serious attempt to evaluate or compare research findings should assess the potential effect of variations in these important dimensions.

Of course, other criteria are equally important in weighting the quality of research findings. The following composite of factors suggested by Zetterberg appears to provide a comprehensive basis for assessing research quality:

1. the validity of indicators ("Validity, ecliptically speaking, is the extent to which an indicator corresponds to a definition.")
2. the reliability of indicators ("Reliability is the extent to which an indicator renders unambigous readings. Reliability is a necessary prerequisite for validity.")
3. the quality of the fit between data trends and trends predicted by propositions:
   a. extent and d rection that the trends coincide (correlation)
   b. likelihood that the trend is chance (test of significance)
4. the control of alternative propositions
5. the representativeness of the sample and scope of the populations
6. the extent to which tested propositions are an integral part of established theory.[46]

A composite such as this serves as a checklist of factors to be considered while evaluating the methodological roots of research findings. An evaluation system that carefully operationalizes these factors would probably help separate the "wheat from the chaff," thereby increasing or decreasing our confidence in certain research findings. But extreme caution must be observed to avoid overzealous economizing in inventory construction. For many of those studies that occupy the middle of the methodological road, meaningful differentiation is extremely difficult unless the evaluator adopts strict and arbitrary cutting-

---

words, Gurr's evaluation approach is a form of multivariate analysis that disregards a basic principle of that technique by attempting to compare coefficients based on a varying number of cases. As an attempt to build parsimonious partial theory, this is a laudable effort. But Zetterberg's warning regarding the use of arbitrary cutting points for acceptance of a proposition is relevant here: "Scientific advance is as much hampered by the error of rejecting something true as by accepting something false" (op. cit., pp. 41-42).

[45] Dennis, op. cit.

[46] Zetterberg, op. cit., pp. 40-66. The factors are illustrated by applying them in an evaluation of one study (Stouffer et al., *The American Soldier*) on pp. 40-41. The quoted definitions of validity and reliability appear on pages 44 and 50, respectively.

points—a potentially risky practice that can lead to rejection or devaluation of important and valid findings.

Zetterberg suggests a cross-tabulation that illustrates the dilemma in evaluating research findings. By means of this cross-tabulation, presented in Figure 2-3, we can rank research studies on the basis of two criteria: the extent to which they control for alternative hypotheses and the method they use to test the hypothesis.

|  |  | TEST OF THE HYPOTHESIS | |
|---|---|---|---|
|  |  | Cross-sectional (0) | Longitudinal (1) |
| CONTROL OF ALTERNATIVE HYPOTHESES | No Control (0) | 0 | 1 |
|  | Pseudo-experimental (1) | 1 | 2 |
|  | Experimental (2) | 2 | 3 |

**Figure 2-3.** Illustration of Evaluation Dilemma[47]

To aid in the ranking, numerical values are assigned to the categories under each criteria. For example, longitudinal studies (value = 1) are more valuable than cross-sectional studies (value = 0). Similarly, studies that employ no controls (value = 0) are less valuable than those that employ only statistical or pseudo-experimental controls (value = 1), which are in turn less valuable than laboratory experiments (value = 2).

By simply adding our arbitrarily assigned values we are immediately confronted with the problem anticipated by Zetterberg: "we know little or nothing about how to evaluate cross-wise combinations of the two criteria. We have no way in which to tell whether a pseudo-experimental longitudinal design (such as a panel with multivariate analysis) is as effective as a cross-sectional experimental design (the conventional laboratory experiment)."[48]

This simple example indicates the complexities we are bound to encounter if we attempt to weight research findings on the basis of multiple evaluative criteria. Yet an inventory that treats a significant body of knowledge without attempting some form of evaluation or without attempting to explain inevitable contradictions in findings paints a unidimensional portrait. To analyze fully and accurately the state-of-inquiry in a given area, an inventory should systematically describe the production (research) process that underlies research findings, particularly when the findings are contradictory. Essentially, this form of evaluation, which Naroll terms "data quality control," follows the spirit and philosophy of content analysis, historical source criticism, and industrial

---

[47]Ibid., p. 66. The cross-tabulation is suggested by Zetterberg; we have assigned the values appearing in the cells.

[48]Ibid.

production control.[49] The general objective of processes such as these is to test regularly "the hypothesis that something is seriously wrong with production methods."[50]

By coupling data quality control with traditional inventory techniques, a broader perspective for understanding research contradictions is established. Some inventories avoid contradictions by reporting only those relationships for which there is substantial agreement in the literature. Other analyses include, but do not explain, contradictions. We suggest the value—particularly in relatively underdeveloped areas of inquiry—of including the contradictions while also noting whether they parallel differences in research approaches and settings. This type of evaluation will not always explain research contradictions but it is a logical first step that should serve both to pinpoint differences that are of method rather than substance and to control for research conditions while reaching an understanding of substantive relationships. Hopefully, the potential contribution of data quality control in accurately describing the stage of development in an area of inquiry will become apparent in our application of that technique described in the following chapters.

## Adapting Principles of the Evaluative Inventory to a Research Case: The Format We Followed

As we stated at the outset, we are interested in two interrelated problems. The first—our substantive concern—centers on attempts to understand increased voter opposition to school financial issues. Our second concern is highlighted by the first. When we looked to the relevant research literature for answers to our substantive questions we found many studies that asked overlapping questions and often produced greatly divergent and conflicting answers. We found a situation accurately described by earlier observers of the same literature:

Samples are generally small, and duplication of effort abounds, with little attempt at integration of results. Although some significant relationships have been found in each study, the differing methods used make it difficult to generalize from these diverse studies. Further there is a lack of consensus on the conclusions that have been reached.[51]

---

[49] The best statement of the need for data quality control is contained in Raoul Naroll, *Data Quality Control—A New Research Technique: Prolegomena to a Cross-Cultural Study of Culture Stress* (New York: The Free Press of Glencoe, 1962). The quality control techniques of content analysis are described by Ole R. Holsti, "Content Analysis," in Gardner Lindzey and Elliot Aronson (eds.), *The Handbook of Social Psychology* 2nd ed. (Cambridge, Massachusetts: Addison-Wesley, 1968), pp. 596-692.

[50] Naroll, op. cit., p. 10.

[51] Beal, et al., op. cit., p. 8.

Thus, before we could solve the first problem, we had to determine some method of using this bountiful but divergent literature.

The preceding pages present arguments for giving increased attention to codification and consolidation of social science research efforts. We think these arguments are relevant for most research areas, particularly for voting in school financial elections. Consequently, we have attempted to codify the findings from a youthful but growing body of literature, representing several academic disciplines and approaches, to create testable empirical generalizations. If some of these broader propositions can be linked with each other and with similar propositions from the general voting behavior literature, then some middle-range theory may evolve.

We do not expect, however, dramatic theoretical breakthroughs. Rather, our effort is based on the assumption that we, and social scientists generally, should spend some time *thinking about the results* of research. Merton contends that the difference between twentieth-century physics and twentieth-century sociology (and by extension, between the "hard" and social sciences) is "billions of man-hours of sustained, disciplined, and cumulative research. Perhaps sociology is not yet ready for its Einstein because it has not found its Kepler."[52] This inventory is undertaken as a halting first step. We are in complete accord with the objective stated by Gurr at the outset of his inventory:

The concepts, hypotheses and models of courses and processes developed in the following chapters are not intended as ends in themselves. Intellectually pleasing filters through which to view and categorize the phenomena of this disorderly world are not knowledge. Systematic knowledge requires us to propose and test and reformulate and retest statements about how and why things happen.... This analysis may demonstrate that too little is known about violence men do one another and that it is known too weakly and imprecisely. It is *designed to facilitate the processes by which that knowledge can be increased.*[53]

Our purposes are to improve the ability to generalize about the determinants of school financial election outcomes and to suggest a vehicle for use in other areas of inquiry. Our relative success or failure will become apparent in the following chapters that report the results of our work. Before beginning that report, we will briefly stipulate some conventions we used in compiling and reporting this inventory.

As we noted earlier (Figure 2-2), the term "proposition" has several meanings. We use the standard meanings of the terms "findings" and "hypotheses" when referring to stated relationships derived from individual research reports. We reserve the use of the term "proposition" for those empirical generalizations in which we have greater confidence than the normal finding or

---

[52] Merton, op. cit., p. 7.

[53] Gurr, op. cit., p. 15.

hypothesis because of corroboration by evidence from more than one outcropping or because of extreme rigor or other factors that markedly increase the inferential capabilities of the generalization.

Following Milbrath's format, we distinguish propositions by levels of confidence. Italicized propositions have been corroborated but warrant less confidence than capitalized propositions. Our format for stating the propositions varies slightly depending on whether the evidence for the propositions is supplied primarily by continuous variables or discrete variables. The individual elements that make up our propositions are included in the same order as illustrated in Figure 2-4.

As is apparent from the examples in the figure, our propositions follow the natural language of the literature and, in most cases, simply relate two variables (independent and dependent) to each other. Of course, problems in the social sciences, including problems associated with success or failure of school financial elections, are complex and consequently require multivariate solutions. Bivariate propositions are presented here on the assumption they are useful "as intermediary steps in theory construction even if they do not tell the whole story. Once formulated they lend themselves to amendments."[54]

Finally, since most of the findings from the surveyed literature are tentative and are derived from statistical techniques based on probability theory, we always intend to state propositions of the stochastic type (if X then *probably* Y). The phrase "likely" will appear frequently, but even when it does not, we are referring to probable relationships.

We stress the use of natural language to avoid, as described earlier, the potentially risky evaluation practice that can lead to rejection or devaluation of important and valid findings. Since different researchers subscribe to various tests of significance and levels of confidence, we accept as significant those findings that are so labeled by individual researchers.

We feel that use of the natural language is also necessary to understand the diversity of meanings that accompany differing operational procedures. Operational definitions play extremely important roles in any theory building effort. In the social sciences we are faced with a multitude of concepts that have been operationalized in many different ways. An example is the concept of alienation. At the same time we have some concepts—for example, intelligence—that are well defined operationally "but so poorly defined conceptually that practically no logical derivation seems possible."[55] We will clearly specify the operational procedures surrounding any variable in this inventory when that variable is stated in the form of a proposition.

Finally, when evidence concerning a relationship is conflicting in several studies, we systematically describe the methodological roots of the evidence in

---

[54] Zetterberg, op. cit., p. 12.

[55] Lewin, op. cit., p. 23.

## I. CONTINUOUS VARIABLES

| Operator | Qualifier | Unit for Analysis | Independent Variable | Operator | Unit for Analysis | Dependent Variable |
|---|---|---|---|---|---|---|
| The greater | a (an) | individual's voter's community's, etc. | X (e.g., education) | the more likely the greater etc. | SAME | Y (e.g., Yes vote) |
| The lesser | a (an) | | | | | |

## II. DISCRETE VARIABLES

| Unit for Analysis | Qualifier | Independent Variable | Operator | Dependent Variable | Operator | Unit for Analysis | Qualifier |
|---|---|---|---|---|---|---|---|
| Individuals | with less than eighth grade | education | are less likely to | vote | than | individuals | with more than eighth grade |

**Figure 2-4.** Sample Format for Statement of Propositions

keeping with our earlier comments on evaluation. We think that the elements of evaluation we describe are important components of the research setting and approach and, as such, might measurably affect the direction of the research findings. At a minimum, we believe that data from the evaluation will assist the reader in making his own judgment, regardless of his ability to resolve specific conflicts in evidence.

# 3

## Voters and Nonvoters: Who and Why

Influenced by the works of such men as John Locke and Thomas Jefferson, the majority of traditional American political philosophers view maximum citizen participation in the governmental decision-making process as a necessary prerequisite to the development of a model democracy.[1] According to these philosophers, the act of voting is inherent in the concept of "civic duty" and therefore a moral issue.[2] It is for this reason that Americans, beginning in their early school years and continuing throughout their lives, are constantly reminded of both their civic duty and their practical role in a representative democracy. In addition to being a fundamental form of political participation,[3]

---

[1] Most traditional introductory texts in American government provide this interpretation in the early pages. These narratives commonly begin by noting that the word democracy is derived from the Greek "demo" (people) and "kratos" (authority), which translates to government by the people, the many, as opposed to government by the few, the elite. Such texts typically move quickly from this ideal to a pluralistic description (model) of American society. See, for example, James MacGregor Burns and Jack Walter Peltason, *Government by the People: The Dynamics of American National, State, and Local Government* (Englewood Cliffs, New Jersey: Prentice-Hall, Inc., 1957), pp. 8-12; Claudius O. Johnson et al., *American National Government* (New York: Thomas Y. Crowell Co., 1960), pp. 4-9; and Carl Brent Swisher, *The Theory and Practice of American National Government* (New York: Houghton Mifflin Company, 1951), pp. 76-80.

Of course the degree of pluralism in American society is open to debate. Among the works that view American society as governed by the few (elite) see: C. Wright Mills, *The Power Elite* (London: Oxford University Press, 1956); Peter Bachrach, *The Theory of Democratic Elitism* (Boston: Little, Brown, and Co., 1967); E.E. Schattschneider, *The Semisovereign People: A Realist's View of Democracy in America* (New York: Holt, Rinehart and Winston, 1960); and Thomas R. Dye and L. Harmon Zeigler, *The Irony of Democracy: An Uncommon Introduction to American Politics* (Belmont, California: Wadsworth Publishing Co., 1970).

[2] Typical among the "civic course" type treatments of voting in a democracy is the one provided by Swisher, op. cit., pp. 81-84, who describes the following five "Responsibilities of Citizenship" in a democracy: (1) participation in elections, (2) public service, (3) paying taxes, (4) law observance, and (5) military service. A penetrating discussion of the varying points of view surrounding the concept of "civic duty" is provided by Robert E. Lane in *Political Life: Why and How People Get Involved in Politics* (New York: The Free Press, 1959), pp. 348-351. Lane discusses the meaning of the "civic duty" attitude on pp. 157-168.

[3] For a thorough discussion of conceptual problems raised by political participation and for a rank-order scheme for classifying political participation activities in a democracy, see Lester W. Milbrath, *Political Participation: How and Why Do People Get Involved in Politics?* (Chicago: Rand McNally & Co., 1965), Ch. 1.

the vote also appears to serve important symbolic and personal benefit functions.[4]

## Participation in National and Local Elections

Despite all the emphasis on the virtues of voting, however, more than one-third of the nation's eligible voters do not vote in the elections for president—elections of highest interest and salience for most voters.[5] Many may choose not to participate because they are unable to envision the connection between their single ballot and meaningful change or improvement in areas of life that are personally important. In other words, political life in general may lack salience for nonvoters, especially at the national level.[6]

Voters themselves, even though they are interested and concerned in the issues surrounding the campaign, are sometimes unable to differentiate meaningfully between two partisan candidates, much less feel confident that their participation as voters will bring about desired political outcomes. Indeed, even political analysts have difficulty tracing the linkage between a voter's partisan choice and policy outcomes in many areas.[7]

---

[4] The most complete treatment of the need reduction function of political participation activities is provided by Lane, op. cit., pp. 101-132.

[5] Angus Campbell et al., *The American Voter,* an abridgment (New York: John Wiley & Sons, 1964), p. 49. These authors report that 62.7 percent and 60.4 percent of the nation's eligible voters cast ballots for president in the general elections of 1952 and 1956 respectively. It is important to be aware of the gross nature of such estimates, which represent the proportion of people estimated by the Census Bureau to be civilians of voting age on November 1 of the year in question. It is not uncommon to find turnout estimates based on lineal interpolation of census data by age group between ten-year census intervals. Obviously, such formulations do not account for the number that would be excluded from the eligible voter population on the basis of such criteria as citizenship, length of residence, illiteracy, etc. Such estimates do tell us that between 35 and 40 million eligible citizens declined to vote in the elections in question, which provides some idea of the scope of nonvoting in American society.

[6] For most Americans, an array of values and concerns supersede those issues and interests generally classified as "political." See Samuel A. Stouffer, *Communism, Conformity, and Civil Liberties* (Garden City, New York: Doubleday, 1955); and Herbert McClosky, "Consensus and Ideology in American Politics," *American Political Science Review,* 58 (June 1964): 361-82. Reasonably, those who are less interested or less involved in political life have been found less likely to vote in partisan contests by a number of researchers, as documented in Milbrath, op. cit., p. 51.

[7] Charles A. Reich provides a powerful explication of this basic flaw in the democratic model as applied to the United States:

> As machinery for translating popular will into political effect, the American system functions impossibly badly. We can hardly say that our political process makes it possible for voters to enforce their will on such subjects as pollution, supersonic planes, mass transportation, the arms race, or the Viet Nam war. On the contrary, if there are any popularly held views, it is impossible for them to be expressed politically; this was demonstrated for all to see in the 1968 presidential campaign, where both candidates

Reasonable doubt thus may be cast on the proposition that citizen participation in partisan elections equals citizen decision-making. Although the pure democratic model provides logical justification for citizens to participate in decision-making by choosing their representatives, experience shows that few citizens act on the basis of the model, at least as it applies to national elections. But what about participation in nonpartisan, local elections, particularly those that ask for voter approval of a variety of financial proposals? These elections seem to adhere more closely to the pure democratic model. The voter, not his representative, is directly involved in decision-making that will have a measurable impact on such important aspects of his life as his child's education, his police and fire protection, and his waste disposal.

Yet turnout for these local referenda is normally substantially less than turnout for national elections.[8] Even in the only American electoral situation that offers the citizen a direct role in making political decisions—"that lionized example of democracy, the New England town meeting"—citizen participation has been found to be substantially short of potential.[9]

The irony of this pattern is apparent. While many citizens choose not to participate in electoral activity of any kind, an even greater number choose not to vote in elections that offer direct access to the community decision-making process.[10]

---

supported the Viet Nam war. (*The Greening of America* [New York: Bantam Books, 1971], pp. 109-110.)

Until recently there was an almost total lack of systematic research attempting to specify the policy-making results of voting in partisan elections. Satisfactory resolution of the pluralist/elitist debate would seem to require greater evidence on this question. An excellent beginning is made by Gerald M. Pomper, *Elections in America: Control and Influence in Democratic Politics* (New York: Dodd, Mead, & Co., 1968). Of course, linking policy outcomes to voting behavior requires explicit treatment of cause and effect. Examples of the analytical perplexities of such an endeavor may be found in Pomper and in William R. Keech, *The Impact of Negro Voting: The Role of the Vote in the Quest for Equality* (Chicago: Rand McNally & Company, 1968). For an important recent study that has an excellent review of the literature, see Benjamin I. Page and Richard A. Brody, "Policy Voting and the Electoral Process: The Vietnam War Issue," *American Political Science Review* 66 (September 1972): 979-95.

[8]Alvin Boskoff and Harmon Zeigler have noted correctly that for these elections "documentation of the prevalence of low turnout can be pursued almost ad nauseam," *Voting Patterns in a Local Election* (Philadelphia: J.D. Lippincott Co., 1964), p. 17. The authors cite several corroborative studies at this point. See also Milbrath, op. cit., p. 106; Edward C. Banfield and James Q. Wilson, *City Politics* (New York: Vintage Books, 1963), p. 225; and for the most frequently cited evidence of low turnout for school financial elections throughout the nation, see Richard F. Carter and William Savard, *Influence of Voter Turnout on School Bond and Tax Elections. Cooperative Research Monograph*, No. 5 (Washington, D.C.: Government Printing Office, 1961).

[9]Charles R. Adrian, *Governing Urban America*, 2nd Edition (New York: McGraw-Hill, 1961), p. 91. The author notes that a 15.7 percent participation rate in a New England town is the finding from an article reported in Roscoe C. Martin, *Grass Roots* (University of Alabama Press, 1957), pp. 60-61.

[10]References to the voter's role as decision-maker in referenda situations are commonplace

Given this fact, the democtatic theorist faces an important question: To what extent is the small population of voters representative of the larger population to whom the voting decision will apply? Walter Lippmann has argued that voters in general elections are not, and never can be, synonymous with the people.[11] He observes that the "mass of voters" frequently does not act in the "public interest" and that "... the enfranchised masses have not, suprisingly enough, been those who have most staunchly defended the institutions of freedom."[12] Since the "public interest" is a nebulous concept, frequently defying agreement or definition, and since it is impossible to compare the voter's decision with the potential decision of some other group or individual,[13] the general debate regarding the ability of voters to exercise "the people's will" is likely to continue for some time.

**Approaches to the Study of Voter Participation**

Several researchers have been able to assess the approximate "representativeness" of voters by comparing them with the general population in terms of a number of characteristics. Others have built models of the voter or the nonvoter based on probability theory.[14] Such comparisons will not, of course, provide

---

in the texts describing "direct" or "grassroots" democracy. Such statements should of course be qualified by noting that the aggregate vote decision in referenda situations represents only the final phase of a decision-making process. The voter can only respond yes or no to a specific proposal that represents the outcome of a more comprehensive decision-making process on the part of an elite (in the case of schools, board members look at alternatives that have been already shaped by staff members, etc.). Robert E. Agger and Marshall N. Goldstein, in *Educational Innovations in the Community, Cooperative Research Project No. 1759* (Eugene: University of Oregon, 1965), p. 276, argue that the superficial nature of the vote in such situations accounts for low participation: "Plebiscites, that is, simple yes-no elections, in fascist Germany and Italy should have made clear by now the hollowness of elections in which the voter has no opportunity to participate in framing the alternatives. Of what value is the right to vote for or against a school budget when the board can within the month place a rejected budget before the voters, almost without change in its form."

[11] Walter Lippmann, *The Public Philosophy* (New York: Mentor Book, 1955), pp. 32-36.

[12] Ibid., p. 38.

[13] It is always interesting to speculate; try, for instance to imagine the voters vs. the FCC and/or the communication industry on matters of "public interest" in broadcasting.

[14] Public opinion polling organizations are, of course, concerned with sorting out voters and nonvoters to predict election outcomes most accurately. The Gallup organization has devised a model based on a variety of attitudinal and behavioral indices, which accomplishes this purpose quite well for national elections. "In eight elections from 1956 to 1970, this index estimated the turnout ratio with a maximum error of 1.5 points." Irving Crespi, "What Kinds of Attitude Measures Are Predictive of Behavior?" *The Public Opinion Quarterly*, 35 (Fall, 1971): 329. See also Harold Mendelsohn and Irving Crespi, *Polls, Television, and the New Politics* (Scranton: Chandler Publishing Co., 1970), p. 76.

answers to the hard questions raised by political philosophers, but they serve to provide an empirical basis for partial theories of interest representation, democratic decision-making, etc.

Table 3-1 lists major correlates of high and low voter turnout as reported in two benchmark studies of voting in partisan contests, and as confirmed in a number of separate studies.[15] The central message of the table for our purposes is that voters differ from nonvoters along a number of dimensions other than their voting habits. Simply stated, most of the evidence from the general voting behavior literature indicates that the population of voters at partisan contests differs significantly from the potentially eligible population in terms of the characteristics listed in Table 3-1.[16]

*Academic Approaches*

It is also important to note from Table 3-1 the different types of characteristics listed. One group, traditionally referred to as "socioeconomic" status (SES) characteristics, can be used to measure an individual's or group's relative position (status) in terms of such variables as income, occupation, and education, which are highly valued by the society. Another group, referred to as "demographic" characteristics, allows us to differentiate between populations on dimensions less directly translatable to status rankings (e.g., sex, race, religion, age). Finally, comparisons can be made on psychological or attitudinal characteristics.

An assessment of voter participation on the basis of socioeconomic characteristics is generally guided by a sociological model for inquiry. Similarly, psychological models make use of attitudinal data. Sole reliance on any one approach is clearly cause for concern. Key and Munger's criticism of the sociological approach that is study of voting behavior applies equally to any approach that is limited to a single set of variables: "In research the answers one gets depend in part on the kinds of questions he asks. If one inquires about social characteristics and political preference, he finds out about social characteristics and political preference."[17]

---

[15] Appropriate citations are provided in Milbrath, op. cit., and Lane, op. cit.

[16] For a systematic examination of the socio-demographic differences among an area's "potential," "qualified" (registered), and actual voters in 1964, see Clifton McCleskey and Dan Nimmo, "Differences between Potential, Registered and Actual Voters: The Houston Metropolitan Area in 1964," *Social Science Quarterly,* 40 (June 1968):103-114. These authors found that, according to several important characteristics, differences between the potential and qualified electorates are greater than differences between the potential and actual electorates. As the authors note, a similar finding was reported in a study of aggregate registration and turnout data for 104 of the nation's largest cities in 1960; see Stanley Keller, Richard E. Ayres, and William G. Bowen, "Registration and Voting: Putting First Things First," *American Political Science Review* 61 (June 1967):359-79.

[17] V. O. Key, Jr., and Frank Munger, "Social Determinism and Electoral Decision: The Case

*Theoretical Approaches*

At the same time, any phenomenon that is subject to cross-disciplinary study, as is voting behavior, is not likely to be fully understood merely by examining a single list of correlates such as those presented in Table 3-1. What is needed is a

**Table 3-1**
**Social/Psychological Characteristics Frequently Correlated with Voter Turnout†**

| *"Voter"*<br>*Higher Turnout* | *"Nonvoter"*<br>*Lower Turnout* |
|---|---|
| high income | low income |
| high education | low education |
| whites | blacks |
| men | women |
| middle-aged people (35-55) | young people (under 35) |
| older people (over 55) | |
| old residents in community | newcomers in community |
| crisis situations | normal situations |
| married people | single people |
| members of organizations | isolated individuals |
| white-collar employees | blue-collar employees |
| (261-63) middle aged (34-64) | young (under 34) |
| | old (over 64) |
| (53) strong partisan preference | weak partisan preference |
| (56) high interest in campaign* | low interest in campaign* |
| (57) high concern about election outcome* | low concern about election outcome* |
| (58) high sense of political efficacy** | low sense of political efficacy** |
| (59) high sense of citizen duty** | low sense of citizen duty** |
| (59) high "political involvement"*** | low "political involvement"*** |
| (252) high education | low education |
| (244) former urban residents | former rural residents—migrated to city |
| (213) urban residents | rural residents |

*short-term attitudes reflecting a person's orientation to a specific campaign

**long-term attitudes transcending a single election

***both short-term and long-term attitudes

†The relationships listed in the top half of this table are adapted from Seymour Martin Lipset, *Political Man* (Garden City, New York: Anchor Books, 1963), p. 189. The second half of the table was constructed from findings reported in Angus Campbell et al., *The American Voter*. Abridged edition (New York: John Wiley and Sons, 1964), page numbers in parentheses.

conceptual referent, a theory, that most efficiently organizes and explains the relationships between the characteristics and voter turnout, regardless of the academic discipline from which the study derives. A number of partial theories for explaining voter participation in general elections should at least be kept in mind while theorizing in the more specific area of school financial elections. Two contradictory theories frequently used in general voting studies appear particularly relevant to our inquiry concerning voting in school financial elections.

One orientation stresses the "economic rationality" of voters.[18] According to this theory, citizens vote when the anticipated benefit of voting exceeds the cost. Reflecting an optimistic view of the nature of man, this orientation is indebted to the academic discipline of economics.

This point of view provides a simple explanation for voting: the citizen casts his ballot when the benefit he perceives as accruing from the voting act exceeds the potential cost of the voting act. According to Anthony Downs, the principal architect of the rational voter model, the chief cost of voting is time—time to register, time to seek out information, time to go to the polls, time to deliberate, and time to mark to ballot.[19] Benefits from voting in any given election are seen as a composite of the value of voting in that election and the general value of voting per se. That is, a citizen's perception of the return he would receive from voting is based on (1) his degree of interest in a specific election, and the impact he believes his vote will have in deciding the outcome; and (2) the extent to which he views his participation as payment in return for long-range values associated with living in a participatory democracy.[20] When these short- and long-term benefits appear to outweigh the costs of voting, the individual will vote.

It is important to note the use of the terms "views" and "believes" and "values," for in the final analysis the cost/benefit equation is solved subjectively

---

of Indiana," in Eugene Burdick and Arthur Brodbeck (eds.), *American Voting Behavior* (Glencoe, Illinois: The Free Press, 1959), pp. 281-99.

[18]For the most explicit statement of a model based on the assumption that voters and political parties act rationally, in their own economic self-interest, see Anthony Downs, *An Economic Theory of Democracy* (New York: Harper and Row, 1957). An excellent review of the literature concerned with rationality and voting may be found in William H. Riker, "Voting and the Summation of Preferences: An Interpretative Bibliographical Review of Selected Developments during the Last Decade," *American Political Science Review*, 55 (December 1961):900-11. For application of economic theory to the specific study of voting behavior in local bond issue situations, see Rene L. Frey and Leopold Kohn, "An Economic Interpretation of Voting Behavior on Public Finance Issues," *Kyklos* 23 (Fasc. 4, 1970):792-804; and James Q. Wilson and Edward C. Banfield, "Voting Behavior on Municipal Public Expenditures: A Study in Rationality and Self-Interest," in Julius Margolis (ed.), *The Public Economy of Urban Communities* (Washington, D.C.: Resources for the Future, Inc., 1965), pp. 74-91.

[19]Downs, op. cit., p. 265.

[20]Ibid., p. 270.

by each individual. Nevertheless, assuming the voter is rational in assessing these costs and benefits, his interest in a specific election and his perception of the value of voting in that election would vary according to certain circumstances. Among the conditions that logically appear likely to stimulate citizen interest in school financial elections are property ownership and parental status. As we see in Table 3-2, any hypothetical population of citizens may be categorized according to these two variables.

Citizens that could be classified in cells 1, 2, and 3 would rationally be directly concerned with a school financial proposal because of anticipated personal benefits and costs that would result from its passage or failure. Property owners are required to pay local property taxes, the amounts of which are frequently affected by the outcome of school financial issues. Similarly, parents of school age children are more directly affected by the outcome of the financial issues in question than their counterparts.

Table 3-2

**A Typology of Potential Voters According to Two Factors That May Affect Citizen Interest in the Outcome of School Financial Elections**

|  | *Property Owner* | *Nonproperty Owner* |
|---|---|---|
| Parent of School Age Children | 1<br>High Interest | 2<br>Normal Interest |
| Nonparent of School Age Children | 3<br>Normal Interest | 4<br>Disinterest |

It should be remembered however, that these conditions, though important, are only two of many that can affect voter interest in school financial elections. Moreover, interest in an election is only one component of an individual's perceived "vote value." For example, a potential voter may care very much about the outcome of an election but feel that his vote will make no difference in that outcome, and consequently abstain.

At first glance this model appears quite simple. Anthony Downs himself describes the model in very simple terms in the introduction to his chapter on "The Causes and Effects of Rational Abstention": "... we assume that every rational man decides whether to vote just as he makes all other decisions: if the returns outweigh the costs, he votes; if not, he abstains."[21] But as we saw in the preceding discussion drawn largely from Downs, the multiplicity of factors involved in reaching a net cost/benefit determination adds complexity to the

---
[21] Ibid., p. 260.

model. The model also contains obvious implications for explaining the direction of the vote that will be explored later. For now it is sufficient to understand that this model posits a *conscious calculation* as the basis for voter participation in elections.

Another theoretical orientation, labeled "psychological," has accompanied the growth of studies of attitudinal correlates of voter bahavior. Primarily derived from the work of researchers at the University of Michigan's Survey Research Center (SRC), this theory advances a more pessimistic view of the nature of man, or at least of his rationality.[22] According to this model, the act of voting or not voting is almost habitual and has little to do with a careful analysis of the situation. Proponents of this theory stress the long-range nature of the attitudinal determinants of voting behavior:

... our inquiry into the determinants of voting turnout is less a search for psychological forces that determine a decision made anew in each campaign than it is a search for the attitude correlates of voting and nonvoting from which they are presently supported . . . some of the dimensions of attitude that are most helpful in accounting for turnout appear to have the character of orientations to politics much more than they do the character of forces acting on a present decision.[23]

Because of their fresh approach and methodological innovation and rigor, the SRC researchers now occupy a position of stature in the voting research field. However, their emphasis on the deterministic nature of the voting act has not been accepted uncritically. V.O. Key argues that because of their lack of attention to the situational element of voting, the SRC researchers convey the impression "that voting behavior can be studied more or less in complete isolation from the events of the campaign."[24] Nevertheless, the attitudinal correlates found by the SRC (listed in Table 3-1) have been repeatedly confirmed by other studies, even while applying rigorous controls.[25]

The psychological model has been applied to nonpartisan local referendum situations in an attempt to explain both turnout and direction of the vote.

---

[22] SRC's researchers describe a partial theory in a number of published sources, perhaps most thoroughly in Campbell et al., op. cit., and Angus Campbell et al., *Elections and the Political Order* (New York: John Wiley & Sons, Inc., 1966). For an excellent critical review of the SRC approach and related literature, see Peter B. Natchez, "Images of Voting: The Social Psychologists" *Public Policy* 18 (Summer 1970):553-88.

[23] Campbell et al., *The American Voter*, p. 52.

[24] In a letter from Key to Campbell, April 8, 1952, as cited in Natchez, op. cit., p. 566.

[25] For example, see Donald Stokes, "Popular Evaluations of Government: An Empirical Assessment," in Harlen Cleveland and Harold Lasswell (eds.), *Ethics and Bigness* (New York: Harper and Row, 1962), pp. 61-72. Stokes finds that frequency of electoral participation in presidential elections is strongly related to the voter's general orientation to government, *while controlling for education.*

Theorists of this persuasion draw heavily on research findings that indicate the relative unimportance of most voters' issue orientations when compared to their party or candidate orientations. From this point of view, most potential voters are apathetic or apolitical. Far from acting on rational, cost/benefit criteria, most citizens, particularly those of lower SES, "require the colorful personality of a political leader to draw them into the political fray."[26] Nonvoters, who constitute the majority of potential voters in most local referenda situations, are characterized by the following orientation:

> Nonvoters (and non-participants generally) are likely to be of lower education, lower income and lower occupational status than voters. These groups are carriers of economic (welfare state) liberalism, but also of intolerance, ignorance of political issues and background information, exenophobia, unwillingness to sacrifice for long-range goals, and authoritarianism.[27]

On the other hand, the minority of citizens who frequently turn out for local nonpartisan elections are viewed as follows:

> Only citizens who are intensely committed to the community are likely to vote in local elections. These are the interested, committed, high status citizens of the "normal" electorate. They feel they have a stake in community decision-making and therefore participate frequently in local affairs. Also, their better education makes it possible for them to comprehend elections that are absent of parties and candidates.[28]

Of course, these characterizations of the voter and the nonvoter are meant to apply to "normal" (i.e., low turnout) local nonpartisan elections. The theory holds that the "voter" segment can be abnormally expanded by a heated or highly emotional campaign that serves to stimulate participation by citizens who would not otherwise vote. However, this increment of new voters, when compared with the normal voting pool, is seen as less concerned about community affairs and more likely to exhibit attitudes of cynicism and alienation toward the local governmental/political systems.[29]

These two theories of voting behavior in part account for the divergent interpretations and explanations of participation patterns in school financial elections. According to the psychological model, voters and nonvoters can be

---

[26]Lane, op. cit., p. 270.

[27]Ibid., p. 341.

[28]Dye and Zeigler, op. cit., p. 167.

[29]Evidence surrounding the effect of "alienation" on voting behavior is murky, largely because of divergent operationalization and definition of the concept. For an attempt to sort out the components of the concept and to assess their meaning for turnout and direction of the vote, see Joel D. Aberbach, "Alienation and Political Behavior," *American Political Science Review* 63 (March 1969): 86-99.

distinguished by long-term attitudinal configurations. The model predicts that in normal local election situations, participants will be those citizens with a strongly held set of beliefs and values that are generally summarized as feelings of "community attachment," "public regardingness," "civic pride," etc. This relatively small group of citizens comprises the participant group in most local elections, the exceptions being those elections accompanied by extreme community controversy. In these unusual situations, voter participation increases in proportion to the increasing emotionalism of the controversy as more citizens are "drawn into the fray."

In contrast, the rational or economic model suggests that electoral participation is largely the result of a conscious determination by each citizen of his economic interest in the outcome of the election.

Both theories owe their development to studies of voting in partisan elections. The theories have received some implicit but little explicit attention in investigations of voting in local nonpartisan issues. Yet most investigations of voting in school and other local financial referenda have proceeded with an apparent lack of concern about the need to test existing partial theory.

We have introduced these theories in an attempt to provide a framework for understanding some of the relationships described in the research findings reported to date. If in the process one theory is confirmed at the expense of the other, or if we are able to merge the theories, well and good. We advocate neither approach. Given the embryonic nature of inquiry in this field, we would not be surprised to find that further evidence is required before any comprehensive theoretical statement can be issued.


**Research Findings**

Those who describe voter behavior as a rational response to costs and benefits frequently begin by stressing the simplicity of their model. Simplicity is an important consideration. Unfortunately, however, simple theories are seldom adequate, except, of course, as explanations of simple problems. Still, they are efficient and do provide a basis for the development of comprehensive theory. Also, the social scientist who uses a simple model avoids criticism that his main concern is for technique and approach rather than for substance.

With these considerations in mind, it seems reasonable to begin our review of research findings with the typology of voter characteristics in Table 3-2. A citizen's parental and property-owner statuses are simple and reasonably objective indicators of interest in school election outcomes. Interest serves as a major component of the vote benefit calculus. Consequently, given assumptions of voter rationality, we would expect these two indicators of election interest to correlate highly with participation in school financial elections.

*Parents*

Two studies (Parnell 1964 and Smith 1968) provide convincing evidence in support of the proposition that *potential voters who have children in school are more likely to vote in school financial elections than those who do not.* Both researchers point to the vote benefit theory as the explanation for this finding. Others have suggested that higher turnout rates among parents may be a consequence of their higher level of information about the schools, brought about by their children's acting as an information channel between school and home. Information in this form may play an important role in influencing the citizen's decision to vote.

*Citizens Interested in Schools*

Some indirect evidence does suggest a linkage between information concerning school affairs and voter turnout. Carter and Ruggels (1966, volume 4) found that the greater the number of citizens' questions answered during a campaign, the greater the voter turnout for a school financial election.

In addition, Parnell (1964) found that potential voters who frequently discuss school matters with others are more likely to vote in school budget elections than those who do not engage in such discussions. In light of the probable correlation between issue familiarity and informal communication, this finding buttresses the explanation that citizens who are more informed about and interested in the schools are most likely to vote in school elections.

Thus indirect evidence exists (Parnell, 1964; Carter and Ruggels, 1966) to support the proposition, established by studies of voting in other election situations, that CITIZENS WHO EXPRESS INTEREST IN SCHOOL AFFAIRS ARE MORE LIKELY TO VOTE IN SCHOOL FINANCIAL ELECTIONS THAN THOSE WHO DO NOT EXPRESS INTEREST.[30]

Despite the implication of these findings we remain uncertain of the impact on voter turnout for school elections of attempts to increase citizens' information levels. We find no evidence to suggest that voter turnout is appreciably increased by the use of various campaign techniques. In fact, two investigations have found no statistically significant relationship between the use of a number of campaign techniques and voter turnout in school bond elections (Beal, Hartman, and Lagomarcino, 1966; Turner, 1968). Of course this lack of

---

[30]This proposition is suggested by the studies of voting in presidential elections conducted by Michigan's Survey Research Center. See Campbell et al., *The American Voter,* pp. 56-57. A similarly strong relationship between interest and turnout is reported in the following recent study of voter participation in a municipal election: Howard D. Hamilton, "The Municipal Voter: Voting and Nonvoting in City Elections," *The American Political Science Review* 65 (December 1971):1137.

evidence may be largely a result of the difficulty of controlling for other influences, a problem inherent in the evaluation of the impact of campaign techniques.

*Interrelationships*

Figure 3-1 describes relationships that have been found among an individual's parental status, his interest in the schools, and his decision to participate in school financial elections. In this and similar illustrations throughout the text each separate line represents an association between two variables. The arrow points to the dependent variable. When linked from left to right, the lines suggest alternative causal explanations—in this case, for the apparent relationship among parental status, interest in the schools, and participation in school financial elections.

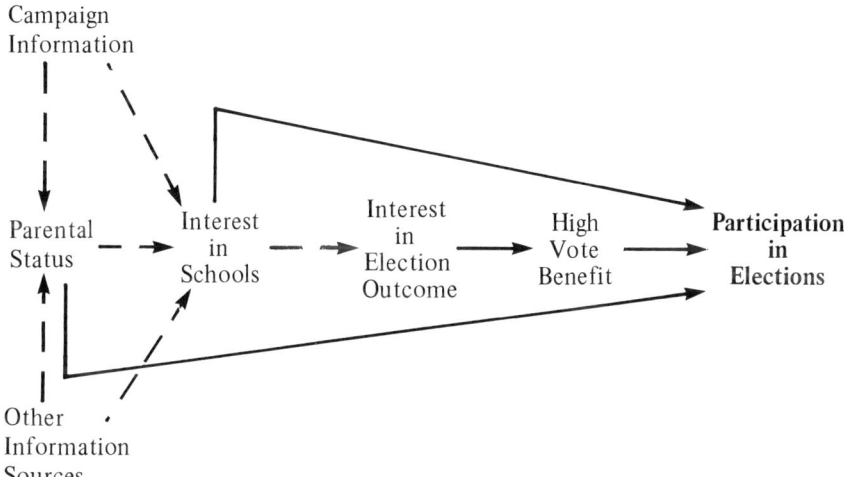

**Figure 3-1.** Alternative Explanatory Paths between Selected Information and Interest Variables and an Individual's Decision to Vote in a School Financial Election

The solid lines indicate relationships for which the evidence, in school financial election settings, is fairly strong and clear. Relationships suggested by the broken lines are either logical relationships that lack empirical verification or points of empirical conflict between two or more studies. The central message of the illustration is that we are fairly secure in asserting that (1) parents of school age children are more likely to vote in school financial elections than are nonparents, and (2) citizens who express interest in the schools are more likely to vote than are citizens who express no interest.

Of course these two findings are only starting points for inquiry. The remaining questions of importance for both the practitioner and the researcher are illustrated by the broken lines: What forces stimulate interest in the schools? How is a generalized interest in the schools related to interest in the outcome of a specific election? Does level of interest in the schools increase proportionately with amounts of information? These and many other similar questions require the attention of researchers simply to clarify this basic model, which helps to understand only why two types of citizens vote (parents and those interested in the schools). The model would have to be expanded to account for the participation of those citizens who cannot be so classified.

*Property Owners*

As we have suggested in Table 3-2, one segment of the potential voting population could be highly interested in the outcome of school financial elections without being particularly interested in the work of the schools. We refer here to local property owners. Regardless of their parental status, members of this group may generally feel that they bear the cost of school financial issues. The evidence does support the proposition that *potential voters who are purchasing their own homes are more likely to vote in school financial elections than renters* (Smith, 1968; Parnell, 1964).[31]

*Middle-Aged Citizens*

One other proposition justified by the evidence is directly relevant to the explanation for voter participation described to this point. The findings of two studies indicate that *middle-aged citizens are more likely to vote in school financial elections than either the very young or the very old* (Parnell, 1964; Carter and Ruggels, 1966).[32] This middle-age group is also the most likely to

---

[31] Homeowners have been found more likely than renters to vote, period; see Milbrath, op. cit., p. 133.

[32] As we see from Table 3-1, data from two major studies of voting in partisan settings—Campbell et al., op. cit., and Lipset, op. cit.—corroborate this finding. A similar curvilinear relationship is reported by Hamilton, op. cit., who notes an important change over time: data from one of the earliest systematic studies of voting suggested a *negative* relationship between age and turnout. See Charles E. Merriam and Harold F. Gosnell, *Nonvoting, Causes and Methods of Control* (Chicago: University of Chicago Press, 1924). For an analysis of all the SRC survey data that reaches a similar conclusion by relating turnout to "life-cycle" stages, see William Klecka, "Applying Political Generations to the

have school age children but might very well be faced with property tax obligations on a fixed income. These senior citizens are probably intensely interested in the election outcome and would be expected to participate if physically able.

Of course age may be a spurious variable. Given proper control for the effects of other variables (e.g., property ownership and parental status), the ability to predict voter participation from age might diminish greatly. However, the variable does serve to summarize important predictive dimensions. From a practical point of view, lack of other data may necessitate use of the age variable even though its predictability is a function of its correlation with other variables.

These findings provide the basis for a more comprehensive model as illustrated in Figure 3-2. Again, the solid lines indicate empirical relationships for which we have some confidence; the broken lines represent possible explanations for the empirical relationships. For example, it has been empirically verified that property owners are more likely to vote than nonproperty owners. Possible explanations for the relationship between property ownership and voting are provided by the broken lines: the property owner is likely to be concerned about school costs and, therefore, to have an interest in the election outcome and to perceive a high benefit from voting. Although the explanations suggested by the broken lines seem logical, it is important to remember that they lack empirical verification and represent questions in need of testing.

By examining the solid lines in Figure 3-2 we see that we can make the

---

Study of Political Behavior: A Cohort Analysis," *The Public Opinion Quarterly* 35 (Fall 1971): 358-73.

Operational definitions of age vary from one researcher to another depending on the researcher's collapsing of data. Until recently most social scientists appeared to have a penchant for ordinal or nominal scales. Although many variables of interest to the social scientist require such treatment, age is not one of them and is, in fact, normally coded as an integer at the beginning of the research process, making the variable perfectly amenable to interval scaling. Researchers' treatment of this variable provides a classic example of both the difficulties and the benefits inherent in attempting to merge research findings. The actual data from the two partisan studies noted in Table 3-1, and from the studies of school elections, are classified as follows:

| *Study* | *middle-aged* | *young/old* |
|---|---|---|
| Lipset | 35-55 | 21-34/56+ |
| Campbell et al. | 34-64 | 21-33/65+ |
| Parnell | 35-54 | 21-34/55+ |
| Carter and Ruggels | interval scale | |

Because of the way the data were classified, we are required to couch our proposition concerning age and voter participation in such relatively soft terminology as "middle-aged," "young," and "old." In other words, we lose some precision due to the researchers' divergent data analysis techniques. But in the case of this specific variable, we probably gain some explanatory power; unless they are of extreme magnitude, *curvilinear* relationships such as this one frequently are reported as "insignificant." At least the simpler scales and associated statistical techniques highlight important empirical differences, and in many cases may be amenable to additivity from study to study.

following four probability statements concerning voters and nonvoters in school financial elections:

| | | |
|---|---|---|
| 1. Parents | | Nonparents |
| 2. Property Owners | are more likely | Nonproperty Owners |
| 3. Middle-Aged | to vote than | Older, Younger |
| 4. Interested in Schools | | Not Interested in Schools |

Simply, any population of voters in a school financial election is likely to be disproportionately composed of citizens who are also parents, property owners, middle-aged, and interested in their schools. The explanation (broken lines) for the overrepresentation of these groups in the school voting pool may be that these citizens are most likely to anticipate a high return from the act of voting. This high valuation of the benefits of participation is seen, in turn, as a direct result of interest in the outcome of the specific election in question. Assuming

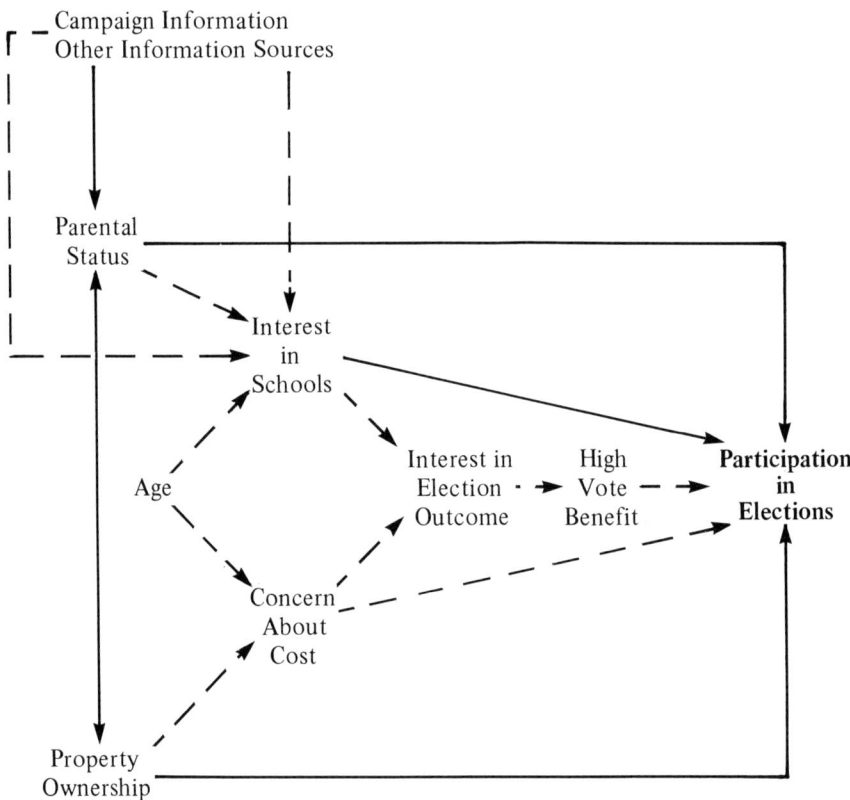

Figure 3-2. Alternative Explanatory Paths among Selected Variables Related to an Individual's Decision to Vote in a School Financial Election

voter rationality, such interest in election outcomes would appear related to high levels of concern about schools, taxes, or both. Property owners would appear more likely than nonproperty owners to be concerned about school taxes, parents of school age children would appear more likely than their counterparts to be interested in school affairs, and middle-aged citizens would be more likely than older or younger citizens to have school age children and property—hence the diagrammed relationships.

It should be emphasized that the researchers who have discovered the links represented by the solid lines do not, by any means, report perfect correlations. Some voters in school financial elections are not parents, property owners, middle-aged, or citizens particularly interested in activities of the schools. Moreover, a number of citizens who could properly be classified as members of one or more of these groups do not vote in school financial elections.[33]

To determine the scope and validity of the model presented in Figure 3-2 we must continue our discussion of research findings concerning who participates in school financial elections. The discovery of more generalizations for differentiating between the voter and the nonvoter will require more rigorous explanation and consequently a more complex model.

It is obvious that forces and conditions other than the ones discussed to this point contribute to participation in school financial elections. However, even if we had a complete list of variables strongly related to turnout for school financial elections we would not necessarily have improved our ability to *explain* participation. The dilemma is an old one—attempts to improve the explanatory power of a fairly simple model frequently result in consideration of a multitude of variables, a situation that contributes to both descriptive realism and theoretical confusion.

*Socioeconomic Status*

Findings concerning the relationship between socioeconomic status and voter participation provide an excellent context for discussion of these complexities. It is not surprising that a number of researchers have investigated the relationship between various indicators of socioeconomic status (SES) and voting.

---

[33] As the authors of the *American Voter,* op. cit., note, some "error" in predicting voter turnout can occur even when individuals rank very high or very low on all known dimensions for predicting their participation. Some of those citizens whom we would have every reason to consider highly motivated to vote, might not vote because of personal circumstances (flat tire on the way to the polls) or legal requirements. The authors found that deviance in the opposite direction (arrival at the polls of individuals who by all known criteria for prediction would normally stay home) was most frequently attributable to interpersonal influence. "Of the twelve voters in 1956 who had the least reason for going to the polls ... nine were women who appeared to respond to the wishes of husbands. ..."(p. 61).

One of the most frequently quoted passages in the recent literature of voting behavior is drawn from the now classic survey of voters in Erie County, Ohio, during the 1944 presidential election campaign: ". . . a person thinks, politically, as he is socially. Social characteristics determine political preference."[34] The frequent appearance of this passage is probably attributable to its "shock value." Certainly the emphasis on a class basis for voting behavior conflicts sharply with values drawn from democratic and individualistic philosophies. Since the study relied on data from a survey of one community taken during one election, the general applicability of its finding is debatable. Other studies, however, have substantiated the correlation between SES and political involvement. Evidence from studies of voting in partisan contests, for example, strongly suggests that higher-class persons are more likely to participate in politics than lower-class persons.[35]

Although many substantive and methodological questions [36] surrounding the role of SES in influencing voting behavior remain unanswered, a strong relationship between indicators of SES and participation in school financial elections has been reported in a number of studies. The following propositions emerge from the literature: THE GREATER A CITIZEN'S WEALTH, THE MORE LIKELY HE WILL VOTE IN A SCHOOL FINANCIAL ELECTION; and similarly, THE GREATER A GROUP'S WEALTH, THE GREATER THE AVERAGE TURNOUT OF THAT GROUP FOR SCHOOL FINANCIAL ELECTIONS (Parnell, 1964; Carter and Ruggels, 1966; Minar, 1966; Smith, 1968; Hatley, 1971).[37] The evidence also suggests that the *greater a citizen's educational attainment, the more likely he will vote in a school financial election* (Parnell, 1964; Carter and Chaffee, 1966).

---

[34] Paul F. Lazarsfeld, Bernard R. Berelson, and Hazel Gaudet, *The People's Choice,* second edition (New York: Columbia University Press, 1948), p. 27.

[35] Milbrath, *Political Participation: How and Why Do People Get Involved in Politics?,* p. 116.

[36] A classic work on empirical approaches to the study of social class is W. L. Warner, M. Meeker, and K. Eels, *Social Class in America: The Evaluation of Status* (New York: Harper Torchbooks, 1960). For an excellent general review of the literature, see Kurt Mayer, "The Theory of Social Classes," *Harvard Educational Review* 23 (Summer 1953):149-57. The initial question facing any researcher concerned with the effects of social status is one of measurement. Should social class be assessed on the basis of objective or subjective criteria? For an understanding of the dilemma see Elton F. Jackson and Richard F. Curtis, "Conceptualization and Measurement in the Study of Social Stratification," in Hubert M. Blalock and Ann B. Blalock (eds.). *Methodology in Social Research* (New York: McGraw-Hill Book Co., 1968), pp. 112-49. Subjective class status is the subject of Richard Centers in *The Psychology of Social Classes* (Princeton, New Jersey: Princeton University Press, 1949). For discussions relating the measurement of social class directly to the study of voting behavior, see Campbell and others, *The American Voter,* pp. 189-90, and Lane, op. cit., pp. 220-34.

[37] Among the indices used to measure this relationship, the most common is income. A less direct indicator, house value, was also assessed by several of these studies. Not surprisingly, the two variables are highly correlated.

Two studies examined the relationship between group variation in SES as measured by a composite index and turnout for school financial elections. One of these (Turner, 1968) confirms the propositions noted above by finding that voters from areas of higher SES are more likely to vote in a school bond election than voters from lower SES areas. However, the remaining study (Jordan) found no significant relationship between aggregate SES and turnout.[38] We have found no evidence to suggest a significant negative relationship between SES indicators and turnout for school financial elections.

Generally, then, available evidence strongly suggests that socioeconomic status (particularly as indicated by wealth, or more narrowly by income and house value) is positively related to voter turnout for school financial elections. This evidence adds complexity since these findings may be explained from both of the previously described theoretical viewpoints. The psychological theory of participation in local nonpartisan elections would anticipate disproportionately greater representation of "higher class" citizens on the grounds that these citizens are likely to have strong positive attitudes toward their community[39] predisposing them to participate in community affairs, including voting. On the

---

[38] Jordan studied voting in one school bond election held in Los Angeles (1963). The units for analysis were the Los Angeles Census Tracts, which were treated by quartile analysis. The 709 tracts were grouped in four quarters of 177 each, which were then ranked from high to low on a composite SES scale. Such a procedure actually leads to only four very heterogeneous units for analysis, an additional weakness for a design based on only one election. Another study, by Boskoff and Zeigler, op. cit., found no significant relationship between aggregate SES and turnout for a local bond election. However, Hamilton, op. cit., p. 1139, found a strong relationship between SES index scores for individuals and turnout for a municipal primary election.

For a general discussion of the utility of indices of social class in the study of voting behavior, see Robert R. Alford, *Party and Society: The Anglo-American Democracies* (Chicago: Rand McNally & Co., 1963), pp. 73-90. Composite indices of SES generally are useful summaries, but as such lack discriminatory ability. Most of these indices are derived from, or similar to, the "Shevky-Bell" index. For an explanation see Eshref Shevky and Wendell Bell, *Social Area Analysis* (Stanford: Stanford University Press, 1959). Useful examples of applications to analysis of voting behavior may be found in Kaufman and Greer, op. cit., and Boskoff and Zeigler, op. cit. For a viewpoint questioning some of the assumptions underlying the Shevky-Bell typology see Maurice D. Van Arsdol, Jr., et al., "The Generality of the Urban Social Area Indexes," *American Sociological Review* 23 (June 1958):277-84. For a general review of SES indices see William H. Gulley and Charles H. Newton, "Methods of Measuring the Distribution of Socio-Economic Conditions," *Socio-Economic Planning Sciences* 6 (April 1972):187-96.

[39] Three local voting behavior studies that are extremely valuable in developing this general line of theory provide the following labels to describe the attitude configurations of citizens of this persuasion: "civic responsibility" in Boskoff and Zeigler, op. cit.; "community conservationism" in Robert E. Agger and Marshall N. Goldstein, *Who Will Rule the Schools: A Cultural Class Crisis* (Belmont, California: Wadsworth Publishing Company, 1971); and "public regardingness" in "Public Regardingness as a Value Premise in Voting Behavior," *American Political Science Review* 58 (December 1964): 876-87. The theory of community conservationism was originally described in the now classic work by Robert E. Agger, Daniel Goldrich, and Bert E. Swanson, *The Rulers and the Ruled* (New York: John Wiley and Sons, Inc., 1964), Chapter 1; the Wilson-Banfield article is reproduced in Richard I. Hofferbert and Ira Sharkansky, *State and Urban Politics: Readings in Comparative Public Policy* (Boston: Little, Brown and Company, 1971), pp. 108-130.

other hand, those who hold to the rational interpretation of voting have avoided the issue of attitudes toward community by accounting for the lack of participation among "lower class" groups as a function of their relatively low level of information, leading them to discount anticipated potential returns (benefits) from voting.[40]

*Attitudinal Variables*

Available research evidence indirectly supports the proposition that *the greater an individual's attachment to the community, the more likely he will turn out for school financial elections.* Parnell (1964) found that potential voters who lived in a community more that three years were more likely to vote in a school budget election than those living in a community less that three years. Similarly, Smith and others (1968) found that the greater a citizen's length of residence in a community, the more likely he will vote in a school millage election. Finally, both Parnell (1968) and Smith and others (1968) have found a strong association between membership in community organizations and participation in school financial elections. The indirect nature of this evidence should be emphasized, along with the fact that the findings represent objective measurement of subjective phenomena—a citizen's attitudes toward his community, its institutions and leaders, etc.

Future research to test the utility of attitudinal variables for differentiating between voters and nonvoters in local elections may help to clarify the effect of an individual's feelings toward his community on his propensity to vote. To date, such evidence is skimpy though highly suggestive. For instance, one study (Parnell 1964) provides data to support the theory that the normal participant in school financial elections holds more conservative politico-economic views than the nonparticipant. [41] Previous theory is less helpful for understanding the finding (Carter and Chaffee, 1966, volume 2) that citizens who regard their general "tax burden" as heavy are less likely to vote regularly in school elections than citizens who view their taxes as not much of a burden. Another irony that has emerged from attitudinal data is the finding that citizens who prefer to settle matters of school district policy by citizen vote are less likely to vote in school budget elections than citizens who prefer to allow the school board and staff greater autonomy.

These three findings suggest the potential importance of attitudes of dissatisfaction and cynicism toward the community, its institutions, and officials

---

[40] Downs, op. cit., p. 265.

[41] The terms *conservative* and *liberal* as used here refer to individual attitudes toward the national government's role in economics—e.g., "carriers of economic (welfare state) liberalism" per Lane, op. cit., p. 341.

(in this case, the schools and school officials).[42] The explanation suggested by the literature on alienation and voting is that these negative feelings toward taxes and school policy are linked with cynicism concerning the individual's ability to do anything about these sources of dissatisfaction.

Feelings of powerlessness and estrangement are often considered causes of apathy toward the social institution in question. If these feelings of political powerlessness are long-lasting and significant, then they corroborate the theory that "to some people politics is a distant and complex realm that is beyond the powers of the common citizen to affect, whereas to others the affairs of government can be understood and influenced by individual citizens."[43] Several studies report that individuals who feel powerless are less likely to vote than citizens who feel politically efficacious.[44] It is hardly surprising, then, that two studies that have investigated the relationship between political efficacy and participation in school financial elections find that *the greater an individual's feeling of political efficacy, the more likely it is that he will vote in school financial elections* (Carter and Chaffey, 1966, volume 2; Parnell, 1964).

## Summary and Conclusions

In this chapter we have examined voter participation in school financial elections as a dependent variable. That is, we have been concerned with empirical evidence for generalizations that can be used to describe who votes in school financial elections and why they decide to vote in those contests.

We have been more successful in answering the "who" question than in answering the "why" question. Briefly, the strongest research findings suggest that the normal voter in school financial elections may be classified as a member of one or more of the groups in the independent variable column of Figure 3-3. Since several of these independent variables are highly interrelated (e.g., wealth, education, and home ownership), we may assume that an individual voter may be classified as a member of several of these groups simultaneously. As the solid line indicates, we know that citizens who fit this profile are more likely to vote in school elections than those who do not.

We are less certain as to *why* citizens fitting this profile are such likely participants in school elections. Two plausible explanations, alluded to throughout this chapter, are listed in the column headed "intervening variables." These explanations vary more in degree than they do in substance. According to the

---

[42] The attitudinal variable cynicism (lack of trust) has frequently been defined as an important component of alienation. For the most explicit treatment of the political cynicism concept, see Robert E. Agger, Marshall Goldstein, and Stanley A. Pearl, "Political Cynicism: Measurement and Meaning," *Journal of Politics* 23 (August 1961): 477-506.

[43] Campbell and others, *The American Voter*, p. 58.

[44] Milbrath, op. cit., pp. 57-58.

first explanation, the citizen meeting the independent variable criteria is more likely to arrive at a favorable cost/benefit determination concerning his participation in a specific election. The second explanation emphasizes the potential deterministic nature of long-term values assumed to be associated with the characteristics frequently found related to participation in school financial elections.

As the broken lines indicate, it is difficult to assess the precise contribution of each explanation to our understanding of participation. Probably both are valuable to varying degrees and are perhaps most valuable when taken together. Yet the differing emphases of the two theories hold important implications for the researcher and the practitioner. Anyone concerned with changing participation rates—such as an expansion of the normal voter pool—needs to know the answer to the questions suggested by the broken lines in Figure 3-3. For instance, clarification of the importance of information as a stimulant to participation holds obvious implications for structuring election campaigns. Of course, the explanation is partly affected by circumstances surrounding the election.

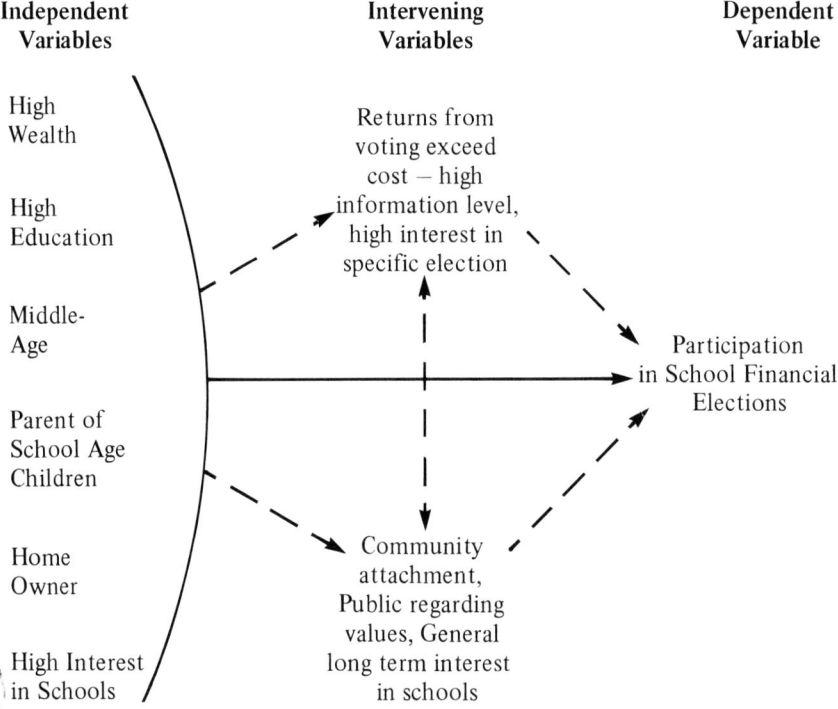

**Figure 3-3.** Alternate Explanatory Paths among Variables That Appear Strongly Related to Participation in School Financial Elections

Throughout this chapter we have been concerned with the correlates of citizen participation in school elections. By focusing our attention on strong correlations we automatically describe the most *frequent* voter. In other words the evidence presented to this point relates to "normal" turnout elections. As we noted earlier in the chapter, the proportion of eligible voters who actually cast a ballot in school and other local financial elections is normally quite small. Yet there is occasional variation in turnout rates. In the next chapter, we turn our attention to the causes and effects of variations in turnout for school financial elections. There we hope to obtain a more comprehensive understanding of citizen participation in school financial elections.

# 4

# Variations in Voter Turnout: Causes and Effects

One of the difficulties encountered in any attempt to generalize about school financial elections is the parochial nature of these elections. The previous chapter's discussion of the correlates of voting and nonvoting was based on the assumption that a smaller proportion of eligible voters turns out for these local referenda than casts ballots in state or national elections (see footnote 8, Chapter 3). Although this generalization is entirely valid, it is important to remember, in reading this chapter, that turnout for school financial elections may be considered low, high, or normal relative to the following circumstances: (1) other types of elections held in that community; (2) previous school financial elections held in that community; (3) various norms—community, regional, national—for the various election types.

## "Normal" Turnout

Figure 4-1 employs six bar graphs to illustrate the potential range of meaning that can accompany the phrases "high" or "low" voter turnout. Each bar represents a different hypothetical but plausible election situation. The turnout percentages in this example (as in all other uses of the term throughout the text unless otherwise specified) refer to the proportion of registered voters that voted in the election in question.

Situation 2 represents the average community turnout (25%) for school financial elections over a period of time. Situations 1 and 3 represent the

**Figure 4-1.** Hypothetical Turnout Rates for Different Types of Elections—Community X

turnout extremes achieved over the same period of time for the same type of elections. Similarly, high, average, and low turnouts for presidential elections are reported in graphs 4, 5, and 6, respectively. Other bases for comparison, not represented in the figure, might include turnout rates for school elections held in nearby districts and national or regional turnout averages. The point to be made here is that a given turnout rate—for instance, one-third of the electorate—can be referred to as low in comparison to presidential contests and at the same time be considered relatively high for a school election.

The findings reviewed in this chaper are from studies that have used two distinct research methods to examine variations in "normal" school financial election turnout rates. The differences between these two types of studies are subtle but meaningful. On the one hand are cross-sectional comparisons of districts or communities to identify factors that may influence turnout variations. Significant associations found in studies of this type provide the basis for confident generalizations. Unfortunately, because of inherent problems of access and comparability of data, the studies leave many potentially important factors unexamined.

The second method compares turnout rates found at different points of time among individuals or aggregates (or samples of either) from one community. Unlike cross-sectional studies, these studies are generally able to analyze problems in depth by asking a greater number of important questions of more reliable and controllable data. The studies face an obvious limitation, however, in that their findings cannot be generalized to other areas.

As the limitation of each of these research methods implies, questions asked in studies of voting in school financial elections often have been at least partly dictated by practical considerations—a situation that occurs frequently in most substantive areas of research. The unfortunate result of this procedure is that unimportant questions are sometimes asked at the expense of more important but less manageable ones. We will see some evidence of this dilemma in the research results described in this chapter. First, however, we will briefly discuss the theoretical considerations that, together with the research approaches described above, have produced the findings on which the chapter is based.

**Explanations of Turnout Variations**

Variations in turnout rates from one community or district to another can be attributed, according to one explanation, to the same characteristics that affect an individual's decision to vote or not to vote. We might assume, for example, that if a group of characteristics allows us to differentiate between voters and nonvoters of a community, that same group of characteristics (for instance, socioeconomic status indicators as described in Chapter 3) should be useful in explaining differences in turnout rates among two or more communities.

This explanation returns us to the problem of determining to what extent people behave rationally in actual voting situations. If a community's demographic composition can be used consistently to predict relative voter turnout rates, we must lose confidence in the portrait of the voter as a rational participant in the political process. Similarly, if deterministic arguments such as the "public-regardingness hypothesis"[1] can be extended to the community level of analysis, we would find that the population characteristics of certain areas would predispose them to relatively high or low turnout levels irrespective of issues and circumstances surrounding particular elections. Situational factors would thus play a relatively unimportant part in stimulating participation and direction of participation in the political process.

It may well be that community or district composition may prove useful in explaining different turnout rates among widely divergent areas. But such an explanation is clearly inadequate for understanding major turnout variations in one community during a short period unless major changes in the community's demographic composition have occurred.

To explain turnout variation among communities only on the basis of characteristics attributed to individuals who normally vote in school elections is to succumb to the "ecological fallacy"[2] and to accept uncritically a deterministic view of voting behavior. Some attempt must be made to account for situational (or structural) factors as well. Only then will we have an analytical framework for understanding large fluctuations in turnout rates from one community to another at one point in time or from one election to another in a single community over a longer period of time. Evidence bearing on situational factors as influencing community turnout rates is reported next.

---

[1] In keeping with our discussion in Chapter 3, we do not mean to limit our discussion of "deterministic" theories of participation in local elections to "public regardingness" as operationalized by Wilson and Banfield. Here, we use the term loosely to designate various hypotheses that posit the existence of a group of citizens that has a more positive outlook regarding the community, its institutions and leaders, etc., and that assume these individuals will normally comprise the majority of the voting population in a local referendum.

[2] The ecological fallacy and related dangers associated with the use of aggregate data are well known and significant. The caution concerning inference from one level of analysis to another has been clearly stated in the following classic essays: Austin Ranney, "The Utility and Limitations of Aggregate Data in the Study of Electoral Behavior," in Austin Ranney (ed.), *Essays on the Behavioral Study of Politics* (Urbana: University of Illinois Press, 1962), pp. 91-102; and W.S. Robinson, "Ecological Correlations and the Behavior of Individuals," *American Sociological Review* 15 (June 1950): 351-57. As Heinz Eulau has noted, inference from one level of analysis to another places one in a precarious position regardless of whether the error is one of "extrapolation" (treating micro units, such as individuals, as analogues of macro units, such as communities, and extending findings from the micro to the macro level) or one of the opposite nature—"personification." See his *Behavioral Persuasion in Politics* (New York: Random House, 1963), pp. 125-26. A similar warning accompanied by an empirical example of the difficulties involved in inferring a positive relationship between educational level and voter turnout in cities on the basis of findings from studies of individuals—is offered by Robert R. Alford and Eugene C. Lee, "Voting Turnout in American Cities," *American Political Science Review* 62 (September 1968): 796-813.

*School District Size*

School district size—as measured by the number of students enrolled in the district—is an easily measured factor that may summarize basic organizational differences among school districts. The steady progression toward centralization of public school districts has not been accomplished without criticism; indeed, contemporary racial issues have served to renew the centralization/decentralization controversy. Despite this and other barriers to centralization, the total number of school districts has declined during the past decade. Apparently, many school officials still consider centralization an effective approach to organizational economy.

It is not surprising that a first step in many comparative studies of school systems is to assess the effect of school district size on variables of interest (in this case, voting in school financial elections).[3]

Evidence produced by the Carter research team (Carter and Sutthoff, 1960) support the proposition that *the smaller the size of a school district the greater the voter turnout in school bond and tax elections.* Carter's subsequent research efforts (Carter and Savard, 1961, and Carter and Ruggels, 1966) generally confirm that proposition.[4]

Carter and Ruggels (1966) also report that the greater a district's rate of population increase, the greater the district's voter turnout. The rate was measured over a ten-year period from 1950 to 1960. This finding did not hold, however, when it was measured during the period 1940 to 1950. Earlier reference to the importance of testing relationships over significant time spans applies here. What, for example, would be the relationship between rate of enrollment increase and rate of voter participation during the decade 1960-1970? Further tests at several points in time are required to verify these findings.[5]

---

[3]The importance of this dimension in studies of educational administration is noticeable in the publications of the NEA Research Division, which typically array their findings by district size (Strata 1 through 4). See for example, National Education Association, Research Division, *Evaluation of Teacher Salary Schedules* 1966-67, 1967-68, and 1968-69 (Washington, D.C.: NEA, 1968).

[4]The following ordinal scale was used to classify district size:

| | | |
|---|---|---|
| 1. | small: | 150-299 |
| 2. | medium: | 300-11,999 |
| 3. | large: | 12,000+ |

[5]As we mentioned earlier, the need to assess observed relationships at different points in time has been stressed frequently by many writers. For an article that underscored this concern in the field of voting behavior research, see Robert R. Alford, "The Role of Social Class in American Voting Behavior," *Western Political Quarterly* 16 (March 1963): 180-94. In their classic study of voting in Elmira, New York, in the 1952 presidential election, Bernard R. Berelson, Paul F. Lazarsfeld, and William N. McPhee emphasize the tentative nature of their findings until they are tested in different settings and *over time.* See their *Voting* (Chicago: University of Chicago Press, 1954), p. xiii.

Evidence concerning the effects of perceived school needs (or perceived need for schools) on citizen participation is skimpy. Turner (1968), however, reports one relevant finding: There is no statistically significant relationship between an area's direct benefit from a bond issue for building additions in area schools and voter turnout in that area.

Enrollment size is only one of many variables that might serve as a surrogate for organizational complexity. A more direct tie to the organizational dimension is the variable the Carter research team labled "board control." Carter and Sutthoff (1960) report that among large districts, those whose boards have greater control are more likely to obtain high voter turnout than districts whose boards have less control. Two of the indicators of board control—the district's use of business procedures, including cost accounting, and the representation of large taxpayers on the school board—were found to be positively related to high voter turnout.

*Type of Election*

Another situational variable that may influence turnout variation is the specific type of election. Minar (1966) found that *voter turnout is likely to be higher for tax than for bond or miscellaneous school financial issues.* This finding is corroborated by the work of the Carter research team (Carter and Savard, 1961). In the absence of evidence to the contrary, the finding takes the form of a tentative proposition. Carter and Sutthoff (1960) also found that the larger the amount of the bond issue, the greater the turnout.

One question raised by a discussion of specific election types involves whether or not areas that exhibit high turnout for one type of election are likely to exhibit similarly strong participation in other types of elections.[6] One bit of relevant evidence is reported by Minar (1966). He found that school districts exhibiting high voter turnout in school board elections are likely to have equally high turnout in school financial elections.

All these findings provide additional definition and some explanation of variations in voter turnout for school financial elections. The factors described in this section represent identified conditions that underlie particular community participation patterns. Unfortunately, descriptive corollaries are of little use to

---

[6]Generally, assessments of turnout among comparable groups and individuals for different types of elections have been limited to the local/national and partisan/nonpartisan dichotomies. The predominate finding has been that turnout is greater for the latter type of election, particularly among lower SES groupings. Milbrath, op. cit., cites several relevant studies on p. 106. Particularly useful evidence and discussion may be found in: Edward C. Banfield and James Q. Wilson, *City Politics* (New York: Vintage Books, 1963); Robert H. Salisbury and Gordon Black, "Class and Party in Partisan and Non-Partisan Elections: The Case of Des Moines, *American Political Science Review* 57 (September 1963): 584-92; and Oliver P. Williams and Charles R. Adrian, "The Insulation of Local Politics Under the Non-Partisan Ballot," *American Political Science Review* 53 (December 1959): 1052-63.

the school administrator and analyst. For a school superintendent of a large district who wishes to increase voter participation in elections, knowledge that large districts' turnout rates are generally smaller than those of small districts is worthless since he cannot reduce the size of his district. Both the practitioner and the theorist need a better understanding of the specific causes and effects of turnout deviations within single communities. Hopefully, such an understanding will be aided by the following section, which attempts to specify the relationship of changing citizen participation patterns to the functioning of the schools as a political system.

**Voter Turnout as a Symptom of System Health**

In Chapter 3 we referred to the concept of "civic duty" and to the notion that maximum citizen participation at the polls is essential to the good health of the American democracy. In comparison to voter participation in other Western nations, recent voter turnout in the United States has been relatively low.[7] In discussing this finding, Seymour Martin Lipset asks the rhetorical question, "What does this lack of participation suggest? An unhealthy apathy and the weakening of democracy, as some liberal rhetoricians suggest?"[8] Certainly if voter turnout is taken to be a direct indicator of a democratic system's viability, then the American democracy suffers in comparison to most European nations. Lipset, however, largely rejects this view. It is possible, he says, that ". . . nonvoting is now at least in Western democracies a reflection of the *stability* of the system, a response to the decline of major social conflicts."[9]

---

[7] Seymour Martin Lipset, *Political Man* (Garden City, New York: Doubleday Anchor, 1963), p. 185.

[8] Ibid.

[9] Ibid. This view is frequently encountered in the literature of political science. For an explicit statement see Bernard R. Berelson, Paul F. Lazarsfeld, and William N. McPhee, *Voting: A Study of Opinion Formation in a Presidential Campaign* (Chicago: The University of Chicago Press, 1954), pp. 314-23. These authors conclude their landmark study by asserting that the stability of the system is dependent on a distribution of citizens that is represented in a normal, bell-shaped curve. This model stresses system equilibrium. Balance is seen as the all-important contribution of the large middle group in the curve, labeled "Political Man." The voter is described as most frequently drawn from this group and as having a certain amount of information, rationality, some principles, and some interest, but ". . . he does not have them in the extreme, elaborate, comprehensive, or detailed form in which they were uniformly recommended by political philosophers. Like Justice Hand, the typical citizen has other interests in life, and it is good, even for the political system, that he pursues them" (pp. 322-23). This model is used to account for relatively low participation rates and is considered highly desirable given the goal of system stability. For additional discussion see Herbert McClosky, "Consensus and Ideology in American Politics," *American Political Science Review* 68 (June 1964): 361-82, who notes that "although political matters are in a sense 'everyone's concern' it is just as unreasonable to hope that all men will sustain a lively interest in politics as it would be to expect everyone to become addicted to chamber music, electronics, poetry, or baseball."

If Lipset's theory is correct, higher levels of turnout may indicate higher levels of tension within the political system. Comparatively low turnout rates, therefore, may not necessarily be undesirable.

Given the divergence between this view and traditional democratic theory, how useful is knowledge of voter turnout in assessing a political system's relative health? The answer is that such knowledge by itself is probably inadequate for assessing the system's progress toward such abstract objectives as "democracy" and "stability." Perhaps higher voter turnout is not always healthy, but, as Robert Lane notes, it is illogical to argue on the basis of some case-study evidence (e.g., Germany during 1930-1933) that higher voter turnout should be avoided at all costs.

Participation is a product of multiple factors; it is imbedded in an area of multiple causation. Because high participation under the stimulus of one set of conditions is associated with revolutionary pressures, or does create dangerous electoral tension, it does not follow that high participation caused by other factors has the same meaning.[10]

In other words, the relative level of nonvoting within a system is an insufficient basis for understanding the general conditions of that system until the reasons for nonparticipation are understood.[11] Donald Stokes has noted that significant increments of nonvoting may indicate widespread hostility toward the political system or government in question. A constant number of nonvoters, however, may be considered a "relatively benign phenomena ... if the millions of people who are free to vote, yet do not, are politically indifferent in a partisan sense, but positively oriented in the system itself."[12]

The evidence cited indicates that voter turnout may be symptomatic of a variety of states of health and that observation of related symptoms is necessary for a valid diagnosis. We must keep in mind, however, that these conclusions are based on voter turnout in partisan contests in large political systems, usually nation-states, and may not accurately define the limits of voter turnout as a variable in our study of school financial elections. Nevertheless, numerous studies have tested these findings in local referenda settings, and the results are useful for our inquiry.

From these studies of local voting behavior, we find substantial evidence corroborating the postion taken in a recent American government text: "When local elections generate a substantial increase in turnout, one can infer that the

---

[10] Lane, op. cit., p. 347.

[11] For a discussion of alternative models for explaining abnormally high voter turnout, see William H. Flanigan, *Political Behavior of the American Electorate* (Boston: Allyn and Bacon, Inc., 1968), pp. 12-20.

[12] Donald Stokes, "Popular Evaluations of Government: An Empirical Assessment," in Harlan Cleveland and Harold Lasswell (eds.), *Ethics and Bigness: Scientific, Academic, Religious, Political, and Military* (New York: Harper and Brothers Publishers, 1962), pp. 62-63.

election is a *symptom* of a deeply felt community conflict."[13] In his classic monograph reporting the results of his research on voting behavior in local referenda authorizing fluoridation of public water supplies, James S. Coleman found that higher turnout rates were positively related to the defeat of fluoridation issues. He developed the theory that these turnout increments mirrored conflict and controversy in the community.[14] The community conflict stimulates many citizens to vote who normally abstain because of negative (or at least neutral) predispositions toward community affairs. A greater percentage of these new voters tend to vote no. Much of the followup research on voting for fluoridation issues has confimed Coleman's empirical finding: increased turnout has been related to defeat in numerous instances.[15]

School financial elections have more in common with fluoridation issues than with partisan national elections. Findings from the fluoridation literature thus are valuable for initial theorizing concerning school financial elections. There are obvious differences between the two issues, however, so we must be careful about applying findings from one to the other. More than one observer has suggested that the specific type of issue may affect the amount, meaning, and direction of voter participation in local referendums.[16] To assess the validity of the community conflict theory[17] for school financial elections, we must turn our attention to the findings of research directly concerned with school issues.

---

[13]Thomas R. Dye and L. Harmon Zeigler, *The Irony of Democracy: An Uncommon Introduction to American Politics* (Belmont, California: Wadsworth Publishing Co., 1970), p. 167. Emphasis added.

[14]James S. Coleman, *Community Conflict* (New York: Free Press, 1957).

[15]See, for example, Thomas A.F. Plaut, "Analysis of Voter Behavior on a Fluoridation Referendum," *Public Opinion Quarterly* 23 (Summer 1959-1960: 213-222; Maurice Pinard, "Structural Attachments and Political Support in Urban Politics: The Case of Fluoridation Referendums," *American Journal of Sociology* 68 (March 1963): 518; Robert L. Crain, Elihu Katz, and Donald B. Rosenthal, *The Politics of Community Conflict: The Fluoridation Decision* (Indianapolis: The Bobbs-Merrill Co., 1969), especially pp. 206-228.

[16]Harlen Hahn and Timothy Almy, "Ethnic Politics and Racial Issues: Voting in Los Angeles," *The Western Political Quarterly* 24 (December 1971): 719-30; Howard D. Hamilton, "The Municipal Voter: Voting and Nonvoting in City Elections," *American Political Science Review* 65 (December 1971): 1135-40; Eugene S. Uyeki "Patterns of Voting in a Metropolitan Area, 1938-1962," *Urban Affairs Quarterly* 1 (June 1966): 65-77; and Clarence N. Stone, "Local Referendums: An Alternative to the Alienated Voter Model," *Public Opinion Quarterly* 20 (Summer 1965): 222. According to Stone, "... it may be hypothesized that the subject matter of some referendum proposals is more conducive to protest voting than is that of others." Along with fluoridation and charter and other forms of government issues, Stone views school bond issues as a type that can easily be converted into "style issues," which "attract large turnouts only if vague, emotion-laden symbols are employed." These "are the referendums in which protest voting rises as turnout increases." Stone contrasts these style issues with other types, such as bond issues for sewers, hospitals, and highways, which are presumed to evoke less emotionalism and more of a cost/benefit orientation.

[17]This label will be used throughout the text to designate the explanation offered by Coleman, op. cit. The theory is not totally original (good theories seldom are), but this

## The Relationship between Voter Turnout and Outcome of School Financial Elections: Research Findings

Measuring the extent and nature of conflict within a community at any given time is not an easy task. Two indicators of community conflict over school election proposals are the amount of individual criticism of the schools and the amount of organized group opposition to the election proposal. Both variables have been found positively associated with voter turnout in school financial elections (Carter and Ruggels, 1966; Jennings and Zeigler, 1970).

These results support Coleman's major tenet that conflict will stimulate greater turnout among some part of the "large passive group" that normally would not vote.[18] Of course, there is need for additional research for corroboration and specification. The first need (corroboration) is obvious: the results from two studies standing alone hardly warrant extreme confidence. But the second need—for research designed to specify the intensity and nature of the conflict/turnout relationship—is even more urgent. Research is needed so that we may see the elements and interrelationships of those elements that combine to result in a significant number of individuals voting that normally would not vote. The term "conflict" is too soft for explanation until it is specified. To borrow from Coleman, we need to be able to explain the causes and consequences of conflict at least to the degree of specificity we employ when explaining that "a boy, a match, and a firecracker combine to set off an explosion."[19]

---

powerful and concise statement is normally, and correctly, cited in any worthwhile discussion of the determinants and results of community conflict.

[18]Coleman, op. cit., p. 8. As is often the case in social science, it is difficult to specify the precise cause and effect relationship between conflict and participation. The theory described by Coleman et al. holds that conflict precedes participation, which is a reasonably logical assumption given the correlation between the two variables. However, it is possible to explain the relationship as one in which participation precedes conflict. For example, for some reason a larger than usual number of voters in a district may indicate their intention to participate in an upcoming election. The activities of these new participants signal "trouble" for the district, which then begins a series of counter maneuvers that themselves increase conflict and polarization within the community during the campaign period, resulting in a high turnout on election day. Further research is needed not only to specify relationships but also to provide tactical guidance for the school official attempting to avoid a conflict escalation process. For a provocative discussion on this point, see Carter and Ruggels (vol. IV, 1966), p. 115.

[19]Coleman, op. cit., p. 7. Theories of social conflict have been expounded that are fairly systematic. An excellent review of this important theoretical literature dealing with social conflict is contained in Lewis A. Coser, *Continuities in the Study of Social Conflict* (New York: The Free Press, 1967), pp. 1-14. Much of this work was stimulated by Coser's earlier classic *The Functions of Social Conflict* (New York: The Free Press, 1954). The not uncommon problem, according to Coser (1967, p. 7), is that little empirical testing of theoretical leads has taken place. Coser cites Raymond W. Mack, "The Components of Social Conflict," *Social Problems* 22 (Spring 1965): 388-97, as being particularly critical of "the lack of empirical work informed by conflict theory."

In the meantime, a number of studies provide evidence related to the second major tenet of the community conflict theory: that the increment of new voters presumably stimulated to vote by the community conflict are more likely to cast negative ballots. Indeed, the findings from the research of the past decade strongly support the proposition that THE LARGER THE TURNOUT, THE SMALLER THE PERCENTAGE OF FAVORABLE VOTES CAST IN A SCHOOL FINANCIAL ELECTION (Carter and Sutthoff, 1960; Carter and Savard, 1961; Carter and Ruggels, 1966; Dykstra, 1964; Wentzel, 1964; Barbour, 1966; Jordon, 1966; Minar, 1966; Spinner, 1967; Crider, 1967; Lieber, 1967; Willis, 1967-68; Marlow, 1970; Goettel, 1971; Banach and Westley, 1972). Significantly, the negative relationship between turnout and favorable voting has been confirmed in divergent research settings in both school tax and school bond issue settings (Carter and Sutthoff, 1960) and while controlling for school district size (Carter and Savard, 1961).

Expectedly, some modifications and qualifications of the proposition have been suggested by a few studies. One important qualification concerns the sequence of the election. Two researchers (Wentzel, 1964; Spinner, 1967) have found a higher correlation between voter turnout and negative voting in *first time* school financial elections. In pursuing this discovery, Spinner found that the greater the turnout for subsequent elections in the same year (following the defeat of the initial budget request), the more likely it is that those elections will succeed.[20]

Most of the studies reviewed for our inquiry did not control for election sequence. In many cases, researchers examined voting behavior in either a single election or a single election from each year. Unfortunately for school districts, the need to hold more than one budget election in a given year has increased dramatically in recent years.[21] The multiple election phenomenon deserves immediate research attention, not only for specification of the turnout/vote

---

[20] A similar finding is reported by Harlan Hahn in his study of a variety of types of local referendums. For school elections, Hahn finds a positive association between yes voting and turnout in second and subsequent elections. His conclusion is that there is basically an element of active support for the schools, but "... as the strains of growing expenses and renewed demands began to intensify, numerous absences at the polls seem to have been related to a reduction in the votes in favor of such proposals." See Harlan Hahn, "Voting in Canadian Communities: A Taxonomy of Referendum Issues," *Canadian Journal of Political Science* 1 (December 1968): 468.

[21] Not all school districts are required to obtain voter approval of their budget on an annual basis. Among those that are, however, the trend (documented in Table 1-1) is clear; for example, in one Oregon county voters passed the budgets of all thirteen school districts at the first election in 1960. By 1970, only three of that county's districts (then totaling sixteen) succeeded in the first attempt, nine issues passed on the second attempt, two required a third election, and two were not resolved until the citizens had participated in the fourth round of decision-making. (Source: Bureau of Governmental Research and Service, School of Community Service and Public Affairs, "Record of Vote on Proposed School District Special Tax Levies to Exceed the Six Percent Constitutional Limitation," Unpublished Report, CSPA, Eugene: University of Oregon, 1971.)

relationship but also for clarification of recent hypotheses that emphasize the importance of a new "bargaining process" between school officials and voters.

The initial proposition suggests a linear (or one-to-one) relationship between higher voter turnout and negative vote. However, one team of researchers, while investigating voting in a large sample of Iowa school bond issues, found that bond elections achieving up to 40 percent and over 80 percent voter turnout were more likely to succeed than elections with turnout rates between 40 percent and 80 percent (Barbour, 1966). Further evidence corroborating this finding would lead to a curvilinear relationship. Such a relationship also has been suggested by Carter and Savard (1961).

Researchers have employed other important controls while testing the turnout/vote proposition. Willis (1967-68) found that increased voter turnout was related to a decreased percentage of favorable votes for school financial elections in inner-city attendance areas. In attendance areas removed from the central city, increased turnout was related to an increased percentage of favorable votes. Evidence from another investigation that employed similar controls, however, contradicts this finding. Marlow (1970) found turnout and favorable vote to be positively related in urban areas. We must conclude that the scanty evidence available for interpreting the influence of urbanism, area of residence, and so forth, on the turnout/vote relationship, is insufficient for modification of the original proposition. Further research to examine these dimensions would seem to require a multivariate design.[22]

Thus, the theory and evidence presented by James Coleman in 1957—that increased rates of community conflict, voter turnout, and negative voting are positively associated—has received substantial empirical support in several studies of voting for school financial proposals, and in studies of voting in other local nonpartisan elections. Yet the basic proposition lacks unanimity. A few studies have found no statistically significant relationship between voter turnout and success or failure in school financial elections (Beal et al., 1966; Murphy, 1966; Stone, 1965; Turner, 1968; Hahn, 1968). [23]

These exceptions to the initial proposition simply hold that turnout makes no appreciable difference—that "election outcomes are unpredictable on the basis of size of turnout."[24] Neither these findings nor those upholding the proposition provide any empirical support for the view—frequently seen in

---

[22] For an example of the type of analysis needed, see the multivariate examination of the effects of the Shevky-Bell indices—social rank, segregation, and urbanization—on participation in and direction of the St. Louis vote for a referendum to establish a metropolitan sewer district and the 1952 vote for president, in Walter O. Kaufman and Scott Greer, "Voting in Metropolitan Community: An Application of Social Area Analysis," *Social Forces* 38 (March 1960): 196-204.

[23] Boskoff and Zeigler, op. cit., come to the same conclusion in their study of voting for civic improvement bond issues. The Stone and Hahn studies both suggest that this relationship varies by type of local issue.

[24] Stone, op. cit., p. 221.

newspaper editorials and educational journals—that those concerned with passing school financial issues should promote greater turnout. Only three of the twenty research reports treating the turnout/vote relationship report significant associations between increased turnout and positive voting, and two of these three findings contradict each other. Marlowe (1970) found turnout and election success rates to be positively related in urban areas of Ohio, while Willis (1967-68) found the opposite relationship in his study of the Akron, Ohio, metropolitan area.

Spinner's (1967) finding that turnout increases are likely to enhance election success for issues that are resubmitted following an original defeat suggests a needed control for future research. If first-time and subsequent issues are not carefully distinguished, findings may tend to cancel out one another, leading to the questionable conclusion that turnout is not significantly related to election outcome.

For the present, we can only concur with the investigators of voting in Iowa bond issues who summarized the research literature as follows:

In examining the literature one may see that the school administrators, in their professional journals, are proposing the use of a multitude of techniques which have not consistently been proven to be either advisable or inadvisable. One of their greatest concerns is getting the electorate out to vote, yet studies have indicated that indiscriminant solicitation of the voters does not necessarily lead to school bond issues passing.[25]

Yet, as we noted in Chapter 1, knowledge of research findings is not necessarily sufficient for explaining success or failure in school financial elections. Despite the near unanimous agreement among researchers that increased voter turnout does not bring success in school financial elections, the studies are in sharp disagreement as to the effect voter turnout does have. Since some studies conclude that increased turnout is related to failure while others conclude that turnout makes no difference, some way must be found to account for the contradictions.

In an affort to reconcile these divergent research findings, we have examined the research approaches and settings that produced the findings. In an area as complex as school financial elections, where any number of variables can affect the research outcomes, data quality control is especially importants.[26] Some of the more important dimensions for control include time period, geographic

---

[25] George M. Beal et al., *Iowa School Bond Issues Data Book* (Ames, Iowa: Department of Sociology and Anthropology, Iowa State University, 1966), p. 12.

[26] As discussed in Chapter 2, the need for such controls provided a central justification for the type of inquiry we have conducted. An excellent statement of the philosophy of data quality control may be found in Raoul Naroll, *Data Control—A New Research Technique: Prolegomena to a Cross-Cultural Study of Culture Stress* (New York: The Free Press of Glencoe, 1962), pp. 11-15.

region, election coverage, and unit for data analysis. In Table 4-1 the two groups of studies that yielded contradictory findings are compared according to these dimensions.

As the table indicates, the studies do not vary significantly in most of the research dimensions for which we have controlled. Data for most of the studies were drawn from the late 1950s and early 1960s. Although settings for the studies varied greatly, both types appear to be geographically representative. Aggregate data from area units of analysis provided the basis for findings regarding turnout in all studies reviewed.

The only significant variations appear in the category "election coverage." One variation involves the types of the election. Of the eleven studies that found a negative relationship between turnout and election success, six investigated both bond and budget elections. On the other hand, of the six studies that found no significant relationship between turnout and election outcome, only one investigated both types of elections. Two of these studies were limited to voting in bond elections, while the remaining three studies investigated voting in a variety of types of local referenda, including school issues (Boskoff and Zeigler, 1964; Stone, 1965; Hahn, 1968). As we noted earlier, one of the overriding questions guiding this inquiry concerns the potential differences in voting in different types of elections. According to the Stone (1965) and Hahn (1968) studies, important differences do exist; the relationship between turnout and election success varies significantly for different types of referenda. An earlier admonition bears repeating at this point: tests of voting differences among various types of elections should be repeated for various regions and over time as a first step in determining the scope of potential voting behavior theories.

Another, perhaps more important, variation among the studies concerns the number of elections covered. Of the twelve studies that corroborate the initial proposition, eleven assessed relative turnout rates in multiple elections. In contrast, two of the six studies that found no significant relationship between voter turnout and direction of vote were based on only one election (Boskoff and Zeigler, 1964; Turner, 1968). Each of these two studies analyzed turnout rates at a number of polling places in a single election. They concluded that variations in turnout did not accompany variations in the proportion of yes or no votes from those polling places. This approach is altogether different from the approach of studies in the first group, which studied variations in turnout rates among the whole electorate in many elections taking place over time or at different locations. Such variations, these studies found, are related to yes or no voting.

The discrepancy between these findings in not surprising if we attempt to account for the relationship between turnout and negative voting on the basis of community conflict or similar theory. It is realistic and logical to assume that the amount of community conflict will vary over time and from region to region. On the other hand, there is little reason for suspecting such conflict to

## Table 4-1
**Comparison of Research Approaches and Settings in the Literature Investigating the Relationship Between Voter Turnout and Success or Failure in School Financial Elections: 1960-1971***

| Control | Group I<br>Greater Turnout/Less Success | Group II<br>No Significant Relationship:<br>Turnout/Success |
|---|---|---|
| TIME PERIOD | 1950-1960 (1); 1950-1970 (1); 1955-1962 (1); 1958-1962 (2); 1957-1966 (1); 1958-1963 (1); 1960-1965 (1); 1960-1966 (1); 1963 (1); 1969 (1); 1965-1971 (1) | 1955-1965 (1); 1957-1962 (1); 1953-1962 (1); 1960-1965 (1); 1961 (1); 1966 (1) |
| ELECTION COVERAGE NUMBER | Multiple (11); Single (1) | Multiple (4); Single (2) |
| TYPE** | All school financial (6); Bond only (2) Budget only (4); Other (0) | All school financial (1); Bond only (2); Budget only (0); Other (3) |
| GEOGRAPHIC REGION*** | Iowa (1); U.S. (1); Michigan (1); New York (2); Los Angeles (1); Cook County, Illinois (2); Ohio (1); Akron, Ohio (1); New Jersey (1); Oakland, Michigan (1) | DeKalb County, Georgia (1); Iowa (1); Canada (1); California (1); Littletown (1); Los Angeles (1) |
| UNIT OF ANALYSIS | Aggregate (12); Individual (0) | Aggregate (6); Individual (0) |

*The studies represented in this table were cited earlier in the discussion of the effect of turnout on voting outcome. The number of studies represented by a given entry in the table is indicated by the number in parenthesis. For this control exercise, repeated analysis of a given data set is not reflected—e.g., the Carter et al. research is designated as only one study here.

**"All school financial" refers to studies that have assessed voting in a mix of school bond, budget, and tax elections. "Other" refers to studies that have looked at a variety of election types but have included some form of school or closely allied type of financial election.

***Refers to largest region covered by the study.

vary between precincts in one community during one campaign. Conceivably, under certain circumstances, for example, a site dispute, conflict could vary between parts of a community in a single election, but such circumstances would be relatively rare. The numerous limitations inherent in a study of voting in only one election have been commented on earlier.

The four remaining group II studies (Stone, 1965; Hahn, 1968) did examine voting behavior in more than one election. Two of these studies, however, examined voting in a variety of types of elections, which included a comparatively small number or school elections.

Two studies that did examine voting in a large number of school elections share a methodological weakness that may be responsible for their conclusion. These studies (Beal et al., 1966; Murphy, 1966) assessed the relationship between subjective measures of turnout, as estimated by school superintendents, and direction of the vote. The difficulty is not simply one of estimation. In both cases data were required for a lengthy time period and responses were measured verbally (e.g., high, low, normal), which may have contributed to the phenomenon of regression toward the mean.

Thus, after examining selected sources of variation in some of the studies, the available evidence still appears to strongly corroborate the proposition that THE LARGER THE TURNOUT, THE SMALLER THE PERCENTAGE OF FAVORABLE VOTES CAST IN A SCHOOL FINANCIAL ELECTION, as long as "larger" or "smaller" turnout rates refer to relative turnout for several elections. For the analyst, this means that in an attempt to understand why one or more of a community's school financial elections have failed while others have passed, he might profitably examine turnout rates for the whole series of elections in question. For the school official, this proposition suggests that, at least for the first time an election is held, indiscriminate efforts to attract voters to the polls may in themselves produce undesirable results. The available evidence also suggests, albeit less strongly, that analysis of precinct turnout levels alone, in the hope of pinpointing areas of support and nonsupport, may prove futile.

## Individual Participation and Aggregate Turnout: Synthesis and Implications

The focus of discussion for this and the preceding chapter has been voter participation in school financial elections. The primary objective of Chapter 3 was to sift from the research literature pertinent evidence for differentiating between voters and nonvoters in school financial elections. This work was motivated by the assumption that if enough evidence could be accumulated to classify school election voters by dimensions other than their propensity to vote in school elections—social, economic, psychological, or whatever—a model of the typical participant could be stated. The quest for such a model, which involved a survey of known correlates to voter participation, seemed initially useful if for no other reason than to determine whether the decision to vote in a school financial election was something more than a random occurrence. Strong and repeated correlates to participation allow classification along dimensions other than voting behavior and, in turn, enhance our ability to explain and predict citizen participation in school elections. In short, by attempting to construct the model voter we hoped to discover whether one exists and, if so, why.

These questions were partly answered in Chapter 3. Several logical correlates to voting in school elections were found to have empirical underpinnings. From this body of evidence we derived a clearer picture of the normal, or at least frequent, school election voter. But this analysis left unanswered several questions regarding the dynamics of participation in school financial elections. Why do turnout rates vary between different communities and in the same community at different points in time? What do we know about the composition of the "normal" school financial electorate at different turnout levels? In other words, under what conditions might we expect variations in turnout rates, and what is the effect of these variations on the outcome of elections?

In an attempt to provide some answers to these questions we began, in the first section of this chapter, by describing correlates to aggregate turnout rates found in comparative studies of districts and communities. Although some of these correlates suggest potentially fruitful paths for future inquiry, the most important questions remained unanswered.

Consequently, the second half of this chapter assessed the contributions of research that has taken a slightly different point of view toward voter turnout. This voting behavior literature suggested the hypothesis that high rates of participation in a political system's elections could signal the ill health of that system. Some direct evidence was found supporting the theory that conflict and dissension within the political system lead to greater voter turnout. Another outcropping of evidence lends substantial inferential support to the community conflict hypothesis: several studies have found that as an independent variable voter turnout is strongly related to negative voting in school and other local financial elections.

Neither this evidence nor sound theoretical interpretation of it allows the conclusion that large turnouts are *always* symptomatic of controversy and dissension within the community. For instance, an increase in participation may occasionally be stimulated by those who wish to see the schools get on with "business as usual" after a series of budget defeats. The role of community acquiescence must be recognized if further support is found for the findings (Spinner, 1967; Hahn, 1968) that turnout and yes voting are positively related in elections subsequent to initial defeats.

Nevertheless, the bulk of evidence we have reviewed firmly supports the interpretation that increases in voter participation rates are *probable* indicators of some level of community conflict. From the material discussed in both this and the preceding chapter, therefore, it seems fruitful to think of *normal*[27] and *abnormal* participation in school financial elections. Figure 4-2 illustrates this distinction. The innermost circle represents a school system's "normal voting pool," made up of the citizens described in Chapter 3 as most likely to vote.

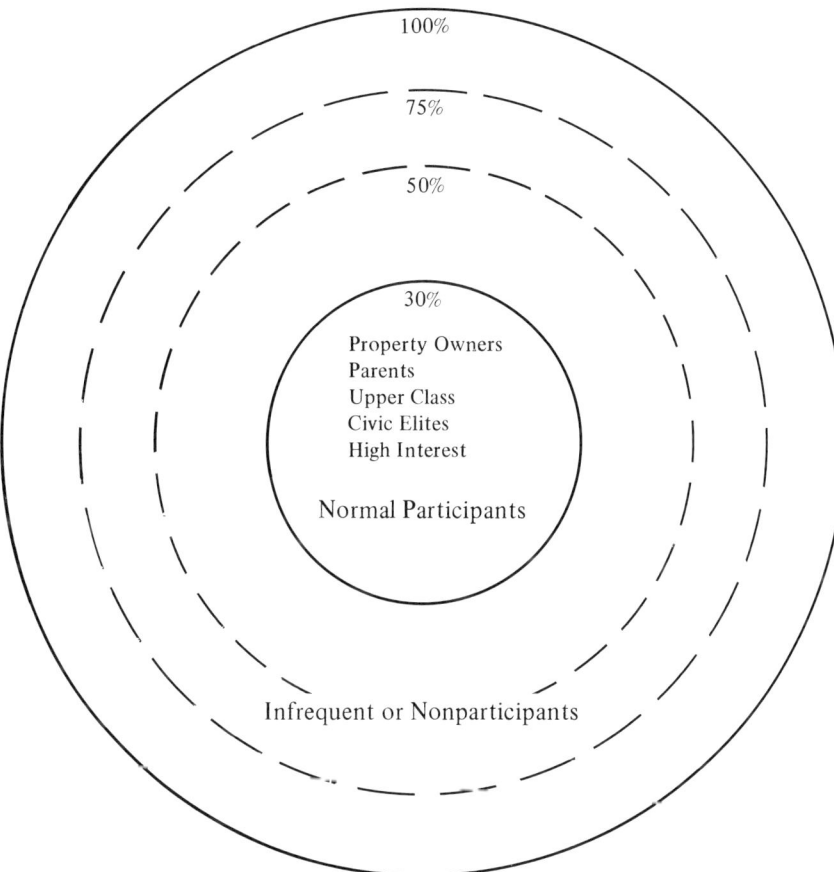

**Figure 4-2.** Probable Participants in "Normal" School Financial Elections

---

[27]The "normal vote" model has been developed by researchers from the Survey Research Center and is central to their explanation of voting in presidential elections. See Philip E. Converse et al., "Stability and Change in 1960: A Reinstating Election," *American Political Science Review* 55 (June 1961): 269-80; Philip E. Converse, "The Concept of the Normal Vote," in Angus Campbell et al., *Elections and the Political Order* (New York: John Wiley and Sons, 1966), Chapter 2; and Philip E. Converse et al., "Continuity and Change in American Politics," *American Political Science Review* (December 1969): 1083-1105.

Under certain circumstances an expansion of that pool takes place and citizens who normally do not vote do cast ballots in a school financial election. As the successive broken-line circles illustrate, expansion of the normal voting pool means a proportionate increase in representation of these infrequent voters. According to the evidence reviewed, this expanded voting pool frequently contains a larger proportion of no voters.

Although the conceptualization presented in Figure 4-2 is based on persuasive evidence, the reader should be reminded that the normal vote model is static and largely based on scholarship of the late 1950s and early and middle 1960s. In the first chapter, we documented a widespread change in national patterns of voter support for the schools during the late 1960s. Unfortunately, correlative participation data that bear directly on the conflict/normal vote hypothesis are not available. However, recent indirect evidence from the Gallup (1969) polling organization indicates a relatively insignificant gap between the a priori choice of *voters* and *nonvoters* in a school financial election. This evidence and its meaning will be considered in greater detail in the concluding chapter during our discussion of future research needs.

At this point, it seems sufficient to note that future research can and should provide a more accurate description of the normal school election voter (and nonvoter) at different points in time. Undoubtedly such descriptions will not always be congruent with community conflict theory, nor will the explanation that some form of community conflict has preceded increases in turnout and negative voting always be sufficient. If conflict stimulates predominantly negative participation among some groups to the exclusion of other groups we need to know why. If conflict and turnout tell us little about outcome in certain election situations we need to be aware of alternative explanations. These and several other questions remain to be answered before we can speak with confidence about the potential for reversing the conclusion—described by Carter and Savard (1961)—that may have been reached by school officials who have read this far: ". . . to do nothing seems irresponsible; to turn out only those voters identified as favorable to the schools seems immoral; and to campaign for full voter turnout seems like gambling against high odds."

In the following chapters we will summarize additional evidence regarding factors that may affect the outcome of school financial elections. Such an analysis should make the dilemma of the practitioner more understandable, if not more palatable.

# 5 Environmental Determinants

Studies of electoral behavior in the United States exhibit differing fundamental premises. Essentially, premises and, to some extent, research results differ because divergent conceptualizations of the malleability of American voters are employed in the studies.

Important research in partisan voting behavior underscores the stable nature of the voting act. This view, which stresses the permanence of voting patterns, is derived from the strong correlations that have been found between a number of long-term and relatively rigid social, psychological, and economic characteristics (including partisan preferences) and direction of the vote in presidential elections. In fact, the institution most responsible for this approach (the University of Michigan's Survey Research Center) has been criticized for developing a model that "threatens to take the politics out of the study of voting behavior."[1]

It may very well be that "normal" voting behavior in school elections is rooted in a maze of historical and contemporary influences that predispose voters to make rather consistent and predictable voting decisions. Nevertheless, the establishment of a theory of "normal" voting[2] —for both individuals and given populations—only increases the importance of a better understanding of voter malleability.

That American voters are adaptive, or malleable, cannot be doubted. Candidates from the nation's majority political party frequently lose. Millions of dollars are spent annually in mass media campaigns. And an increasing number voters refuse to register as partisans. Of those who do claim a partisan preference, many split their tickets.[3] These and similar indicators demonstrate that if voting behavior "norms" can be identified, so can changes or deviations from those norms.

---

[1] V.O. Key and Frank Munger offer this critique of the "sociological approach" in "Social Determinism and Electoral Decision: The Case of Indiana," in Eugene Burdick and Arthur Brodbeck (eds.), *American Voting Behavior* (Glencoe, Ill.: The Free Press, 1959), pp. 281-99.

[2] The Survey Research Center has done most to advance a theory of the normal vote in presidential contests. See, for example, Philip E. Converse, "The Concept of the Normal Vote," in Angus Campbell et al., *Elections and The Political Order* (New York: John Wiley and Sons, 1966), Chapter 2.

[3] The recent trends of increased independent affiliation and split-ticket voting are documented in Walter De Vries and Lance Tarrance, Jr., *The Ticket-Splitter: A New Force in American Politics* (Grand Rapids, Michigan: William B. Eerdmans Publishing Co., 1972).

Although certain "nonpolitical"—social and psychological—factors may prove most useful in explaining "normal" voting in partisan contests, the static nature of these factors prohibits their explaining deviations from the norm (e.g., large numbers of Democrats voting for the Republican candidate, as was the case in the presidential elections of 1952 and 1956). For this reason, analysts and strategists must look to the environment—to those directly political factors that the SRC researchers label "short term forces"[4] and that Anthony Downs considers "short run vote value"[5] considerations. The preeminent theoretical and practical question about voter malleability is, What are the controllable and noncontrollable factors that stimulate individual voters and groups of voters to *change* their habitual or "normal" voting patterns?

Although it seems evident from the partisan voting literature that some voters are both malleable and manipulatable some of the time, a partisan campaign manager must still determine who is most malleable and how to use this information most effectively. Similarly, a school election strategist is interested in the effect of short-range forces on the outcome of school financial elections. The following pages discuss research findings on the relative importance of certain environmental (or situational) factors on school financial election outcomes.

## School District Characteristics

A number of findings concern the effect environmental forces have on the success or failure of school financial elections. School districts vary greatly in organizational patterns and personnel characteristics. Assuming that these patterns and characteristics affect a district's ability to communicate with and influence the community, then we may anticipate a strong relationship between these qualities and election outcomes. The findings discussed immediately below clarify the relationship between "resource characteristics" and election success and provide indirect evidence concerning the potential of environmental determinants.

### *Organization*

School districts differ greatly from one another in important organizational, financial, and personnel resources. These differences in organizational capacity may well be reflected in different communication patterns and levels of support

---

[4]Campbell et al., op. cit.

[5]Anthony Downs, *An Economic Theory of Democracy* (New York: Harper and Row, 1957), p. 270.

for the schools. For an initial analysis of the effect of organizational complexity on communication and support factors, school districts may be classified by size and type.

The research literature frequently cites school district size as an indicator of organizational complexity and a useful control variable in comparative studies. A majority of the studies available find there is NO SIGNIFICANT RELATIONSHIP BETWEEN SCHOOL DISTRICT SIZE AND ELECTION OUTCOME (Beal et al., 1966, Minar, 1966; Dykstra, 1964; Hicks, 1967; New York State Education Department, 1970; Wentzel, 1964; Crider, 1967). However, three studies based on exceptionally comprehensive data sets (Carter, 1960, national data; Davidson, 1964, 217 Illinois elections; Saalfeld, 1972, 250 Oregon elections) report strong positive relationships between school district size and negative election outcomes. Beal et al., (1966) and Barbour (1966) report a curvilinear relationship: districts classified as "large" and "small" were more likely to succeed than those classified as medium-sized. The effect of controlling for school district size on several other relationships will be apparent in other findings reported in this section.

Another plausible indicator of school district organizational climate is the teacher/pupil ratio. The New York State Education Department (1970) reports finding no significant relationship between a district's professional staff to student ratio and voter choice in school financial elections. On the other hand, data from the Iowa research project conducted by Beal et al. (reported in Beal et al., 1966; and in Barbour, 1966) suggest there is no significant relationship between the differing teacher/pupil ratios of school districts and the success or failure of their school bond elections.

Finally, Davidson (1967) found that Illinois elementary districts were more likely to have successful financial elections than were high school or unit districts in that state.

*Characteristics of School Officials*

The personal qualities and characteristics of school officials are, at least potentially, among a school district's most important resources for influencing voter behavior. Often, the only significant difference between one district's financial election campaign and another district's campaign is the salesmen—principally school officials—attempting to justify the need for voter approval of new issues.

As the chief executive officer of a school system, the superintendent attempts to respond to and influence both the board of education and the public. Although superintendents are normally deeply involved in school elections, the evidence concerning their actual impact on election outcomes is inconclusive. Barbour (1966) found no statistically significant relationship between the experience of a district superintendent and approval or disapproval of a bond issue. Carter and Ruggels (1966) found, however, that school districts whose superintendents have experience teaching in that district are more likely to pass school elections than are districts whose superintendents are without such experience. Carter and Ruggels also report a positive relationship between a superintendent's aspirations and election success: School districts whose superintendents aspire to future administrative duties outside education are more likely to succeed in passing school financial elections than are districts whose superintendents aspire to other future goals.[6]

A number of questions have been asked—primarily by the Carter et al. research team—that shed some light on the association between school board characteristics and election outcome. Some of the questions appear more directly related to the structure of the market place (the local political system) than to the attributes of the salesmen (board members). For example, in their national sample Carter and Sutthoff (1960) examined the relationship between length of board members' terms of office and election success. They found that medium-size school districts whose board members' terms exceed four years were more likely to pass tax elections than were districts whose terms are four years or less. No such relationship was evident among districts classified as "large" or "small."

When the setting was changed to school *bond* elections, a different pattern became evident: large school districts whose terms of office exceed four years were more likely to pass bond elections that were districts whose terms are four years or less. No significant relationship was found among medium and small districts.

Regardless of the importance (or lack of importance) of length of term, board stability has been associated with election success while controlling for district size (Carter and Ruggels, 1966).[7]

Few sound conclusions can be drawn from the above evidence alone, but it can be noted that an individual's role as a school official might be more important in large communities where communication channels are formal and complex. If one is to be influential in a large community, it may be necessary to have had access to formal communication channels and/or "public official" status for a longer time. The assumption is that sheer size may be a significant barrier to communication and influence.

Other factors pointing to the potential influence of school district organization and personnel are suggested in the following findings concerning board of education contributions to election outcome:

1. The greater the occupational and educational status of the school district's

---

[6]"Other future goals" are defined as teaching in higher education, educational administration other than the superintendency, or superintendency in other districts.

[7]Board stability is defined as the number of years needed to change the majority composition of the board.

board of education members, the greater the probability of success in financial elections (Minar, 1966).

2. School districts whose board members are appointed are more likely to pass *bond* issues than are districts whose board members are elected. Selection procedure is not related to *tax* issue outcome (Carter and Sutthoff, 1960).
3. Medium-size school districts whose boards have sole authority to approve budgets are likely to pass bond and tax elections that require voter approval. This relationship did not hold for "large" and "small" districts (Carter and Ruggels, 1966).
4. School districts whose board members consider the "preparation of children for citizenship" the most important goal of their schools are less likely to pass school financial issues than are districts whose board members consider other[8] goals more important (Carter and Ruggels, 1966).
5. Districts whose board members disagree over the desirability of a bond issue are less likely to pass school bond issues than are districts whose board members agree on the need (or lack of need) for the bond issue (Crider, 1967).
6. The more board members agree on the factors affecting school community relationships, the greater that district's portion of favorable votes in a school financial election (Carter and Ruggels, 1966).
7. School districts whose boards have a legally sanctioned potential for greater fiscal control[9] are more likely to succeed in passing school bond issues than are districts whose boards have a lesser potential for fiscal control. However, there is no statistically significant relationship between the degree of board fiscal control and success or failure of school tax elections.

These findings tentatively suggest a profile of a school board that appears to accompany election success. This profile provides clues for understanding the effects of less tangible but probably more important environmental factors such as "community atmosphere." The relatively greater success rates of districts governed by appointed board members who have (in medium-size districts) authority to approve budgets without referral to the electorate appears to reflect (or may be one of the factors affecting) an atmosphere of deferral to expertise and a consequent (or subsequent) relatively tranquil community decision-making process.[10] Additional evidence for assessing this possibility is available, as we shall see in the following sections.

---

[8]"Other goals" that were selected include "preparation for problems of adult life," "development of intellectual ability," and so forth.

[9]Degree of fiscal control is measured by an index of several variables, some of which have been mentioned in the above list of findings.

[10]This interpretation introduces the concept of "community conflict," which is treated at length by Carter and Ruggels, particularly pp. 1-24, and will be treated in detail in another

## Community Conflict

The nebulous concept "community atmosphere" reintroduces community conflict theory. Chapter 4 outlined a theory of community conflict developed to explain the positive relationship between increased voter turnout and negative voting levels that is often noted in studies of local elections in general and local school elections in particular.[11] The evidence points out that "rising tension in a political system results in increased voter participation"[12] and that general increases in participation signal decreases in the magnitude of group differences in the total voter population (Tingsten's "law of dispersion").[13]

Significant questions surrounding the exact kinds and meanings of community conflicts remain. Is a conflict situation a simple stimulate causing a large number of normally apathetic individuals who harbor latent negative attitudes toward the schools to participate in an election? Or is the substance of a conflict responsible for increased dissatisfaction that cuts across the voter population at the same time that participation is increased?

The literature does not contain specific answers to these questions. Nevertheless, partial theory surrounding the study of community conflict and the relationship between voter turnout and negative voting supports a number of inferences.[14]

*Issues*

Studies of the process of community conflict indicate that the specific issue that "causes" or "stimulates" a given controversy may exhibit great qualitative variation. In an average school district, it seems reasonable to assume that a significant number of individuals are dissatisfied with some of the things the

---

section. An excellent model for discussions such as this is contained in Robert L. Crain, Elihu Katz, and Donald B. Rosenthal, *The Politics of Community Conflict: The Fluoridation Decision* (Indianapolis: The Bobbs-Merrill Co., 1969). These researchers find a strong relationship between "type of community" and the outcome of fluoridation decisions.

[11] For a list of the studies that report this relationship see Chapter 4, p. 107.

[12] Clarence N. Stone, "Local Referendums: An Alternative to the Alienated Voter Model," *Public Opinion Quarterly* 29 (Summer 1965):213.

[13] Herbert Tingsten, *Political Behavior: Studies in Election Statistics* (London: P.S. King & Son, Ltd., 1937).

[14] The key citation to the concept of community conflict is James S. Coleman, *Community Conflict* (New York: The Free Press, 1957). For further discussion of relevant research and theory see Chapter 4, particularly notes 17 through 19. For a concise theoretical discussion directed at school election voting see Goettel (February 1971, pp. 24-27, or September 1971, p. 4).

schools are doing (or not doing) or at one time felt sufficiently dissatisfied to develop some negative attitudes toward the schools or education in general. These attitudes may remain dormant as long as the schools are noncontroversial.

The sudden emergence of an emotional school-related issue, however, may awaken dormant attitudes, values, and predispositions that prompt an immediate evaluation of the schools and education. The content of the precipitating issue is probably important only to the extent that some issues may prompt a greater emotional or "gut-level" reaction than others.

Certain issues—e.g., sex education, desegregation, and district boundary disputes[15]—seem to have the greatest potential for eliciting responses from individuals and coverage by the news media, and for increasing the community's level of concern over and awareness of the schools. As informal and formal communication networks begin to carry more "news" about the issue, borderline individuals—those who hold negative opinions and attitudes toward the schools but normally do not vent them—may receive enough reinforcement to prompt action (in this case, a negative vote).

According to Coleman, community conflicts blossom from specific issues in the manner described above, though "the issues which provide the initial basis of response in a controversy undergo great transformations as the controversy develops."[16] The community conflicts Coleman observed tended to exhibit a uniform pattern of issue transformation as the controversy developed from its beginning to its apex: (1) specific issues become more general, (2) issues that are new and quite different from the original ones emerge, and (3) dispassionate disagreement over issues becomes generalized as emotional antagonism and hostility.[17] In other words, community conflict theory posits a spiraling stimulus over time. As the issue becomes more general it gains appeal for more individuals who in turn become activists. The participation of these activists raises the general community "heat" and increases the pressures to polarize those individuals who remain borderline cases so as to draw them into the conflict.

This pattern of controversy development suggests that the content of the conflict-stimulating issue is relatively unimportant except as it serves to highlight the schools: "Certainly the increased level of communication created by an originally unrelated issue or conflict can serve as a catalyst for the expression of negative attitudes toward the schools."[18]

---

[15] A number of case studies describe the growth of a single school issue into a full-blown community conflict. For the best such accounts see Louis H. Masotti, *Education and Politics in Suburbia* (Cleveland, Ohio: The Press of Western Reserve University, 1967); and Agger and Goldstein (1971).

[16] Coleman, op. cit., p. 10.

[17] Ibid.

[18] Goettel, February 1971, p. 27.

*Interest Groups and Leaders*

Community groups and leaders appear to have an important effect on the outcome of community controversies. In general, *the greater a community's level of organized opposition, the more likely is defeat of school financial elections* (Jennings and Zeigler, 1970; Crider, 1967; Carter and Ruggels, 1966).[19]

In some kinds of conflict the organized opposition is likely to grow with the controversy. In other cases, the membership and pressure of the organizations that are in opposition remain predictably the same from issue to issue and from campaign to campaign (e.g., taxpayer's associations and local financial elections). In either case, organizations serve as clearinghouses for selectively important information concerning election issues. Organization pressures also serve to reinforce existing predispositions among those individuals for whom group ties are most important and consistent. The seemingly inevitable result of these pressures is the surfacing of latent negative feelings toward the schools, increasing polarization of opinions, and increasing antagonism and "heat" within the community.

Although the role of opposition groups in community conflict is generally understood, the effect of group leaders is not. Coleman, however, describes a typical pattern of leadership emergence that is useful in understanding the growth of community controversies. He labels the leadership that emerges during community controversies the "Ideologically Committed":

A few active oppositionists, men who are continually in opposition, oppose the administration. These men are sometimes motivated by the hope of power, but often they are ideologically committed to a 'cause'. In the recent school controversies, these have often been men who are sincerely convinced the schools are subversive, men who are against all modern trends in education, or whose whole political philosophy is far to the right of present-day parties. Though their 'causes' may differ, the men are fully dedicated.[20]

According to Coleman, these men come from a group of potential leaders that is more-or-less ever-present. Frequently, they are isolated and marginal men who change into group leaders when a large and normally inactive group of citizens are activated either by a change in the general climate of opinion or by a series of administration blunders in matters that are salient to the "passive majority."[21] Once the passive majority is activated,

---

[19] Each of these studies actually measured the level of group activity within a community. Similar measurement techniques and results are reported in William S. Berner, "Campaign Conduct and the Outcome of Library Bond Referendums," in Guy Garrison (ed.), *Studies in Public Library Government, Organization, and Support* (Urbana, Ill.: Illinois University, 1969), p. 213. For the one study that takes exception to this proposition see Beal, 1964.

[20] Coleman, op. cit., p. 8.

[21] Ibid.

The ideologically-committed, active oppositionist is now able to use this new hostile atmosphere to gain his ends. He can now lead the large, mobilized group against the administration and its supporting minority. Seldom are his objectives and values those of the majority, but he uses them for his own purposes while they are active and in opposition of his adversary. Unfortunately, perhaps, these mechanisms suggest manipulation of the masses by 'evil' opposition.[22]

By definition, these new leaders are not likely to be pragmatists. Their ideology calls for a "with us or against us" posture. The demand that clear-cut ideological positions, or "sides," be taken may immobilize the traditional community groups and leaders who are more pragmatically inclined and, hence, subject to internal conflict. At the same time, the inexperience and self-righteousness of the new leaders and groups frees them "from some of the usual shackles of community norms and internal cross-pressures which make pre-existing organizations and leaders tend to soften the dispute."[23]

Although many local issues—fluoridation and charter revision are good examples— seem vulnerable to this kind of ideological opposition, school issues appear uniquely susceptible to *group-based* attack. School issues also receive the brunt of the organized opposition to taxes in general. The dilemma that the schools face is probably compounded by the diffuse nature of their traditional sources of support. Even if the immobilization process described above does not take place, the nature of school-based group conflict in many communities appears to create a bias toward the negative forces. Agger and Goldstein (1971), for example, compare one community's reception of a federally funded, locally implemented program for urban renewal with its reception of a similar program for a teaching innovation. While both programs received similar opposition from the "radical right," urban renewal appeared to have the advantage of particular and powerful group support (e.g., downtown merchants). On the other hand, proponents of an innovative education program

have had a more loosely woven network of supporting groups than have community conservationists who favor urban renewal. And they have been faced with a vigilant set of taxpayer associations and other citizens concerned with rapidly mounting local property taxes, especially for local school systems, as well as with local radical-right groups. (pp. 23-24)

In summary, for some time the schools have been surrounded by issues that are likely to create emotional debate within a community. Recently, the potential for emotional conflict has been increased by the addition of such issues as school busing, teacher strikes, and student activism to the traditional disputes over site location, facilities utilization, teaching innovations, and so forth. More important, however, than the conflict issues per se are the attitudes and values of both the general citizenry and the leaders produced by the issue of the moment.

---

[22] Ibid.

[23] Ibid., p. 12.

This is the case because the conflict process often spirals to the point at which the original issues are lost in the perceptual smoke screen referred to as "polarized opinion."

*Conflict Management*

The relationship between the intensity of community group activity and negative voting in school elections is in harmony with the persistent finding that chances of election success tend to decline with increases in voter turnout (reported in Chapter 4). Together these findings buttress the community conflict explanation of election defeat: a full-blown community conflict loads the case against a school election.

Coleman observed full-scale conflicts and then worked deductively to identify initial issues in deriving his "reciprocal causation" model of community conflict. The reciprocal and escalating nature of the conflict process raises an important question:

... if all these forces work in the direction of increasing intensity, how is it that community conflicts stop short of annihilation? After all community conflicts are inhibited. ... Forces do exist which can counteract these processes and bring the dispute into orderly channels.[24]

Coleman attributes variation in conflict intensity among communities to a "third force" or "governor" that exists in the form of a set of *"preexisting community characteristics."*

Some important evidence does suggest that certain kinds of communities are more successful than others in controlling and minimizing conflict.[25] Minar (1966) found that low conflict and school election success are related to high community status. Minar's explanation of this finding is that high status communities have fewer conflicts with the schools because the individuals in those communities respect technical expertise.

Although a community's net conflict management resources may be difficult to define, the voters evaluation of technical expertise appears important from clues provided by research on the relationship between cynicism and voting. For example, *individuals who express confidence in the ability of school officials to make decisions are more likely to vote in favor of school financial elections than are individuals who are cynical about the decision-making ability of school*

---

[24] Ibid., p. 14.

[25] Relevant earlier literature is cited in ibid., pp. 16-25. For more recent corroborative evidence and discussion see Maurice Pinard, "Structural Attachments and Political Support in Urban Politics: The Case of Fluoridation Referenda," *American Journal of Sociology* 68 (1963):513-26; and Crain, Katz, and Rosenthal, *The Politics of Community Conflict: The Fluoridation Decision* pp. 227-28.

*officials* (Agger and Goldstein, 1965 and 1971; Milstein and Jennings, 1970). Attitudinal correlates to voter choice are described more fully in Chapter 7.

Obviously, the net evaluation of a community's officials by the individuals (or voters) of that community is a product of the interaction between the officials and the citizenry at large. If Minar's hypothesis provides an accurate method of differentiating environments (communities) that are more-or-less susceptable to conflict and, in turn, more-or-less likely to pass school issues, then school supporters must look for means of improving both the community's conflict management skills and its acceptance of expertise. This quest must begin by entertaining the traditional question: What can the concerned school official or citizen do to direct the outcome of an election? Or, phrased more generally, what are the effects of environmental inputs on a school election?

## Communication, Information Flow, and Campaign Techniques

Theories of communication and of information flow may suggest methods of directing election outcomes. Myriad plausible techniques designed to inform and influence voters are in use. Because these techniques are in such widespread use in various campaigns, their impact on voters must be determined. Not surprisingly, the general theories of communication are useful only to a limited extent because, as one reviewer has noted, such theory tends to deal "with psychological processes after the individual has been engaged or involved in the message. To get him to attend to the message is, however, another story."[26]

Unfortunately, however, the well-known studies of the effectiveness of various campaign techniques used in partisan elections also provide information of limited value—relatively few minds are changed by use of traditional techniques.[27] That is, campaigns have traditionally been interpreted as attempts

---

[26] Daniel Katz, "Psychological Studies of Communication and Persuasion," in Leslie W. Kindred (ed.), *Communications Research and School-Community Relations* (Philadelphia: College of Education, Temple University, 1965), pp 58-79. Several articles useful in understanding the application of communication theory to school public relations efforts are contained in this reader.

[27] This was the surprising direction of findings that emerged from the early voting research conducted at Columbia and reported in Paul F. Lazarsfeld, Bernard R. Berelson, and Hazel Gaudet, *The People's Choice.* Second Edition. (New York: Columbia University Press, 1948), and in the sequel to that work by Bernard R. Berelson, Paul F. Lazarsfeld, and William N. McPhee, *Voting* (Chicago: University of Chicago Press, 1954). These studies provide the basis for the "floating voter hypothesis," which asserts that those voters most likely to change their vote—from the candidate of one party to the candidate of the other party—are among the least informed segment of the voting population. In general, this hypothesis has been supported by a number of studies reviewed and cited in H. Daudt, *The Floating Voter and The Floating Vote: A Critical Analysis of American and English Election Studies* (Leiden, Holland: H.E. Stenfert Kroese, 1961). More recent support for that hypothesis is reported in Edward C. Dreyer, "Media Use and Electoral Choices: Some Political Consequences of Information Exposure," *The Public Opinion Quarterly* 35 (Winter

to activate voters' existing partisan predispositions in an effort to polarize them along partisan lines. The direction of these techniques, together with most voter's selective perceptions of campaign information, tends not to influence choice so much as to reinforce existing preferences.[28] Thus, from the systemic viewpoint, the essential purpose of a campaign appears to be to invigorate "politics of a democracy in which otherwise most people are apathetic most of the time."[29]

Recent research, however, has found an important, though limited, increase in both the number of voters who consider themselves "independents" and the number of voters who behave independently by splitting their tickets both in the same election and between elections.[30] According to researchers in the area, this erosion of partisan influence suggests an increase in the importance of campaign techniques and strategies as methods of influencing voter choice.[31] If this reasoning is accurate, campaigning should have great value in nonpartisan contests such as school elections.

---

1971-1972):544-53. Dreyer's analysis is based on Michigan Survey Research Center data for the presidential election year surveys from 1952 through 1968. Although he finds that the "floating voter pool" has expanded somewhat during that time—perhaps partly because of short-term forces including mass media—its composition as reflected by certain attitudinal and socioeconomic characteristics remained the same relative to other segments of the voting population. This analysis partly conflicts with Philip Converse's revision of the floating voter hypothesis. Converse posits a curvilinear relationship between information exposure and stability of partisan preference on the basis of a hypothesized link between political involvement and the qualitative impact of new political information. See Dreyer's comments in op. cit., particularly pp. 548-51, and Philip E. Converse, "Information Flow and the Stability of Partisan Attitudes," in Angus Campbell et al., *Elections and the Political Order* (New York: John Wiley, 1966), pp. 136-58.

[28]The classic treatment of the effect of mass media in influencing public opinion may be found in Joseph T. Klapper, *The Effects of Mass Communications* (Glencoe, Ill.: The Free Press, 1960). Klapper underscored both the minimal effect of mass media on direct opinion persuasion and the importance of selective perception. However, several experimental studies that "force" exposure to media have found evidence of substantial attitude change. For a review of those studies see C. I. Hovland, "Reconciling Conflicting Results Derived from Experimental and Survey Studies of Attitude Change," in Maria Jahoda and Neil Warren (eds.), *Attitudes* (Baltimore: Penguin Books, 1966), pp. 287-304.

[29]Ithiel De Sola Pool, "Mass Communication and Political Science," in Kindred (ed.), op. cit., p. 136.

[30]The trend toward a growing independent electorate is evident in surveys taken periodically during the last twenty years. The trend is documented in various editions of the Gallup Opinion Index. The growth of the split-ticket and floating voter pools in recent years is documented in Walter De Vries and Lance Tarrance, Jr., *The Ticket-Splitter: A New Force in American Politics* (Grand Rapids, Mich.: William B. Eerdmans Publishing Co., 1972), and in Dreyer, op. cit., respectively.

[31]This assumption underlies much of what is tactically new in political campaigns. A number of provocative articles that are based on assumptions of increasing voter volatility are contained in Ray Hiebert et al. (eds.), *The Political Image Merchants: Strategies in the New Politics* (Washington, D.C.: Acropolis Books Ltd., 1971). For particularly relevant sections see Oliver A. Quayle III, "Charting the Volatile and Shifting Electorate," pp. 131-33; and Matthew Reese, "Locating the 'Switch-Split' Vote," pp. 162-64.

*Campaign Techniques*

The major problem in attempts to assess systematically the effect of various campaign strategies is controlling for variables. Despite this problem, a few studies have attempted to measure the relative effect of various campaign techniques and strategies. Turner (1968) found no significant relationship between the use of a variety of techniques and the proportion of favorable votes in a Los Angeles school bond election. A similar study[32] that attempted to trace the effect of various "personal contact" campaign techniques on the outcome of library bond elections reached a similar conclusion: there is no significant relationship between the use of the different campaign techniques studied and the outcome of a library bond issue.

The only significant finding reported by studies attempting to compare the relative merits of different campaign techniques stresses the importance of message content as opposed to the particular communications vehicle. Carter and Ruggels (1966) found that the greater a school district's emphasis on specific school needs during a campaign, the lesser the district's proportion of favorable votes in a school financial election. This finding, however, points to the problem of controlling for the effects of extraneous variables. Perhaps, as Carter and Ruggels suggest, school district personnel may decide to emphasize district needs after it becomes apparent that the campaign is going against them. In such situations school officials may react to symptoms of voter disapproval by increasing the intensity of the campaign effort (including stressing specific school needs). This effort, in turn, created increased resistance to the campaign. The result is in keeping with the "reciprocal causation" model described in the community conflict section of this chapter.

Again the problem may not lie with the campaign effort itself but with the timing of that effort. To the degree school officials are correct in assessing serious negative forces within the community, the officials will probably signal the election failure through well-meaning but futile and short-term campaign responses. This explanation should be considered as we look at the following findings, which, ironically, show no relationship between school district efforts to obtain voter approval and actual success rates in school financial elections.

*Information: Source and Amount*

Four studies based on relatively comprehensive data sets find *no significant relationship between school district campaign use of mass media and success or failure of school bond or tax elections* (Whisler, 1965; Barbour, 1966; Beal et al.,

---

[32] William S. Berner, "Campaign Conduct and the Outcome of Library Bond Referendums," in Guy Garrison (ed.), *Studies in Public Library Government, Organization, and Support* (Urbana, Illinois: Illinois University, 1969).

1966; Turner, 1968). Although their operational definitions varied slightly, these studies attempted to assess the effectiveness of TV, radio, and newspaper publicity along with the more specialized school media such as pamphlets, specially prepared sound tracks, and brochures. Most of the evidence collected by these researchers is quantitative. For example, Beal found no statistically significant relationship between the *number* of district press releases on a school bond election and the success or failure of that issue.

Similarly, Carter (1960) and Whisler (1965) found they were unable to differentiate between successful and unsuccessful districts on the basis of the *amount* of information (measured differently) supplied by the district to the voters.

In their study of voting for several local bond issues, Boskoff and Zeigler[33] found official campaign efforts to be generally ineffective in changing voter attitudes. Their explanation for this finding may be useful in interpreting the lack of a positive relationship between mass media campaign efforts and election outcome. According to these researchers, the government communication source served as a symbol for strengthening already hostile attitudes on the part of most negative voters. For many positive voters, on the other hand, it dissipated doubts on specific aspects of the election.

The authors conclude that "both sets of voters followed their own perceived notions of their own and the county's needs. It is true, however, that the resistance to information is more characteristic of the negative voters with their firmer 'set' of attitudes."[34] Thus, to the extent that Boskoff and Zeigler's theory is generalizable, normal campaign efforts may do more harm than good by reinforcing existing attitudes.

Similarly, Carter (1960) concludes there is "little to be gained from any simple attempt to increase the informational output of schools." In explaining his conclusion, Carter notes two conditions that he feels are necessary for the school's use of mass media campaign techniques to be effective: (1) values in the audience that turn constructive attention toward the schools and (2) a social environment that facilitates participation. Chapter 4, however, provided evidence that raises questions as to the strategic wisdom of school attempts to change the second condition.

*Techniques to Increase Participation*

Techniques designed to increase voter participation in school financial elections may accomplish that objective but appear unlikely to lead to victory on election

---

[33] Boskoff and Zeigler, *Voting Patterns in a Local Election,* pp. 85-94.

[34] Ibid., p. 91.

day. Carter and Ruggels (1966) report that the more a school district uses telephones and mail correspondence to increase voter participation, the less that district's proportion of favorable votes in school financial elections.

Similar findings are reported by the researchers who reviewed Iowa school bond issues (Beal et al., 1966). These analysts report no statistically significant relationship between a district's use of such techniques as providing babysitters on election day and making absentee ballots available and success or failure in a school bond election.

Another unrewarding campaign technique is evident from the findings that school districts providing voters with transportation to the polls on election day are more likely to fail in a school bond election than those who do not (Beal et al., 1966). Although the use of these "get out the vote" techniques represents an admirable faith in the "democratic model," they may well cause a net increase in negative voting.

As was suggested above, new publicity and increased campaign activity almost always increase the polarization of public opinion and escalate the intensity of community conflict. Thus, in keeping with the evidence from Chapter 4, efforts to increase participation among the general citizenry may frequently prove self-defeating from the school proponent's point-of-view.

The boomerang effect of the schools' promotion of democracy may also be at least partly attributable to the fact that many campaign techniques do not actually promote general—that is, randon—increases in citizen participation. For instance, by providing voters with transportation to the polls a school district invites a very select portion of the population to participate: those who normally would not be able to vote because their age or income level makes transportation a problem. These two categories of citizens can normally be expected to oppose tax increases for the schools (as we shall see in the ensuing chapter).

Indeed, few techniques that are not ultimately "selective," either by design or by the nature of the technique, can be imagined. As the "floating voter" hypothesis (see footnote 27 of this chapter) suggests, the use of mass media to increase voter turnout for presidential elections exerts a selective effect by "raising the turnout rates of the less involved groups more than the rates of the more involved."[35] In other words, effective media campaigns serve to insure the operation of Herbert Tingsten's "law of dispersion."[36]

Media use brings turnout differences slightly closer together between men and women, between the rich and poor, and between the better educated and the less educated. Thus, media stimuli might bring into the electorate a larger

---

[35] William A. Glaser, "Television and Voting Turnout," *The Public Opinion Quarterly* 29 (Spring 1965):82.

[36] Herbert Tingsten, *Political Behavior: Studies in Election Statistics* (London: P.S. King & Son, Ltd., 1937), pp. 230-31.

*number* of the politically less involved than of the population groups more interested in politics.[37]

If the law of dispersion holds true for partisan elections, it would reasonably apply even more strongly to nonpartisan elections because (as was suggested in Chapter 3) the normally small voting pool in local nonpartisan contests is even more likely than a presidential electorate to be a nonrepresentative sample of the larger population. Media activity prior to a school election may thus serve to attract new participants who, on the basis of evidence to be reviewed in Chapters 6 and 7, are unlikely to favor school financial proposals.

Even without considering group and attitudinal correlates of receptivity to mass media, available data suggest that citizens who normally do not vote in school financial elections are more inclined to vote no than are citizens who normally do vote. Data from a panel study of four random samples of populations drawn from four New York communities (N=1,280, evenly divided between voters and nonvoters) yield the following cross-tabulation (Milstein and Jennings, 1970, p. 19):

|  | *Voter* | *Nonvoter* |
|---|---|---|
| For | 56% | 51% |
| Against | 44% | 49% |

Similarly, evidence from a national random sample survery (Gallup 1969, pp. 18-19) suggests a slightly greater negative response from those who did not participate in school elections during 1969:

|  | *Voter* | *Total Sample* |
|---|---|---|
| For | 47% | 45% |
| Against | 47% | 49% |
| Don't Know | 6% | 6% |

It is difficult not to conclude that general or "unfocused" techniques designed to improve the participation of individuals who normally do not vote are, inadvertently, directed toward one segment of the population just as much as "selective" campaigns are directed toward another segment. Therefore, the morality of selective campaigns aimed at a predefined supportive audience may not be a real question.[38] Those who support the schools may rightly think, on the basis of this and similar evidence from the communication literature, that many accepted campaign techniques are, in fact, selective of negative voters. If the school supporter or official is still troubled by perceived infidelity to the

---

[37]Glaser, loc. cit.

[38]For an excellent and detailed case study of a selective campaign see William J. Banach and Lawrence Westley, "Public Relations, Computers, and Election Success," a paper prepared for presentation to the Association for Educational Data System, May 19, 1972.

democratic way, he will have to console himself with pragmatic considerations based on the likely voting direction of voters and nonvoters.

*Planning and Implementing the Campaign*

The preceding section has, of course, presented a bleak picture for school officials who may have been contemplating use of mass media and related techniques to generate support for school issues. Reasonably, those attempting to encourage greater positive voting in school financial elections must at this point ask if any positive campaign action can be taken to achieve their objectives.

A more optimistic evaluation of campaign efforts follows from the proposition *that the longer the campaign,*[39] the more likely is approval of school financial issues (Beal et al., 1966). The evidence is not unanimous, however. Murphy (1966) found no significant association between length of campaign and election outcome. More importantly, this proposition tells us nothing about the variety of forms—the multitude of specific techniques—that a campaign may take. We suspect that the most important factor the length of a campaign indicates is the planning and concern of the school officials in charge of the election.

Finally, two other techniques frequently advocated by the "how to win through improved communication" school of thought appear to be equally unimportant determinants of election success or failure. One technique is the use of a citizen's advisory committee to help formulate and implement election campaigns. The rationale behind this technique is that involvement of acknowledged community leaders will lend legitimacy to the campaign, improve communication channels, and generally enhance school-community relations.

Theoretically, advisory groups should provide the opportunity for greater agreement among school and community leaders on the goals of the schools and on factors affecting the attainment of those goals. This portion of the rationale has been labeled "understanding" by Carter et al. (1966), who found it strongly related to success/failure rates in school financial elections. Nonetheless, most available evidence suggests the proposition that *the use of a citizen's committee in an election campaign has no influence on the success or failure of a school financial election* (Carter and Chaffee, 1966; Crider, 1967; Beal et al., 1966).

---

[39] In two of these studies, length of campaign is treated as a nominal variable. Hence, the actual findings are as follows: Districts that spend more than six months preparing for bond elections are more likely to obtain voter approval than districts that spend less than six months (Barbour); and districts that allow seven or more months to pass between the time the public is first informed of a bond proposal and election day are more likely to succeed in passing school bond issues than districts that allow less time to elapse (Beal et al.). Crider treats the variable in a linear fashion: therefore, it is correctly stated in the "greater or lesser" form of the proposition.

Two researchers, however, report that citizen's committees did make a difference in elections they studied. According to Barbour (1966), districts that did not use citizen's advisory committees were more likely to obtain voter approval for bond issues than districts that were assisted by such committees. Davidson (1967), on the other hand, reports a significant positive relationship between use of citizen's committees and bond election success in Illinois school elections.

The same rationale used to support citizen's advisory committees also applies to involving other potentially favorable groups in the campaign planning and implementing process. The only available relevant study suggests the futility of such involvement: Barbour (1966) found no statistically significant relationship between active PTA participation in the preparation and presentation of a bond proposal and approval or disapproval of the proposal.

Questions on the influence the second technique—hiring "outside consultants"—might have on election results are not definitively answered in the literature. Beal et al. (1966) found no significant difference in the success rates of districts that employed such help, whereas Barbour found that school districts that *did not* use professional consultants were more likely to obtain voter approval than those that did. Future research on the potential return from such services should try to answer at least two questions: (1) What kind of consulting help is involved (that is, what is the expertise of the consultant, etc.)? and (2) What other factors associated with the use of consultants may affect election success or failure? It may be, for example, that district officials call upon consultants because they have already encountered signals of opposition. If that is the case, the consultants must wage a campaign that from the start has a less than average chance of being successful.

*Measurement Questions*

The preceding discussion on the influence of several communication and campaign techniques suggests a bleak outlook for the schools. The evidence does not, however, automatically require a fatalistic attitude. In the first place, existing evidence is meager and mixed (e.g., the "length of campaign" findings). Second, any comprehensive theory must account for the finding that high information levels among the potential voters in the general communication-receiving audience are strongly associated with positive voting.[40] In the third place, much more evidence is needed on the qualitative impact of various communication efforts.

---

[40] The relationship between information level and support of local issues is confirmed by Carter (1960), Boskoff and Zeigler op. cit., and Tebbutt (1965). As we noted in Chapter 3, information levels have also been frequently and positively associated with participation in both partisan and nonpartisan elections.

The need to distinguish between quantity and quality of campaign efforts in assessing media influence in future research designs is apparent from the evidence surrounding the one media variable that appears most strongly related to election outcomes—newspaper support. The results of three studies *suggest that districts receiving "favorable newspaper support"*[41] *are more likely to succeed in passing school issues that those not receiving such support* (Beal et al., 1966; Lieber, 1967; Tebbutt, 1968). The relevant literature does not, however, unanimously support this proposition. According to Barbour's (1966) analysis, there is no statistically significant relationship between the attitude a district's newspaper takes toward a proposal and election success.

Of course, even if the positive relationship between general newspaper support and election success continues to appear in future research, Beal's finding that there is no significant relationship between the number of district press releases concerning a school bond issue and the success or failure of that issue may still be valid. Beal's finding may still hold because the causes of election success or failure may be beyond the control of school officials. For example, a stream of press releases from a district public relations office cannot counteract a newspaper's accurate reporting of a busing controversy. In such a case, "lack of support," as defined operationally for content analysis research, may at least partly be the result of accurate reporting of community controversies or other negative elements that already spell defeat for the issue of the moment.

**Election Characteristics**

In the preceding sections of this chapter, we reviewed a number of environmental or situational factors that could plausibly affect the outcome of school elections. Although the dedicated school proponent or opponent might examine this review in hope of finding methods for developing a "grand strategy" to influence the outcome of elections, several strands of evidence suggest the manipulation of any school financial election at any given time may prove extremely difficult. A number of factors entirely controllable by school officials may, however, have some bearing on an election outcome. Most of these factors refer to the actual presentation of specific election issues to the public.

*Election Timing*

Many have speculated that the time the election is held influences the outcome.

---

[41] This judgment was made by researchers on the basis of content analysis and survey techniques. In practice, a relatively small amount of newspaper coverage was evaluated as "unfavorable." For instance, in the Beal et al. (1966) study, superintendents were asked to

Available evidence, however, shows there is NO SIGNIFICANT RELATIONSHIP BETWEEN THE TIME OF THE YEAR IN WHICH THE ELECTION IS HELD AND SUCCESS OR FAILURE OF A SCHOOL FINANCIAL ELECTION (Murphy, 1966; Kean, 1964; Beal et al., 1966; Barbour, 1966; Crider, 1967). To test the proposition, these researchers used several operational definitions of timing, including season, month, day, and quarter of the year.

The extensively documented negative relationship between voter turnout and election success suggests that school elections are likely to be defeated when they are combined with other elections that draw a large turnout. Studies analyzing pertinent data report mixed and inconclusive results.

Four studies of school district voting patterns conducted in four distinct areas of the country reached four separate conclusions. Surprisingly, Marlow (1970) reports that any given year school tax issues are more likely to pass when offered at a general election than when offered at a primary or special election. He also found that school tax issues are more likely to pass when held in a presidential election year than when held in congressional elections or off years.

Kean's (1964) findings are more in keeping with the turnout/vote relationship described earlier: districts consolidating a tax override issue with state or national elections are less likely to obtain voter approval than are those who do not consolidate.

Similarly, Murphy (1966) reports a negative association between election success and first attempts to pass bond issues when the bond election is consolidated with other elections. This relationship does not appear to hold in subsequent elections. Finally, Crider's (1967) analysis reveals no significant relationship between election consolidation and outcome.

Another aspect of election timing is election frequency. Beal et al. (1966) found that districts reporting the highest bond election success rates also reported the fewest election attempts over a five-year period. Despite this finding, the same researchers report no statistically significant relationship between the time elapsed since a district's last bond election and the outcome of that district's most recent election.

*Issue Cost*

The most conspicuous aspect of a school financial issue is, of course, its dollar value. Hicks (1967), Dykstra (1964), and Varden, (1973), however, found no significant association between the amount of an issue and success or failure of tax and bond elections. The only finding that conforms to a picture of self-interest voting is Barbour's. He found that the smaller a bond issue the

---

evaluate the general attitudes of local papers toward 195 election issues. Results were as follows: Favorable–142; neutral–27; no coverage–24; and unfavorable–2.

greater its chance of approval. Crider (1967) offers the unique and interesting finding that in large school districts (over 3,000 enrollment) large bond proposals (over one million) have a greater chance of passing than similar size proposals in small (under 3,000) school districts.

In most cases, however, the total dollar amount of an issue is probably less important to voters than its effect on their tax bill. In Chapter 6 we will examine the differential impact of property taxes on voters having different incomes and different perceptions of the worth of public services. Until then it is sufficient to review the research that tests the hypothesis that both the amount of personal tax and the rate of increase in that tax for the schools are directly, positively, and linearly related to the size of the negative vote on school issues.

This hypothesis assumes cost, as a determinant of voting direction, is equally important to most voters; consequently, as the cost of a tax issue increases, more voters are presented with a personal cost/benefit equation that can only be solved rationally by voting against the tax increase.

The hypothesized positive relationship between issue cost to the voter and negative voting will be confirmed if a progressively greater number of voters recognize and respond to tax rate increases in a random and linear fashion. Of course, tax rate increases are at least partly controllable by school policy. Nevertheless, it is possible that less manipulatable factors—either economic such as ability to pay, or noneconomic, such as level of community conflict—might have a greater influence on a particular election outcome than would an increase in tax rates.

The effect of these unalterable factors calls into question the validity of the linear model of the cost hypothesis. The manner in which the hypothesis is usually stated and tested would lead one to expect that a huge tax rate increase of $20.00 per thousand would make the cost issue so salient that many voters would decide to vote no because of their individual cost/benefit determinations and the issue would be handily defeated. But when the change in tax rates is small, the result cannot be so easily anticipated, especially when other factors affect the election outcome. Suppose, for example, a community is engaged in an intense debate over school busing? What would be the net effect on the outcome of a school financial election in that community of a proposed $2.00 decrease in the tax rate?

Further, if every voter "has his price," what is the price of the average elderly, fixed-income voter? If a cost decrease would reduce negative voting, could any school district afford a decrease of sufficient size to change meaningful numbers of votes?

All these questions point to the importance of "real world" factors that can contaminate the one-to-one relationship between dollars and votes. The evidence simply does not suggest overwhelming support for an economic explanation of school financial election outcomes when the most common indicators of cost differences—per pupil property assessment tax rates—are used.

Four studies (Murphy, 1966; Beal et al., 1966; Hicks, 1967; Crider, 1967), representing a large sample of school districts in four separate areas, found *no significant relationship between per pupil assessed valuation rates and election outcome.* One study of Illinois school districts did report a significant positive association between per pupil assessed valuation and election success (Davidson, 1967). However, a similar study of Iowa districts (Barbour, 1966) found precisely the opposite relationship.

Some studies have used multivariate techniques to determine whether various indicators of issue cost can be used to predict school financial election outcomes (Lawrence, 1966; Hicks, 1967; Davidson, 1967; Goettel, 1971; Saalfeld, 1972; Varden, 1973). Of the variables tested, school tax rate emerged as the most important for discriminating between successful and unsuccessful districts. The relationship between a district's tax rate and its election success has, however, been found to be positive and sometimes negative. For instance, school tax rate was the most important predictor variable among thirteen employed in Davidson's (1967) rather powerful model, but the direction of that relationship is positive (the greater the school tax rate, the greater the chance of success). The logically based hypothesis, which was confirmed by the findings of two other models (Goettel, 1971; Saalfeld, 1972), is, of course, that greater tax rates produce greater probability of issue defeat.

The multivariate inquiry done to date has not answered the fundamental questions surrounding the linear economic model: To what extent do issues of cost penetrate a voting population in a linear (as related to a dollar amount) and random fashion? Are other kinds of explanations required (at least for some segments of the electorate) in the majority of election cases where cost increases and decreases appear within *normal limits* (difficult as these may be to define)?

These kinds of questions are at the heart of an improved understanding of voting behavior in school financial elections and will require additional multivariat inquiry. The models derived from the studies mentioned above do, however, provide important evidence, which is included in the summary presented in Table 5-1.

As we see from the table, the amount of explanation and prediction provided by these models varies greatly from a high of 77.9 percent to a low of 13.0 percent. Statistical purists will note that comparison of these percentages violates the traditional prohibition against comparing apples and oranges. For studies that employ discriminate statistics, the percentages simply refer to the proportion of districts that are correctly classified as passing or rejecting school issues on the basis of multiple criteria. Studies that used multiple regression techniques were pursuing a more elusive objective: the attempt to explain and predict the linear differences (variance) in the amount of yes or no voting among the sample of districts. However, for both types of analysis, the percentages represent the optimum amount of explanation and prediction achieved by the researcher's model, which ideally would reach 100.0 percent in all cases.

## Table 5-1
Multivariate Models of Voting in School Financial Elections: Percent of Variance in Direction of Vote and Percent of Success in Discriminating Between Winning and Losing Districts Accounted for by Selected Financial Variables

| Study | Type* | Number of Variables | Scope of Model** | Amount of Explanation/Prediction |
|---|---|---|---|---|
| Lawrence 1966 | Discriminate | 34 | Financial only | 77.9% |
| Lawrence 1966 | Discriminate | 14 | Financial only | 71.4 |
| Lawrence 1966 | Discriminate | 7 | Financial only | 57.1 |
| Hicks 1967 | Regression | 13 | Financial only | 13.0 |
| Davidson 1967 | Discriminate | 13 | Financial, Demographic, Political | 75.0 |
| Nelson 1968 | Regression | 13 | Financial, Demographic | 72.0 |
| Goettel 1971 | Regression | 10 | Financial only | 47.0 (N.Y. City SMSAs) |
| Goettel 1971 | Regression | 10 | Financial only | 53.0 (Upstate N.Y. SMSAs) |
| Goettel 1971 | Regression | 10 | Financial only | 23.0 (Rural N.Y.) |
| Saalfeld 1972 | Regression | 4 | Financial only | 18.9 |
| Saalfeld 1972 | Regression | 6 | Adds District size and turnout rates to financial variables | 29.2 |
| Varden 1973 | Regression | 6 | Financial and Past Voting | 40.0 (for entire N.Y. sample) |

*Models of the "discrimination" type have been used to *predict* the probability of *success or failure* in school elections on the basis of multiple criteria that have been associated with election outcomes. Drawn from biology, these models can be used to refine the researcher's ability to correctly classify any complex or questionable binary phenomenon. For methodological instruction see Paul G. Hoel, *Introduction to Mathematical Statistics* (New York: John Wiley and Sons, 1947), p. 121.

Models labeled "regression" have been used to *explain* the proportion of variance in yes or no voting that can be accounted for on the basis of multiple criteria. For discussion see Huber M. Blalock, *Social Statistics* (New York: McGraw-Hill Book Co., 1960), pp. 346-58.

**By "financial" we refer to those variables that reflect differences in the district's fiscal capacity and needs (e.g., tax rate, bond amount, assessed valuation, bond indebtedness, etc.). Other studies have arrived at multivariate explanations without attending to such factors (Carter and Ruggels, 1966, and Nelson 1968).

The differences in the amount of variance accounted for by these five studies is not surprising considering the number and type (scope of the model) of variables considered by the different researchers. Although some measure of issue cost (usually tax rate or tax rate increase) was included in each of the financial models, the *total* amount of explanation provided by those models (e.g., tax rate *plus* others) leads one to agree with Goettel. After noting that approximately one-half the variance in electoral dissent was *not* explained by the fiscal and economic variables used in his study, he concluded: "While it may be possible to explain more of the variance in electoral behavior with fiscal variables that were not used ... the evidence at hand suggests that attention be devoted to two other sets of factors" (Goettel, 1971, p. 22).

The studies that discriminated only between winning and losing districts were most successful, though Davidson's model extended beyond economic considerations and Lawrence's financial model lost a good deal of predictive power in his final attempt to deal with multicolinearity.[42] The economically based multiple regression models were clearly less successful. To some degree, however, their explanatory value is a matter of interpretation. For Goettel, the 50 percent explanation rate (dropping to 23 percent among rural New York districts) simply suggests the need for a better model. On the other hand, Saalfeld expresses pleasure that his model explains 29.2 percent of the variance in voting direction among Oregon districts: "Rarely do indicators in aggregate data analysis achieve a much higher percent of the variance explained unless a very large number of independent variables are utilized" (Saalfeld, 1972, p. 104).

We would tend to agree with Goettel that a more complex model is warranted in interpreting the evidence of these studies taken as a whole. Sole reliance on financial or economic models appears to leave us unnecessarily short of the desirable explanatory mark. Among economic variables, however, two surrogates for issue cost—tax rate and tax rate increase—appear relatively important, especially when compared with the other independent variables used in the financial models. The usefulness of these two indicators suggests that they be retained in future models that consider nonfiscal variables as well.

**Miscellaneous Findings**

According to Barbour (1966) and Carter (1960), the purpose of proposed construction is not related to a bond issue's chances of success or failure. However, Crider's (1967) data indicate that bond issues for construction needed

---

[42] A common problem of multivariate research, multicolinearity refers to the overlapping or duplicating nature of independent variables. To understand the problem see Hubert M. Blalock, Jr., "Correlated Independent Variables: The Problem of Multi-colinearity," *Social Forces* 42 (December 1963): 233-37; and D.E. Farrar and R.R. Glauber, "Multicolinearity in Regression Analysis: The Problems Revisited," *Review of Economics and Statistics*, (February 1967): pp. 92-107.

to replace old facilities were more likely to succeed than issues for other purposes.

One factor controllable by a school district involves the actual wording of a ballot proposal. The varying degrees of precision that can be used in wording an issue have prompted at least three researchers to classify issues as either "general" or "specific." Barbour (1966) found that in small districts (less than 750 students) general bond proposals were more likely to succeed than were specific bond proposals. Kean (1964) found that districts that specify the duration (number of years) of the proposed tax increase are more likely to obtain approval in tax override elections than are districts that do not. Finally, according to the study by Beal et al. (1966), the relative specificity of the language used in school financial proposals appears unrelated to their outcome.

Finally, a finding concerning one election variable that is—unfortunately for school officials—not controllable should be mentioned in closing this section: the greater the majority required for school bond issue approval, the greater the chance of bond issue defeat (Cooper, 1967).

**Summary and Synthesis**

This chapter emphasized the relationship between the environment of an election and its outcome. We noted that elections take place in communities that are divergent in many respects, including organizational and personal dimensions. In addition, we suggested that because of their visibility schools are often attacked by individuals concerned about broad political and social issues; frequently, schools are the institution most subject to involvement in community controversies. Finally, we noted a number of techniques available to partisans (both positive and negative) who wish to change the existing situation and thereby affect election outcomes.

Some findings suggest that school districts and communities differ significantly in their capacity to control potential conflicts and that these differences are related to their varying rates of school election success. However, this evidence is far from overwhelming.

Most of the correlations reviewed leave enough unexplained variance in election success rates to suggest that future research (1) examine other situational variables and (2) continue and refine examination of the theories stressing long-term determinants of voter behavior.

The potential importance of voter predispositions (long-term forces) in affecting the outcome of most elections was also suggested by studies that assessed the impact of various campaign techniques. Although exceptions were noted, tacit corroboration of theories stressing long-range forces was supplied by a number of findings showing that various school district campaign efforts, ballot terms, and issue costs are not related to the outcome of school financial elections.

If the situational elements most easily controlled by school districts—information, general campaign efforts, and, within certain limits, cost—continue to be found ineffective in changing the course of election outcomes, and if less easily controlled environmental influences—conflict, district characteristics, and base costs—continue to leave a significant amount of unexplained variance in election outcomes, then the main hope for improving our ability to explain election outcomes seems to rest with our understanding of voter attitudes and predispositions (long-range forces). Whether certain determinants of voter behavior can be isolated that frequently override situational variables, thus providing a superior explanation of financial election outcomes, provides the theme for the analysis of the next two chapters.

# 6   Socioeconomic Determinants

This chapter sets forth propositions useful in understanding the importance of a variety of social and economic background factors that may influence the direction of a voter's choice in school financial elections. The chapter is organized in two major sections, the first of which describes the relationship between voter choice in school financial elections and a number of objectively classifiable economic group affiliations. The second section, introducing the concept of social class, offers empirically based propositions useful in understanding the relationship between class and voting in school financial elections.

## Economic Determinants

In Chapter 3 we began our review of correlates to voter participation with obvious indicators of interest in the schools. In that chapter we presented a typology of four categories of citizens based on two characteristics—parental status and property ownership (see Table 6-1). Given the assumption that individuals vote rationally in the pursuit of their own self-interests, we used the typology to predict levels of citizen interest in the schools. Now, given the same assumption, we would like to use the same typology to predict the probable *direction* (yes or no) of citizen's votes. Table 6-1 shows the four categories of citizens.

In this typology, we assume that even though the renter may indirectly pay an equitable (indeed, in some instances an inequitable) share of tax increases for the schools, it is the homeowner who, through his direct payment of property taxes, is most conscious of the costs of school financial issues. We also assume that whatever benefits accrue from schools are more visible to parents of school age children than to nonparents or parents of children not in school.

**Table 6-1**
**A Typology of Voters in School Financial Elections According to Two Factors that May Affect Direction of the Vote**

|  | *Property Owner* | *Renter* |
|---|---|---|
| Parent of School Age Children | 1<br>? | 2<br>Yes |
| Nonparent of School Age Children | 3<br>No | 4<br>? |

From this economic point of view, with all other factors constant, we would expect the renter who is also a parent of school age children (cell 2) to be the most likely "yes voter" and the nonparent property-owner to be the best candidate for the "no voter" label. The parent who is also a property owner (cell 1) may be in a situation that parallels the familiar approach-avoidance conflict.[1] A variant of another form of conflict—avoidance-avoidance—may be operative for the voter portrayed in cell 4 (the nonparent renter).[2] This important topic will be treated more thoroughly in Chapter 7: "Psychological Determinants." For now we simply note that although a reservoir of interdisciplinary partial theory touches on conflict[3]—its causes, effects, and means of resolution—we know little about effects of conflict on the individual voter's choice, particularly at the level of local nonpartisan elections.

The one existing empirical test of the Table 6-1 typology (Dillingham, 1969) confirms our expectations for cells 2 and 3; a disproportionate number of yes voters were both parents and renters, and a large majority of no voters were property owners without school age children. Importantly, this study also found that the two groups that appear most vulnerable to conflict (cells 1 and 4) were most likely to change their vote in a subsequent school budget election.[4]

The remainder of the evidence relevant to understanding the simple cost/benefit alternatives presented in Table 6-1 is bivariate.

*Parental Status*

The association between parental status and voting is quite strong and persistent throughout the literature, providing one necessary, though not sufficient, condition for validation of the model presented in Table 6-1. VOTERS WITH CHILDREN ENROLLED IN THE PUBLIC SCHOOLS ARE MORE LIKELY THAN VOTERS WITHOUT CHILDREN TO APPROVE OF SCHOOL FINANCIAL ISSUES (King, 1963; Fish, 1964; Smith, 1964; Schoonhoven and Patterson, 1966; Carter and Ruggels, 1966; Tebbutt, 1968; Gallup, 1969;

---

[1] For conflict to occur we assume that the two opposing forces are approximately equal in strength. Lewin's conceptualization of conflict is described in most introductory psychology texts. For more extended and authentic treatment, see Kurt Lewin, *A Dynamic Theory of Personality* (New York: McGraw-Hill, 1935), pp. 104-123; or Dorwin Cartwright (ed.), *Field Theory in Social Science: Selected Theoretical Papers by Kurt Lewin* (London: Tavistock Publications Ltd., 1952), pp. 260-69.

[2] Ibid.

[3] Elton B. McNeil (ed.), *The Nature of Human Conflict* (Englewood Cliffs, New Jersey: Prentice-Hall, Inc., 1965).

[4] In this second election, the district proposed a reduction in school services. Dillingham concludes that this proposal was a "reinforcement of the benefit vector" that leads to greater positive voting among those whose conflict was partly attributable to their parental status.

Hatley, 1970). Although the relationship has been reported persistently, its strength has varied greatly among the different studies. For example, Wilson and Banfield (1971), in their sample of Boston homeowners, found that "those with children in the public schools are *only slightly* more likely that the others to favor increased expenditures for the schools" (p.1061). At the same time, their finding of a strong positive relationship between income level and affirmative voting was virtually unaffected by controlling for parental status. This evidence strongly suggests the need for stringent controls while assessing this relationship in the future. The need for controls is also shown by the most recent Gallup survey (1972), which suggests that the increase in total voter dissension has been accompanied by a decrease in the relative difference between parents and nonparents (see Table 6-2). For each survey, the question was worded as follows: "Suppose the local public schools said they needed much more money. As you feel at this time, would you vote to raise taxes for this purpose, or would you vote against raising taxes for this purpose." The questionnaire and results for each year are contained in Gallup 1969, 1970, 1971, and 1972.

If the trend suggested in Table 6-2 continues, we will be forced to take a skeptical view of the influence of parental status on direction of the vote in school elections. Related findings suggest that whatever the magnitude of that relationship, it is a transitive one.

Tebbutt found that voters who have children in grades 10 or under are more likely to approve a tax rate issue than are voters who have children in higher grades. Similarly, Fish (1964) found no statistically significant difference between the approval rates of voters without children in school at the time of a budget election but who previously had children in school and voters who never had children in school. Apparently, parental status does not influence most voters to take a lasting and philosophical view of the voting act.

*Homeownership*

Although the benefit side of our cost/benefit model is well supported by the literature, the cost side is not. A majority of the studies report findings indicating *there is no statistically significant relationship between homeownership and voting for or against a school financial election* (Wentzel, 1964; Cooper, 1967, Hicks, 1967; Tebbutt, 1968). The Cooper study also found there was no significant relationship between limiting the school election vote to property owners and approval or disapproval of a bond issue. Two other studies, however, report different findings. Smith (1964) and McKelvey (1966) found that renters are more likely than homeowners to vote in favor of school financial issues. Finally, a curvilinear relationship emerges from Jordan's (1966) quartile analysis: voters from Los Angeles areas in the lowest and highest quartiles for percentage of homeownership were more likely to approve school bond issues

Table 6-2
Proportion of Adults that Should Vote Yes on Issues to Increase Taxes for School Purposes: 1969-1972*

| | Percent Yes | | |
| Year | Total Sample | Nonparents | Public School Parents |
| --- | --- | --- | --- |
| 1972 | 36% | 35% | 37% |
| 1971 | 40 | 37 | 44 |
| 1970 | 37 | 35 | 43 |
| 1969 | 45 | 41 | 51 |

*These data are from national probability samples taken annually by Gallup since 1969.

than voters from areas ranking somewhere between the high and low owner occupancy rates.

As originally conceived, the owner-renter/parent-nonparent cost-benefit equation was intriguing. If the evidence on the cost side of the equation had been as persuasive as the evidence on the benefit side, we would have been well on our way to developing a model, based on a verifiable yes or no answer to two simple questions, that would help predict the direction of a school financial election vote.

Before abandoning the cost/benefit formulation, we should examine our operational treatment of it. Although the owner-renter dichotomy makes a neat 2 by 2 cross-classification with parental status, it may oversimplify the concept of cost. Property ownership, while indicating the existence of the property tax, tells nothing about the amount and burden of that tax. Owners of $10,000 and $40,000 homes, who pay widely varying taxes, are lumped together in the same classification. To obtain a more accurate measure of the actual cost to voters of school financial proposals, we must look to other variables. Two more objective indicators of the cost of school taxes are house value and property assessment (or assessed valuation) rate.

*House Value*

As the basis for financing school issues, property values are a direct indicator of an issues's cost to the voter. The use of house value in a cost/benefit formulation for analyzing voting behavior in several different kinds of local bond issues has been justified as follows: "Most expenditures . . . confer about the same benefits on large properties as on small, whereas of course the taxes to pay for the expenditures are levied (in theory at least) strictly in proportion to the value of the property."[5] We should emphasize, however, that although property values and assessment rates serve as excellent indicators of tax burden they do not necessarily reflect ability to pay, a dimension that is more accurately measured by income.

Income and house value can also be used as overlapping indicators of socioeconomic status. In that case, as we shall see in the following section, some existing theories predict a positive relationship between house value, income or other indicators of wealth and direction of vote in school financial elections. However, if we treat house value as an indicator of tax burden and assume rational self-interest on the part of the voter, we would expect a negative relationship between the two variables (house value and positive voting). Relevant research findings are inconclusive. McMahon (1966) found the greater a precinct's average value of owner-occupied housing, the greater that precint's negative vote for three different types of school financial elections (tax, bond, and junior college creation). Paralleling the relationship he found between owner occupancy rate and voting, Jordan (1966) found that Los Angeles voters from census tracts in the lowest and highest quartiles for median property valuation were more likely than voters from tracts in the low-middle and high-middle quartiles to approve a school bond issue.

*Property Assessment Rate*

The voter's actual property assessment rate is, of course, an even closer indicator of his tax burden than his property value. Two studies found no significant relationship between a voter's property tax rate and his approval or disapproval of a school budget (Fish, 1964) or bond (Tebbut, 1968) issue. Six other studies examined the relationship between assessed valuation and election success, using school districts as the units of analysis and standardizing the variable on a per student basis. Four of these studies (Murphy, 1966; Beal et al., 1966; Hicks, 1967; Crider, 1967) found *no significant relationship between the two variables.* One study of Illinois school districts reported a significant positive association between per pupil assessed valuation and election success (Davidson, 1967),

---

[5] James Q. Wilson and Edward C. Banfield, "Public-Regardingness as a Value Premise in Voting Behavior," in Richard I. Hofferbert and Ira Sharkansky (eds.), *State and Urban Politics: Readings in Comparative Public Policy* (Boston: Little, Brown, and Company, 1971), pp. 112-13. The same article may be found in *The American Political Science Review* 58 (December 1964):876-87. Although the authors provide a strong justification for the theoretical utility of house value, they measure tax liability with median family income. Although the two variables are normally highly correlated, they are neither theoretically nor empirically synonymous as is evident in an innovative multivariate reexamination of the "public-regarding hypothesis" that controls for multicollinearity between these and other key variables. See Frederick C. Collignon, "Public Regardingness in the Behavior of the Voters in the Baltimore Metropolitan Area," Cambridge, Massachusetts, Harvard–M.I.T. Joint Center for Urban Studies, Unpublished paper, 1971, pp. 13-14.

whereas a similar study of Iowa district (Barbour, 1966) found precisely the opposite relationship.

Although these findings do not allow any definitive conclusion, they point to a devaluation of the voter benefit hypothesis. Several elemental cautions are in order, however, before deciding that individuals do not react in their own self-interest to the size of their tax bill. Researchers have used variables such as house value, assessed valuation, tax rate, and income because these variables are objective and comparatively easy-to-measure surrogates for tax burden. For taxes to be burdensome, however, they must be so perceived. We do not know if voters are aware of the relative amount of their tax contribution nor can we be sure that individuals do not immediately compensate for their actual burden by taking other values into consideration—such as their ability to pay. One study more attuned to the subjective nature of the tax burden (Fish, 1964) found voters who experienced a property tax increase of more than 25 percent for the year immediately preceding a school budget election were more likely to cast negative votes in that election than voters who did not experience such an increase. Research on the voter's perception of his taxes relative to former and anticipated tax rates, as well as relative to his current and future ability to pay, is needed.

*Age*

Clearly, additional, more discriminating research on the cost/benefit equation illustrated in Table 6-1 is needed before we can make definitive statements about voting as a response to immediate individual and group interests. We may be able, however, through the indirect indicator of age, to gain some idea of the effect of consistent and multiple cost/benefit influences on voting in school financial elections.

It seems reasonable to assume that large numbers of elderly citizens see school issues as costly and of little or no personal benefit. At we noted earlier, the influence of parental status on voting appears transient: parents vote disproportionately in favor of school issues *until* their children leave the school system. Whether or not an older voter has at one time had children in school makes no appreciable difference in school election voting. At the same time, most elderly citizens must meet any cost increases with fixed, and, in many cases, limited, resources. Assuming rational self-interest, the unanimity of research evidence supporting the following proposition is hardly surprising: YOUNGER VOTERS ARE MORE LIKELY THAT OLDER VOTERS TO VOTE IN FAVOR OF A SCHOOL FINANCIAL ISSUE (King, 1963; McKelvey, 1966; Carter and Ruggels, 1966; McMahon, 1966; Jordan, 1966; Smith, 1968; Tebbutt, 1968; Gallup, 1969).[6] We could find no conflict concerning this

---

[6] One study reported that voters from age forty to sixty were more likely than younger or

## Length of Residence

We do not mean to imply that voter benefit theory is the only plausible explanation for this relationship between age and voting.[7] It may be that a set of attitudes defined as "civic responsibility" and "community attachment" are both more likely to be found among certain age groups and more important in determining a positive reaction to local financial proposals.

A variable closely related to age and important in this context is "length of residence" in a community. The findings on this variable are not extensive. One study (Smith, 1968) reports a linear relationship paralleling the age/vote relationship: the longer a potential voter has resided in a community, the less likely it is he will support a school millage proposal. Indirect corroboration is provided by Milstein and Jennings (1970), who found that as a citizen's length of residence increases his favorable perceptions of school board activities decreases; and by Boskoff and Zeigler (1964), who found that recent residents provided more consistent support for several bond issues that did long-term residents.

Objective measurements of age or length of residence, of course, only allow us to infer the extent of subjective motivations such as civic responsibility. This finding should not be surprising, since a number of hypotheses suggest that feelings of "community attachment" are less salient in Southern California. Jordan (1966) found no significant relationship between length of residence and voting in a school bond election in Los Angeles. Tebbutt (1966) discovered that voters who have resided in a district for five to ten years are more likely to approve school tax issues than those who have resided there for a shorter or longer time. This finding suggests that voters with residencies of from five to ten years have had time to gain any community pride or civic attachment that they are going to gain but have not yet encountered the negative costs, statuses, and attitudes associated with old age.

## Ethnic Background

Finally, several findings that concern other "group membership" correlates to

---

older voters to vote in favor of five different types of bond issues. See Alvin Boskoff and Harmon Zeigler, *Voting Patterns in a Local Election* (Philadelphia: J.B. Lippincott, 1964), p. 44. The substance of footnote 32, Chapter 3 is relevant here, though the obvious strength of this relationship precludes concern over divergent operational definitions of age.

[7]We have emphasized economic justifications for negative voting among the elderly. Of

local voting have been interpreted in light of the rational self-interest voting model. By virtually every indicator, minority ethnic groups have received less than a proportionate share of "societal benefits." Frequently, members of these groups have the most to gain in both short-term (improved school conditions) and long-term (improved status) benefits that may accrue from the passage of a school issue. At the same time, their proportionate cost is likely to be low. Accordingly, we find support for the proposition that BLACKS ARE MORE LIKELY THAN WHITES TO VOTE IN FAVOR OF A SCHOOL FINANCIAL PROPOSAL (Smith, 1968; Wilson and Banfield, 1964; Jordan, 1966; Hahn and Almy, 1971; Wirt and Kirst, 1972).[8] Blacks do not, of course constitute all minority groups though assimilation has been least extensive and relative deprivation probably most extensive for this group. The well-known "public-regardingness" hypothesis[9] suggests that descendants of immigrants from certain European countries are more likely to oppose public expenditures because of a predominant private-regarding ethos among members of that group. Two proponents of this hypothesis contend that their data indicate a large number of citizens vote "against their self-interest narrowly conceived and that a marked ethnic influence appears in the vote."[10] Although this would appear to be a

---

course, a similar argument can be made for greater positive voting among younger citizens, which may be an important component in this total relationship. In any event the onset of the eighteen-year-old vote raises interesting and strategically important questions concerning participation and direction of the youth vote.

[8]Studies of precinct voting in elections for other types of local financial issues confirm this relationship. See M. Kent Jennings and Harmon Zeigler, "Class, Party, and Race in Four Types of Elections: The Case of Atlanta," *Journal of Politics* 28 (May 1966):400-401; and Edward C. Banfield and James Q. Wilson, *City Politics* (New York: Vintage Books, 1963), p. 237.

[9]This provocative hypothesis, which has stimulated a good deal of discussion and research, was originally offered in ibid, and most concisely stated in Wilson and Banfield, op. cit. (footnote 5, this chapter). The authors have now modified the public vs. private dichotomy to read "unitary vs. individualist ethos"; see James Q. Wilson and Edward C. Banfield, "Political Ethos Revisited," *American Political Science Review* 65 (December 1971):1048-62. The all encompassing nature of their formulation has made criticism inevitable. For a thorough critique based on original research of one element of the hypothesis—the relationship between the independent variable of ethnicity, the intervening variable of ethos (public or private regarding), and the dependent variable of local governmental structure—see Raymond E. Wolfinger and John Osgood Field, "Political Ethos and the Structure of City Government," in Richard I. Hofferbert and Ira Sharkansky, (eds.), *State and Urban Politics: Readings in Comparative Public Policy* (Boston:Little, Brown and Company, 1971), pp. 194-231. The article originally appeared in *The American Political Science Review* 60 (June 1966):306-26. As Wilson and Banfield correctly point out, Wolfinger and Field do not assess the relationship between ethos and the independent variable that is of most interest to us—voting in local elections. On the basis of their respective data sets, the debate between the two teams is not likely to be resolved. For an excellent example of advocates "talking past each other," see the exchange of letters between Banfield and Wilson and Wolfinger and Field appearing in *The American Political Science Review* 60 (December 1966):998-1000.

[10]Wilson and Banfield, "Public-Regardingness as a Value Premise in Voting Behavior," p. 125.

reasonable conclusion based on their data from predominantly Polish and Irish precincts, it is of no use in interpreting data regarding the black vote in school elections:[11] the finding that blacks are much more likely to favor such expenditures can hardly be considered a rejection of that group's self-interest.

It is probably true, however, that some voters habitually favor local financial proposals because they are concerned about the "public good" or "community benefit" that is expected to accrue from the issues. Although some citizens may reject issues because of narrow private interests, it is obvious that this does not exhaust the logical reasons for a negative vote. It is possible that sincere public benefit concerns motivate some negative votes.[12] Just how much space on a continuum of eligible voters is occupied by individuals who adhere to a "pure" public or private—or in the case of their reformulation, "unitarist" or "individualist"—position we cannot say.[13] Nor do we know how strong these predispositions are in shaping voter choice in different situations. Although we probably will not be able to answer these questions, we will raise them periodically when we consider other social and psychological explanations of voting in school financial elections.

*Religious Affiliation*

Wilson and Banfield have suggested that public-regarding voters are predominantly Protestant whereas private-regarding citizens express predominantly Catholic religious preference.[14] If this relationship is valid, we would expect many Catholic voters to cast negative ballots in school financial elections. The well-established Catholic parochial school system is supported by the Catholic parishioner who is also a taxpayer. Regardless of his parental status, the Catholic who supports his church and pays his taxes pays a higher price for educational benefits.

Available research tapping this relationship is limited. Smith et al. (1968) found that Catholic residents of Detroit's central city were less likely to support a school millage proposal than Protestants. However, in that city's suburban areas, no significant relationship was found between religious affiliation and voter support in school millage elections. Among the plausible explanations for this finding is one suggesting greater assimilation in areas removed from the more

---

[11] Ibid., particularly the last column in Table 7.

[12] In their excellent study of fluoridation controversies, Robert L. Crain, Elihu Katz, and Donald B. Rosenthal suggest that the no vote may well be perceived as rational action toward the "public good." See their *The Politics of Community Conflict: The Fluoridation Decision* (Indianapolis: The Bobbs-Merrill Co., 1969), pp. 9, 63-70.

[13] In their survey of Boston residents, "About one fifth of the respondents displayed one or the other ethos and had in addition the predicted personal attributes." Wilson and Banfield, "Political Ethos Revisited," p. 1062.

[14] Ibid., p. 1061.

tightly drawn ethnic boundaries of the central city. However, a study of a small suburban community in Illinois found no statistically significant relationship between religious affiliation and approval or disapproval of a bond or tax issue (Tebbutt, 1968).

*Sex*

One final demographic classification can also be seen as providing a rational basis for differing vote decisions in school elections. Although a myriad of other factors would seem more directly relevant to voter choice, a voter's sex may sometimes be influential.

We might hypothesize, for example, that many mothers would regard the schools as performing important educational and babysitting functions and therefore emphasize the benefit side of school financial proposals.[15] Fathers, on the other hand, would be more likely to be aware of the cost of school issues. If this hypothesis is true (and that is a big if), we might expect more positive voting by women. Although one study does find that women are more likely than men to support local bond issues,[16] three studies refute the proposition.[17] Among these three, Mahon (1968) and Tebbutt (1968) report there is no statistically significant relationship between sex and voting in school elections. At the same time, Smith et al. (1968) report men are more likely to support school millage proposals than women.

*Economic Interests: A Synthesis*

We began this section with a very simple cost/benefit typology (Table 6-1). The typology served as a referent in the ensuing discussion of the relationship

---

[15] Even if this factor is operative, it may prove less of a boon to school administrators than it appears at the outset. Although motherhood may be associated with greater positive voting, it has also been found to deter participation rates in age groups ranging from twenty-one to fifty-four, even while controlling for levels of involvement. "The presence of young children requiring constant attention serves as a barrier to the voting act," Campbell et al., *The American Voter,* p. 258. The same basic paradox confronts the school official who examines our findings concerning black voting direction (positive) in light of reported lower turnout levels of blacks in both the North and South in national elections, ibid., p. 153.

[16] Boskoff and Zeigler, op. cit., p. 44.

[17] To the extent that local voting patterns parallel national voting patterns, this finding is to be expected. Campbell et al., op. cit., p. 261, note that differences in partisan preference between men and women are slight (women are 3 to 5 percent more Republican in presidential elections), and those differences can be accounted for by differences in other characteristics between the sexes.

between various economic characteristics of voters and direction of their votes in school financial elections.

This perspective seemed quite useful as we reviewed the evidence concerning the relationships between two characteristics—parental status and age—and vote direction. The findings strongly suggest disproportionately positive voting patterns among parents and disproportionately negative voting among the elderly. A majority of parents and elderly citizens who participate in school elections apparently make voting choices that are dictated by their perception of their personal self-interest. These findings square well with the predictions of many objective observers who assume rational responses to obvious group needs or interests. The group interest in these cases was fairly clear.

Not surprisingly, findings became less unanimous as we examined other research classifications of voters—groups whose "self-interest" was less easily defined. The evidence surrounding various indicators of tax burden, which has in turn been used as an indicator of "cost," was mixed and inconclusive. Either the cost of school issues is relatively unimportant to some groups studied or existing research has failed to accurately operationalize the concept of cost as perceived by these voters.

**Social Determinants**

The questions raised in the preceding section are some of the most pervasive and difficult questions that face social scientists: What is the relationship between an individual's group affiliation(s) and his perceptions of self-interest? How valid are objective indicators of subjective phenomena? What can we predict about individual *behavior* even if we gain a much clearer understanding of how the individual weighs self- and public-interests? This section, which continues to entertain these perpelxing questions about group and individual interests, considers interests other than the more-or-less economically based interests we have just considered.

*Voting and Social Class*

One cannot profitably discuss the political impact of economic interests of groups and individuals without turning to the concept of socioeconomic status (SES) or class. Ranking with such concepts as alienation and power in scholarly attention, SES has been correlated with activities ranging from music preference to presidential voting. Social class is, of course, at the center of the theories of society suggested by Karl Marx and Max Weber. Contemporary social science research continues to use these analytical constructs in the study of social structure.

A review of the relevant literature shows that the terms "social class," "social stratification," and "socioeconomic status" have been used interchangeably to:

... denote all those individuals (or families) who possess within the framework of some society or community relatively the same amounts of power, income, wealth, or prestige or some loosely formulated combination of these elements.[18]

Class differences mean that some citizens receive more of the highly valued goods of a society than do other citizens. A most important component of social class—beyond economic benefits—is prestige. "Status or class differences imply not only that some persons have more of the goods of life than others, but also that some persons are *looked up to more than others.*"[19]

Because differences in class status, by definition, mean differences in the distribution of physical and psychological benefits, it is not surprising that social theory predicts some degree of conflict and competition between the classes. The means for allocating societal benefits (or rewards and punishments) is the political process. For these reasons, it is assumed that the classes will have divergent political preferences and opinions.

There is general agreement that social class stratification and conflict are present in all societies as long as the qualifying phrase "to some degree" is added. The extent of class differences and the importance of those differences for understanding the political processes of a society and the political behavior of individuals within a society can vary greatly depending on the society being studied, the theoretical predisposition of the study, and the method used to measure social class.

The theoretical and methodological orientations for studying the relationship between SES and political behavior in the United States allow a wide range of interpretation. Note the wide variation in the importance assigned to social class in the following quotations taken from noteworthy and systematic studies of American political behavior:

1. There is a familiar adage in American folklore to the effect that a person is only what he thinks he is, an adage which reflects the typically American notion of unlimited opportunity, the tendency toward self-betterment, etc. Now we find the reverse of the adage is true: a person thinks, politically, as he is socially. Social characteristics determine political preference.[20]
2. ... if domestic politics are related to a distribution of rewards and punishments on a socio-economic basis and the parties favor different

---

[18] Julius Gould and William L. Kolb (eds.), *A Dictionary of the Social Sciences* (New York: The Free Press, 1964), p. 684.

[19] Lester W. Milbrath, *Political Participation: How and Why Do People Get Involved in Politics?* (Chicago: Rand McNally & Co., 1965), p. 114, emphasis added.

[20] Paul F. Lazarsfeld, Bernard R. Berelson, and Hazel Gaudet, *The People's Choice,* Second edition (New York: Columbia University Press, 1948), p. 27.

status-groups, as most observers believe, the fact that the proportion of the working class voting Republican is larger than the proportion of the middle class who vote Democratic suggests (but does not prove) a lower visibility of objective group interests in the working class.[21]

3. With regard to class, we have developed the thesis that status voting patterns established in the 1930's have been eroding since that time.[22]

The study quoted first concluded that social class accounted for a rather large proportion of voting variance. The second quote suggests a differential impact of class consciousness on voting, while the third reflects the contention that social class is becoming a relatively unimportant variable in explaining American voting patterns.

These differences in the degree of importance assigned to SES center on the salience and reality of class ties for individuals in modern Western society. As with intelligence, no one doubts the existence of the concept; the question is how to define and measure it. The essence of the problem has been stated by the authors of *The American Voter:*

Status differences exist, and these differences are related to differences in attitudes and behavior. They do not, however, assure us that the social class has *reality* as a group, or that class 'members' come to behave distinctively because they take the class as a reference point in decisions about behavior. Thus, the argument comes to rest on the nature of the class as a group. It is our thesis that the 'group' reality of the social class is variable.[23]

The lack of agreement on ways to define and measure social class has resulted in two distinct kinds of indicators—objective and subjective—of social class. Studies in the "objective" tradition often have used variables such as income, occupation, and education, or a combination of the three.[24] to place individuals or groups in stratification systems. This placement is made on the basis of available "hard" demographic data (e.g., census reports). Although this information tells us something about the "power, income, and wealth" components of the previously cited definition, it tells us nothing about the perceived importance of class position and little about the "prestige" compo-

---

[21] Robert E. Lane, *Political Life: Why and How People Get Involved in Politics* (New York: The Free Press, 1959), p. 226.

[22] Campbell et al., *The American Voter,* p. 202.

[23] Ibid., p. 185, emphasis added.

[24] For an excellent discussion concerning use of objective indicators, see Elton F. Jackson and Richard F. Curtis, "Conceptualization and Measurement in the Study of Social Stratification," in Hubert M. Blalock and Ann B. Blalock (eds.), *Methodology in Social Research* (New York: McGraw-Hill Book Co., 1968), pp. 112-149. A vareity of SES indices have evolved that provide summary SES scores for areas. Most of these follow or represent simplified versions of the Shevky-Bell index. For a discussion and explanation, see Eshref Shevky and Wendell Bell, *Social Area Analysis* (Stanford: Stanford University Press, 1955). For examples of application, see note 38, chapter 3.

nent. Most importantly, objective data do not indicate whether an individual identifies with a given class and the assumed objectives of that class. One can even quarrel with the use of the term "objective" because selection of the specific indicator(s) and delineation of categories used in the analysis are subjective choices made by the researcher.

On the other hand, "subjective" studies are based on the individual's perception of his position in a stratification system.[25] By tapping the individual's subjective sense of class identification, these studies come closer to determining the reality of social class. Yet it is still difficult to evaluate the extent of true class consciousness because such awareness is inevitably stimulated to some degree by the interviewer's questions.[26]

Although the debate concerning the most appropriate approach continues, advocates of each approach have used the other's indices and methods.[27] This dichotomy in research approaches should be recognized for its potential effect on theories stressing group influences on political behavior. For our purposes, however, it is equally important to note that the development of pockets of theory pertaining to the effect of class on voting behavior has proceeded with contributions from both objective and subjective studies. The contributions of both types of studies have been apparent in the literature that links SES to voter choice:

The extensive modern literature on social class and political behavior has shown persistently that individuals of higher status (subjectively or objectively) tend to give 'conservative' responses on questions of economic policy and tend as well to vote Republican. . . .[28]

The differences in research approaches have not had any apparent effect on the outcome of studies tracing the relationship between social class and participation in elections: *No matter how class is measured,* studies consistently show that higher class persons are more likely to participate in politics than lower class persons."[29]

---

[25] For a classic study of subjective class status, see Richard Centers, *The Psychology of Social Classes* (Princeton, New Jersey: Princeton University Press, 1949). For discussions relating the subjective approach directly to the study of political behavior see Campbell et al., op. cit., pp. 188-90; and Lane, op. cit., pp. 220-34.

[26] For instance, in the Survey Research Center's 1956 presidential election study, one out of every three respondents could not voluntarily identify himself as a member of a particular class group but would subsequently place himself in one of the groups mentioned by the interviewer. Campbell et al., op. cit., p. 190.

[27] Gould and Kolb, op. cit., p. 697. Although dated, an excellent review of the literature in light of this distinction is Kurt Mayer's "The Theory of Social Classes," *Harvard Educational Review* 23 (Summer 1953):149-57.

[28] Campbell et al., op. cit., p. 191.

[29] Milbrath, op. cit., pp. 115-16, emphasis added.

These introductory remarks are offered as a backdrop for the discussion to follow, in which "class," "social class," and "SES" will be used interchangeably. As we shall see, studies of SES and voting in school elections share the objective and subjective approaches found in the wider literature. Many researchers would probably accept the following assessment of the relationship between traditional indicators of social class:

Class status is indicated by objective criteria (such as income, occupation, and education), *plus* a network of social relations, *plus* a person's conception of his own place in society.[30]

The "objective criteria" normally used to measure social class are often highly interrelated. The relationship between any one of the three major SES criteria (income, occupation, and education) and voting seems to be as strong as the relationship between all three variables combined (as in summary indices) and voting. The pool of school voting studies that we have examined contains findings based on the variables defined both objectively and subjectively.

The specific effect social class has on direction of the vote is open to some conjecture. Depending on one's a priori theoretical predispositions or one's post factum explanation skills, the concept of social class and the specific indicators of that concept can be used to predict divergent voting patterns in school financial elections. Specific and plausible hypotheses will be elaborated in our discussion of each variable. By way of introduction, the research findings can be viewed in light of two general hypotheses that suggest contradictory effects of social class on voting patterns.

First, some strict economic interpretations of local voting patterns suggest that if SES is related to direction of the vote in local elections, higher SES is related to negative voting. Briefly, these theories hold that the cost of many issues increases with higher social class while the benefits from the issues may be distributed equally among the classes or disproportionally to the lower strata. Seldom (as in the case of a recreation issue) will these public expenditures confer increased benefits on the upper class.[31]

Second, a more frequent interpretation of local voting suggests the opposite hypothesis: SES and positive voting in local elections are positively and persistently related. Closely related partial theories stressing this view can be subsumed under the general "central-peripheral" classification scheme.[32] This

---

[30] Lane, op. cit., p. 220, emphasis added.

[31] For this interpretation, with some empirical justification, see Rene L. Frey and Leopold Kohn, "An Economic Interpretation of Voting Behavior on Public Finance Issues," *Kyklos* 23 Fasc. 4 (1970):792-805. See also the discussion in James Q. Wilson and Edward C. Banfield, "Voting Behavior on Municipal Public Expenditures," in Julius Margolis (ed.), *The Public Economy of Urban Communities* (Washington, D.C.: Resources for the Future, Inc., 1965), pp. 74-91.

[32] For a discussion of the concept and citations to related literature, see Milbrath, op. cit., pp. 110-14.

theory begins with an economic interpretation: higher status citizens have more of the benefits (e.g., goods, prestige, and power) of society. More important than the benefits (which may vary *greatly* when measured objectively in different settings at different times), however, are the feelings toward the community— community attachment, community identification, etc.—that appear to accompany higher levels of SES. Thus, higher status individuals may be considered closer to the center of their society and more interested in and concerned about "social progress" than their lower class counterparts. Those on the bottom of the SES ladder are considered on the periphery of their community and, hence, hold attitudes toward the community that are largely cynical and negative. This central-peripheral theory links a broad economic interpretation of voting to a predominant set of attitudes, or "world view," that, as we shall see in the next chapter, may be considered the most direct influence on voting direction in school financial elections.

*Income*

During our earlier discussion of house value as an indicator of tax burden we noted that normally income and house value are strongly correlated. Indeed, income has been explicitly verified as a measure of tax burden.[33] If we assume that voters cast their ballots on the basis of economic self-interest, other things being equal, we would predict a negative relationship between income and positive voting. There is little empirical evidence for this hypothesis. Only one study reports a negative relationship between median family income and positive voting in school financial elections (McMahon)[34]

On the other hand, income can be viewed as an indication of ability to pay. This view, coupled with the central-peripheral interpretation of status to which we referred earlier, suggests a positive association between income and yes voting in school financial elections. The evidence supports this interpretation: THE GREATER A VOTER'S INCOME, THE MORE LIKELY IT IS HE WILL VOTE IN FAVOR OF A SCHOOL FINANCIAL ISSUE (Fish, 1964; Milstein and Jennings, 1970; Gallup, 1969; Hatley, 1970; Smith et al., 1968; Schoonhoven and Patterson, 1966; Wilson and Banfield, 1971).[35]

---

[33] Wilson and Banfield, "Public-Regardingness as a Value Premise in Voting Behavior," pp. 114-15, particularly footnote 4; and Collignon, "Public Ragardingness in the Behavior of Voters in the Baltimore Metropolitan Area," pp. 13-15.

[34] This relationship was found for a number of public expenditures (though no school issues) that would favor the lower income groups in Switzerland. See Frey and Kohn, op. cit., pp. 800-803.

[35] This finding is corroborated in several studies of voting in other (than school) types of local financial referenda, most notably in Boskoff and Zeigler, *Voting Patterns in a Local Election*, Chapter 3; and Wilson and Banfield, "Public-Regardingness as a Value Premise in Voting Behavior," pp. 114-15.

The findings of all the studies listed immediately above are based on survey data, with individuals serving as the unit for analysis. Thus, in most cases researchers were able to examine the effect of subjective or perceived class status on individual voter responses to school issues. A closer examination of the findings would appear instructive, particularly to those who agree that "these personal interpretations of status constitute a link between the superficial opportunities and limitations of a given status and the ways in which persons behave in specific situations."[36]

Several researchers report findings that provide insight into the ways a voter's subjective view of his income affects his ballot choice. According to Boskoff and Zeigler, the higher a voter's income the more likely it is he will offer a positive reason for his vote in a local bond election.[37] Milstein and Jennings (1970) found that the lower a citizen's income the more likely it is he will perceive the tax bill resulting from a school bond issue as excessive. In these cases, the voter's capacity to pay appears to affect his perceptions of the benefit and cost of the issue. Another important dimension of the voter's perception was tapped by Smith et al. (1969) who found that the greater a person's "income satisfaction"[38] and the better his job outlook the more likely it is he will support a school millage proposal. Closely related to the voter's subjective satisfaction with his income is income stability. Fish (1964) found that voters who have experienced family income increases immediately preceding an election are more likely to approve school budget elections than voters whose income has remained stable or decreased.

The picture emerging from this examination is hardly surprising. A voter's subjective assessment of his relative income is an important part of the objective correlation between income and voting. The question these findings raise (which has received little direct empirical attention) centers on the perceived importance of two potentially conflicting economic concepts: tax burden and tax capacity. Among voters concerned with the cost of an issue, the objective variable of income allows us to rank-order both their required payment and their ability to pay. The question is, which consideration is overriding? The dearth of findings indicating a relationship between income and negative voting in school financial elections suggests that the use of the income variable as a surrogate for tax burden is misleading.

As an indicator of ability to pay (tax capacity), however, income appears to have greater theoretical promise. The concept of the "diminishing marginal utility of income" holds that the value of the dollar decreases as the individual accumulates more of them. Simply stated, wealthier individuals may be willing

---

[36] Boskoff and Zeigler, op. cit., p. 57.

[37] Ibid., p. 60.

[38] This scale is simply the result of the respondent's answer to the question "Is your family income above average, average, or below average?"

to spend more money for taxes than less fortunate voters because they have more money to spend. A straightforward exposition of this point of view is provided by Agger and Goldstein:

Why should people whose only property is their home, and a home which is comparatively inexpensive at that, offer the most resistance to what is for them a rather small dollar tax increase? Such a question could only be raised by a middle-class person for whom $10 or $20 a year is a small sum, and not by a lower-income person for whom every extra dollar is noticeably important in maintaining a current level of living. For the low-income family, increased taxes may necessitate postponing the purchase of a new automobile, or new clothes for the children,. . . or simply a few drinks with the boys. (1971, p. 116)

As persuasive as this explanation of the income/positive vote relationship appears, it needs supplementation. Wilson and Banfield suggest the following limitation to the "diminishing marginal utility" explanation:

Differences in the value of the dollar to voters at different income levels account in part for the well-to-do voter's relatively strong taste for public expenditures. They can hardly account for it entirely, however. For one thing, they do not rationalize the behavior of those voters who support measures that would give them only trivial benefits while imposing substantial costs upon them.[39]

In other words, a missing part of the explanation is suggested by the question: why should a rational individual choose to spend money—regardless of how little a dollar is worth to him—on schools when no immediate, tangible return can be anticipated from the investment? The income/affirmative vote relationship requires testing under more rigorous control conditions including multivariate designs that can adequately weigh the impact of the voter's perception of his relative income (as well as occupational and educational) status. The type of question that needs to be answered, for example, is whether marginal utility of income can be considered a viable explanation for the higher proportion of yes votes found among nonparents in the high, as opposed to low, income brackets? As a stimulant for future inquiry, we suggest the following logically based proposition: To the extent that the relationship between status variables and positive voting in school financial elections holds *while controlling* for obvious benefit ("narrow self-interest") variables (e.g., number of children in the public schools), the "marginal utility of income" or other economic explanations must be devalued in favor of explanations that stress the psychological, or at least extremely long-range benefit, correlates of class behavior.

Although the majority of the studies in our sample reported a strong positive association between income and affirmative voting in school financial elections,

---

[39]Wilson and Banfield, "Public-Regardingness as a Value Premise in Voting Behavior," pp. 116-17.

the finding is not unanimous. One study found a negative relationship between the two variables (McMahon, 1966, as noted earlier) while another (Tebbutt, 1968) found no significant relationship between a voter's income and the direction of his vote.

The results are mixed when the relationship is tested among aggregates. Davidson (1967) and Minar (1968) both found income positively related to the successful outcome of school financial elections held in certain Illinois school districts. Similarly, Hahn and Almy (1971) report a positive relationship between income and support for school financial elections among Los Angeles precincts. However, a study by Hicks (1967) that analyzed Ohio school districts found no significant relationship between the variables. Finally, Jordan (1966) again reports a curvilinear finding in his study of Los Angeles; voters from census tracts in the lowest and highest quartiles for median family income are more likely to approve bond issues than voters from tracts in the low-middle and high-middle quartiles.

*Education*

The strong correlation normally found among income, education, and occupation leads us to expect positive associations between education and occupation on the one hand and yes voting on the other, at least at the individual level. We began with a discussion of income as an indicator of status because it serves to bridge key debating points suggested by economic and sociopsychological theories. Compared to the other two status indicators, income has received the most research attention. Educational achievement (or level) is, however, a variable attracting more unanimous theoretical support than income. Indeed, other things being equal, it is difficult to imagine alternatives to hypotheses that predict positive relationships between education and yes voting in these elections. The general status-related attitudes and behaviors we have discussed up to this point should be as predictable from educational level as they are from income. Education is directly related to levels of information and involvement, which in turn are fairly direct potential avenues (as is income standing alone) to the "center" of society.

It is reasonable to assume that the higher an individual's educational level, the more likely he will feel that education is generally beneficial. By correlation, the highly educated individual has received more of society's goods and prestige, to say nothing of less tangible rewards, than a person with less education. To the claim that lower class citizens should favor education as a means of upward mobility for their children, Agger and Goldstein (1971) respond that many of the innovative programs stimulating increases in school expenditures may actually widen the gap between classes.[40] Hence, there is a rational basis for

---

[40] For instance, these authors argue that the certain teaching technique innovations may

those in the lower educational status category to discount educational benefits.

Aside from relatively complex explanations of behavior such as those suggested by status inconsistency[41] and upward mobility, we have little reason to expect anything other than a positive association between educational attainment and positive voting in school elections. That has been the predominant finding, leading to establishment of the following proposition: THE HIGHER A VOTER'S EDUCATIONAL LEVEL, THE MORE LIKELY IT IS HE WILL SUPPORT A SCHOOL FINANCIAL ELECTION (McKelvey, 1966; Schoonhoven and Patterson, 1966; Tebbutt, 1968; Gallup, 1969; Hatley, 1971; Hahn and Almy, 1971; Wilson and Banfield, 1971). The research leaves little doubt concerning the strong relationship between an individual's education and his support for the educational system. The significant question that remains involves specifying the independent nature of the variable. In the most tightly controlled study mentioned above (McKelvey), individuals who had received at least some college education were much more likely to vote in favor of a school financial issue than those with less education, regardless of their ranking on several other dimensions (both status and attitude).

When we examine research undertaken at the aggregate level of analysis, again we face a paradoxical reversal of the direction of a relationship. Although one study (Hahn and Almy 1971) confirms the positive association between educational attainment and yes voting at the aggregate level, and another study (Minar 1966) reports a weak but positive correlation, three studies have found a

---

function to reinforce tracking systems which in turn are blamed, in part, for forcing disadvantaged children out of the school system. This is a much simplified version of the argument made by Walter Schafer, "Rural and Small-Town Delinquency: New Understanding and Approaches," paper read to the National Outlook Conference on Rural Youth, Washington, D.C.: October 24, 1967 (mimeo.), as cited in Agger and Goldstein. A more recent version of the argument accompanied by persuasive data may be found in Walter Schafer and Carol Olexa, *Tracking and Opportunity: The Locking Out Process and Beyond* (San Francisco: Chandler, 1971).

[41] Status inconsistency is the result of a high rank on one status dimension (in this case, education), accompanied by low ranks on other dimensions (e.g., income and occupation). An individual in such a situation might, on the basis of his own experience, entertain reasonable doubts toward the general validity of the educational experience. It has also been suggested, in the context of other partisan elections, that these inconsistencies could lead to a sense of "relative deprivation." These feelings of relative deprivation may foster frustration that under certain conditions can only be vented by some form of "protest." In the 1968 presidential election, status inconsistency and consequent feelings of deprivation appear strongly related to support for George Wallace: See D. S. Eitzen, "Status Inconsistency and Wallace Supporters in a Mid-western City," *Social Forces* 48 (June 1970):493-98; and Thomas Pettigrew, Robert T. Riley, and Reeve D. Vannemann, "George Wallace's Constituents," *Psychology Today* 5 (February 1972):47-49+. In recently completed and unpublished research on precinct voting in Eugene, Oregon, John Hall finds a strong and persistent relationship between Wallace support and negative voting patterns in school elections, while controlling for a number of other social, economic, and political variables. Of course a "protest" vote need not necessarily be linked to personal feelings of deprivation. Other plausible stimulants will be considered in the following chapter.

strong negative relationship between educational level and positive voting.[42] In his study of precinct voting in Austin, Texas, McMahon (1966) found that the greater a precinct's median educational level, the greater the proportion of negative voting in school financial elections. Davidson (1967) reports a similarly strong negative relationship between a community's median educational level and success in school financial elections. Finally, Jordan (1966) found that Los Angeles census tracts ranking in the lowest quartile on the educational attainment dimension were most likely to *support* a school bond issue. However, census tracts from the next highest quartile of educational attainment were most likely to oppose the school bond issue. This may be an important clue for understanding these apparent anomalies in aggregate voting patterns. The potential curvilinearity suggested by this and similar status relationships might also be found among surveyed individuals if sufficient representation were given to the very highest and lowest ranking individuals in a sample (random sampling techniques usually preclude this).

*Occupation*

The third variable in the traditional SES triad is occupation. The definitions offered in the introduction to this section suggest the theoretical importance of this variable, which is, of course, strongly correlated with income and education. Occupation, however, presents greater validity problems for the researcher than do the other two variables. The typical scale ranks occupational status along the lines of the objective classification scheme used by the Census Bureau. These are normally very broad categories that cover a wide range of occupational titles. Such classifications do not normally reflect the wide status differences that exist *within* jobs and professions. Attempts at comparing and synthesizing such research findings are inevitably frustrated by operational difficulties. The problem is pronounced in the case of occupational status.

Partly because of these measurement difficulties, few studies have reviewed the relationship between occupational status and voting. Despite the small number of relevant studies, accurate synthesis is impossible. Of two studies of

---

[42] Fairly well established propositions found at the individual level are subject to mixed evidence at the aggregate level in studies of voting in other situations. An excellent discussion of this phenomenon is contained in one such study that finds, in contradiction to the individual level norm, a negative relationship between educational level and voter turnout for mayorality and councilmanic elections among a national sample of cities. See Robert R. Alford and Eugene C. Lee, "Voting Turnout in American Cities," *American Political Science Review* 62 (September 1968):796-813.

For a study that reports a positive relationship between median precinct educational level and support for a state constitution referenda, see Norman C. Thomas, "The Electorate and State Constitutional Revision: An Analysis of Four Michigan Referenda," in Hofferbert and Sharkansky (eds.), *State and Urban Politics* pp. 149-62. Reprinted from *Midwest Journal of Political Science* 12 (February 1968):115-29.

individual voting behavior, one (Gallup, 1969) found that individuals employed in "business and professional" categories were more likely to vote in favor of school financial proposals than individuals in other occupational categories, whereas the other (Tebbutt, 1968) found no relationship between a voter's occupational status and his vote.[43]

Two studies conducted at a higher level of analysis also reached contradictory conclusions. McMahon (1966) found that the greater a precinct's percentage of males engaged in professional occupations, the greater the precinct's negative vote for school financial elections. On the other hand, Carter and Ruggels (1966, Vol. 4) found that the greater a district's ten-year increase in the percentage of citizens employed in professions and administration, the greater that district's proportion of favorable votes for school financial elections.[44] A corroborative finding from the same study indicates that the greater the percentage of a district's citizens employed in manufacturing (1960), the smaller that district's favorable vote in school financial elections.

*Summary Measure of SES*

In this section so far we have discussed the relationship between specific variables most frequently treated as indicators of SES and direction of the vote in school financial elections. We have noted conflict within groups of findings that (particularly in the case of education) may be attributable to variations in research focus, specifically in the unit of analysis. Now we examine other research approaches that have been used in attempts to provide a better summary of the concept of social class. Several investigators have examined the relationship between socioeconomic status and voting by operationalizing SES as an index of objective factors such as the ones we have just discussed (e.g., income, education, and occupation).[45] Statistical summaries such as these indexes have the same advantages and disadvantages as any other summary; they provide a convenient capsule of important information, yet they may sometimes blur important distinctions among the parts composing it. For example, an SES index score tells us nothing about the potentially important phenomenon of status inconsistency.

Defined in these summary terms, available evidence suggests that the higher an area's SES the greater that area's positive vote in school financial elections.[46]

---

[43] A similar finding for other types of local elections is reported by Boskoff and Zeigler, op. cit., p. 47.

[44] The ten-year period is 1940 to 1950.

[45] Index descriptions and computational techniques may be found in works cited in footnote 38, Chapter 3, and footnote 24 this chapter.

[46] Other studies of the "class"—as measured by objective indices or subjective questions—in-

Minar (1966) found that the greater a district's aggregate social rank (measured via the Shevky-Bell index) the less strong is voter dissent in that district. Willis (1967-68) found that school district attendance areas (units similar to precincts) exhibiting the following *combination* of characteristics were more likely to oppose a school bond or tax election than those that do not: (1) a large proportion of school enrollment in nonpublic schools, (2) a high percentage of persons with relatively low levels of education, and (3) a large proportion of blue-collar workers.

However, two other studies that examined SES in summary terms report contradicting evidence. Turner (1968) and Jordan (1966) both found that Los Angeles areas scoring lowest on the Shevky-Bell social area index were likely to be more supportive of school financial issues than some of the city's higher ranking areas. These two studies are both based on quartile analysis, which, in an area the size of Los Angeles, suggests significant heterogeneity of populations within each area. On the other hand, these findings point to the potential importance of ethnic influences described in the first section of this chapter; the areas ranking lowest on the SES scales of these studies are predominantly black. A revision of the SES/positive vote proposition that controls for ethnic influences may be required, particularly for large urban areas.

## Socioeconomic Determinants: A Synthesis

The evidence reviewed in this chapter has proved helpful in our attempt to identify categories of individuals most likely to favor or oppose school issues under normal election circumstances. From this evidence we were able to construct a portrait of the model voter—positive and negative—that appears in Table 6-3. Although we have discussed several other correlates to voter choice, the ones appearing in Table 6-3 have received the most support from empirical research.

Several important cautions apply to interpretation of Table 6-3. First, a number of other factors may be equal to or more important than these determinants of voter choice. Many plausible variables either may not have been strongly correlated with voter choice or may not have received adequate research attention. Second, a *ceteris peribus* clause should be read into each dichotomy established by the table. For example, all other things being equal, parents of school age children are more likely than nonparents to support school financial issues. Third, there is little empirical evidence available for assessing the additive

---

fluence on voting for other types of local issues support this proposition. For support based on the Shevky-Bell index, see Walter C. Kaufman and Scott Greer, "Voting in a Metropolitan Community: An Application of Social Area Analysis," *Social Forces* 38 (March 1960):196-204; and Eugene S. Uyeki, "Patterns of Voting in a Metropolitan Area, 1938-1962," *Urban Affairs Quarterly* 1 (June 1966):65-77. Corroboration based on subjective data may be found in Boskoff and Zeigler, op. cit., pp. 55-57.

**Table 6-3**
**Characteristics of Voters Most Likely to Favor or Oppose School Financial Issues**

| *Yes* Voters | *No* Voters |
|---|---|
| Parents of school age children | Nonparents |
| Higher income | Lower income |
| Younger | Older |
| Blacks | Whites |
| Higher education | Lower education |

nature—the multiple correlation—of these variables. And finally, these relationships have frequently been asserted, tested, and explained on the basis of conflicting (or at least different) theories.

As severe as these restrictions are, Table 6-3 represents a distinct improvement in our ability to understand school financial election voting behavior. In the first place, the evidence that led to these models of the yes and the no voter has strengthened the case for a theory of normal voting in school financial elections. As we had grown to suspect from the evidence presented in earlier chapters, the direction of the vote cast in school elections is frequently a result of longstanding, "nonpolitical" forces that are, in themselves, uncontrollable by those who would like to affect the outcome of school financial elections. In addition, the model improves our ability to describe the normal voting population and to predict normal voting behavior.

Nevertheless, the models raise more theoretical questions than answers. Why are status variables related to voting behavior in school elections? Although we have discussed some plausible answers, others, not yet mentioned, are suggested by previous research in electoral behavior. Boskoff and Zeigler have suggested that the last twenty years of voting research—taken as an aggregate of knowledge—have identified a

> ...theoretical trio of voting analysis: socio-enonomic status in its various objective and subjective forms, influence and persuasion processes as a source of either maintenance or change of political orientations, and a complex set of primarily non-ideological attitudes that reflect alienation from or commitment to social environments from the neighborhood to the nation.[47]

Thus far, we have reviewed evidence from two of the three branches: "influence and persuasion processes" were examined in Chapter 5 and socioeconomic influences occupied much of our attention in this chapter. Before proceeding to more complex explanations, we must review the evidence surrounding the third theoretical branch mentioned by Boskoff and Zeigler: attitude sets.

---

[47] Boskoff and Zeigler, op. cit., p. 139.

# 7
## Psychological Determinants

By now it is apparent that studies of voting behavior have considered a wide variety of forces—and a consequent multitude of specific variables thought to represent those forces—that affect a citizen's decision to vote. Researchers from the University of Michigan's Survey Research Center have suggested a unifying conceptual scheme to show how this variety of factors affects voting decisions. This conceptual scheme, labled the "funnel of causality," is presented in Figure 7-1.

This model attempts to depict the causal relationships among various independent and intervening variables that may affect voter choice in presidential elections. Borrowing from Kurt Lewin's field theory of social psychology,[1] the funnel of causality superimposes some order on the totality of forces and experiences that could conceivably affect a voter's choice. The order is established through the concept of immediacy: variables at the broad end of the funnel have a minimal or indirect effect on a voter's specific choice while variables at the narrow end of the funnel have a more immediate and salient effect.

According to this concept, the economic and social influences we have discussed previously are of less immediate importance to voter decision-making in partisan situations than individual psychological attributes, specifically party identification. As we indicated in Chapter 3, this model has not been accepted uncritically;[2] nor has it been systematically applied to voting in local nonpartisan situations. But even if their origins may be traced to class and group affiliations, variables that we label "attitudinal" or "psychological" may be potentially important for understanding voting patterns in school financial elections.

The most important attitudinal determinant of choice in presidential elections, intensity of party identification,[3] seems less likely to provide an equally clear division among the local electorate. The nonpartisan nature of school financial elections suggests that other attitudes would occupy the

---

[1] See Dorwin Cartwright (ed.), *Field Theory in Social Science: Selected Theoretical Papers by Kurt Lewin* (London: Tavistock Publications Ltd., 1952), particularly the classic "Behavior and Development as a Function of the Total Situation," pp. 238-303.

[2] A recent and thoughtful critique that provides references to earlier reactions, most preeminently those of V. O. Key, is Peter B. Natchez, "Images of Voting: The Social Psychologists," *Public Policy* 18 (Summer 1970):553-88.

[3] Campbell et al., *The American Voter*, pp. 79-83 et seq.

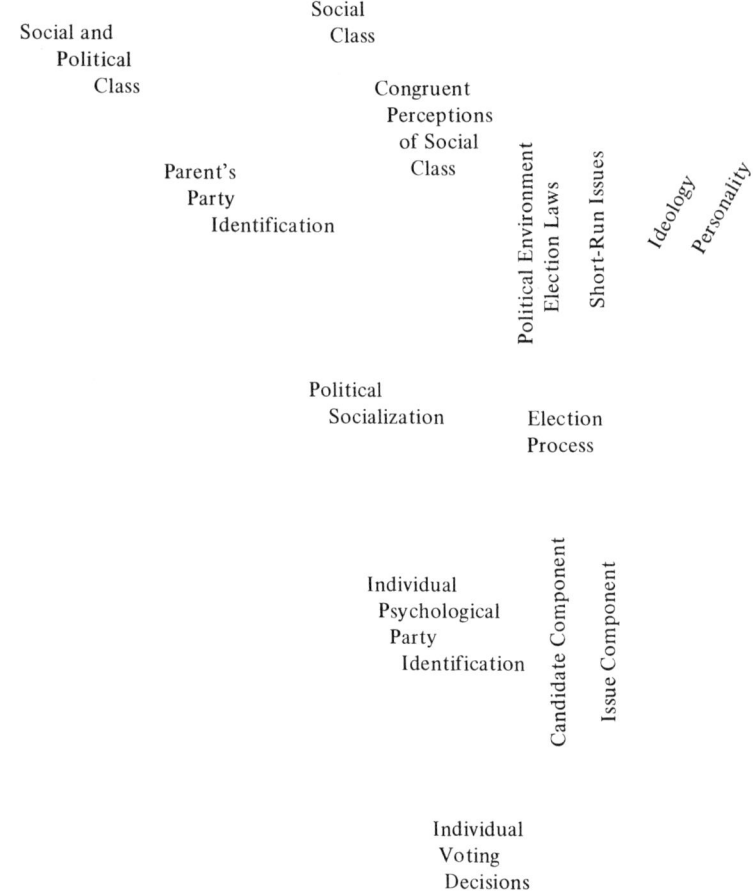

**Figure 7-1.** The "Funnel of Causality" Leading to Voting Decisions*

*Reproduced by permission from Peter Natchez, "Images of Voting: The Social Psychologists", *Public Policy* 18 (Summer 1970): 562.

narrowest end of the funnel of causality. Several researchers have suggested that attitudes toward schools, taxes, community, government, and governmental officials generally, are central correlates to voter choice in school financial elections. In this chapter, we examine the literature in an attempt to assess the importance of these attitudes.

**Partisan and Nonpartisan Attitudes**

At the outset, we should not dismiss partisan attitudes as potential predictors of nonpartisan voting. Partisan attitudes might summarize attitudes toward government, taxes, and even the schools. This possibility raises old and unanswered questions in American political theory: How permanent (or malleable) is the set of attitudes that comprise a voter's view of the political world? To what extent is a voter's decision a "standing" one? What is the link, if any, between a voter's choice of national candidates and his decision on local issues? To what extent do individuals and groups exhibit continuity in their voting for different offices and issues? And, as Frederick Wirt has asked, "do voters retain an almost subconscious Madisonian democracy concept of balancing the factions of society, and so vote for different parties for various offices?"[4] Because our theory, and the evidence for it, is drawn largely from studies of presidential elections, we face these and similar questions with limited empirical information.

The first step toward measuring the pervasiveness of political attitudes is to compare voting records of groups and individuals over time and in various kinds of elections. The problem has been well stated by Boskoff and Zeigler:

Since in many local elections party labels are absent, the problem is to ascertain the extent to which 'national' Democrats or Republicans vote in local elections in a manner consistent with their national inclinations, even without the image of the party as a guide. Are there correlations between national and local voting patterns?[5]

We have seen no direct evidence bearing on the relationship between voting in school financial elections and a voter's partisan predisposition. There is, however, some indirect evidence that may allow us to draw tentative conclusions concerning this relationship. Mahan (1968) found no significant relationship between voters' value orientations[6] and direction of the vote for a school bond issue. Several researchers have found that voting for partisan or nonpartisan offices was an inadequate predictor of voting direction in school financial elections (Templeton, 1966; Jordan, 1966; Hahn and Almy, 1971).

In their study of voting for local financial issues other than school elections, Boskoff and Zeigler found no significant relationship between a voter's "political orientation"[7] and either his socioeconomic status or his vote for local bond issues. Given this clue, we are hardly surprised by their finding that there is no

---

[4]Frederick M. Wirt, "Suburban Patterns in American Politics" (unpublished address delivered at the 1960 annual meeting of the American Political Science Association, New York, Statler Hilton Hotel, September 8-10, 1960). The same basic point is stressed, along with an excellent treatment of differential attitudes of both voters and office holders toward various types of public office, in Joseph A. Schlesinger, *Ambition and Politics: Political Careers in the United States* (Chicago: Rand McNally and Co., 1966), pp. 69 et seq.

[5]Boskoff and Zeigler, op. cit., p. 21.

[6]Establishes a dichotomy between those voters whose value orientations are primarily "traditional" as opposed to "emergent."

[7]Mahan establishes a dichotomy between voters whose attitudes toward government are primarily ideological and voters whose attitudes are primarily "personal-moral."

significant relationship between a voter's choice in a presidential election and his choice in a local bond election.[8]

We have no direct evidence on the relative permanence of *individuals'* voting decisions in school financial elections at different points in time. The importance of voter predispositions in these specific election situations is underscored, however, by researchers who have examined the effect of previous school financial election voting patterns at the aggregate level. Their findings support the following proposition: AN AREA'S PAST VOTING BEHAVIOR IN SCHOOL FINANCIAL ELECTIONS IS A SIGNIFICANT INDICATOR OF ITS PRESENT VOTING BEHAVIOR (Beal et al., 1966; Nelson, 1968; Willis, 1967-68; Saalfeld, 1972; Varden, 1973). This proposition lends substantial corroboration to the broader one suggested by several of the findings in Chapter 6: particularly within the confines of the school financial election situation, the voter's decision is frequently a "standing decision." The remainder of this chapter explores some more plausible explanations for that situation.

Methods of analyzing political attitudes frequently tap economic attitudes that bear a close, though potentially confusing, relationship to political ideology. Only two studies (Fish, 1964; Mahan, 1968) have assessed the relationship between "liberal" or "conservative" economic attitudes and voting in school elections; neither found any significant relationship. Fish did, however, find that a voter's opinion concerning the "state-of-the-economy"[9] was not related to the direction of his vote in a school budget election. This evidence is inadequate but presents an interesting point of departure for future research capable of directly assessing attitude permanence/instability over time, since such research could parallel changes in objective economic conditions. One example of such research would be panel studies, which survey one group of respondents at several points in time.

---

[8]Other studies that have examined the relationship between the voting patterns of diverse social and partisan groupings in partisan and nonpartisan elections offer mixed conclusions: Significant associations are reported in Jennings and Zeigler, op. cit.; and Oliver P. Williams and Charles R. Adrian, "The Insulation of Local Politics Under the Non-Partisan Ballot," *American Political Science Review* 53 (December 1959):1052-63. The findings from one study suggest the existence of parallels between partisan and local nonpartisan elective office situations, though similar relationships between voting for referenda and partisan office are not evident; see Robert H. Salisbury and Gordon Balck, "Class and Party in Partisan and Non-Partisan Elections: The Case of Des Moines," *American Political Science Review* 57 (September 1963):584-92.

V.O. Key found that voting in local elections frequently is unrelated to voting for partisan office. As a possible explanation for this finding, he suggested that long established patterns of local political behavior facilitate voter differentiation between local and national electoral situations. See V. O. Key, Jr., "Partisanship and the County Office: The Case of Ohio," *American Political Science Review* 47 (June 1953):525-32.

[9]The author simply asked respondents "Which of the following best describes the state of the economy: recession, stable, or expanding?"

## Attitudes toward Taxes

The evidence suggests that voters' feelings about taxes—their general level, need, and impact—influence voting more than their views of the economic situation in general. Accordingly, *citizens who express positive attitudes toward taxes are more likely to support specific school financial issues than those who do not* (Agger and Goldstein, 1965 and 1971; Carter and Ruggels, 1966; Milstein and Jennings, 1970).

This proposition is almost tautological in its simplicity. Clearly, additional explanation is necessary. Why, for example, do some individuals tend to have more favorable attitudes toward taxes than others? Boskoff and Zeigler found no statistically significant relationship between a voter's social status and his opinion that tax rates are excessive, about right, or too low.[10] Further, these researchers found no statistically significant relationship between a voter's income, occupation, or perceived status and his preference for methods of raising taxes for county services. This lack of association led the authors to conclude that "the values and motives associated with different voting patterns of our status categories are *not primarily economic* or utilitarian in nature."[11] Although Agger and Goldstein (1971) found that educational level is associated with positive attitudes toward taxes, the relationship appears far from perfect and virtually disappears when controls for social-psychological variables such as alienation are employed (p. 149).

There is, then, both direct and indirect evidence suggesting that, to many voters, attitudes associated with broad (e.g., politico-economic philosophies) or narrow (e.g., taxes) considerations of cost are at best only as important as other attitudes. In addition, we have reviewed some findings suggesting that broad classifications of voters on the basis of their party preference for national office or their ranking on various ideological scales do not summarize attitude sets that are valuable in predicting the direction of the vote in school financial elections.

## Attitudes toward Community

Several theorists have suggested that a voter's attitude toward his community is a more precise predictor of whether he will normally vote yes or no in school financial elections. These theorists contend that long-range and general benefit

---

[10] Boskoff and Zeigler, op. cit., pp. 64-66. One recent national survey found that 45 percent of the U.S. public considers the local property tax as "least fair" among tax alternatives. No significant difference is apparent in responses from various income and occupation categories, though homeowners were more likely than renters (47 percent to 40 percent) to oppose the property tax. For these and other current data reflecting attitudes toward taxes and tax options, see Advisory Commission on Intergovernmental Relations, *Public Opinion and Taxes,* Washington, D.C., May 1972.

[11] Ibid., p. 66.

considerations—as indicated by a voter's attitude toward, and perceived relation to, his community—provide overriding predispositions that determine the vote in a local election. The previously mentioned "center/periphery" continuum may be the best device for assessing the relevance of these attitudes.

In this regard, the evidence strongly suggests the following proposition: *the more favorable a citizen's "generalized civic improvement orientation," the more likely it is he will vote in favor of a school financial issue* (Agger and Goldstein, 1964 and 1971; Wilson and Banfield, 1964 and 1971).[12] Indicators of this orientation have varied among researchers, as have labels of it, such as "public vs. private-regardingness" (Wilson and Banfield, 1964), "unitary vs. individualist ethos" (Wilson and Banfield, 1971), and "civic responsibility" (Boskoff and Zeigler, 1964). But aside from differences in terminology, the studies usually find that some individuals are more likely than others to favor community improvements and that these individuals are also more likely to express feelings of identification with and pride in their community. Not surprisingly, individuals who feel this way are much more likely to vote in favor of school issues than those who do not, regardless of other important social and psychological characteristics. The findings suggest that some individuals feel more closely allied to their community and feel they have a stake in the outcome of community decisions, including financial ones such as school bond or budget elections.

This proposition is also favored by objective evidence suggesting that attachment to the community and its institutions may serve to motivate "progressive" voter reactions: Smith et al. (1968) found that the greater a potential voter's participation in formal associations the more likely it is he will vote in favor of a school millage election.

If strong community identification feelings lead to a propensity to support local financial issues, then opposite feelings should lead to negative voting. A large body of theory and research suggests that a significant proportion of individuals living in modern "mass societies"[13] are psychologically on the periphery of those societies. The concept most frequently used to describe these individuals is alienation. As one of the central concepts in contemporary social science, alienation has been used to explain wide varieties of human behavior, including voting.[14] Accompanying this wide use of the concept is a divergency

---

[12] For excellent theoretical treatment and supporting evidence from voting for other types of issues, see ibid., Chapter 5, and James S. Coleman, *Community Conflict* (New York: The Free Press, 1957), pp. 18-19.

[13] For the classic treatment of the relationship between "mass society" and alienation, see William Kornhauser, *The Politics of Mass Society* (Glencoe, Illinois: The Free Press, 1959). For one of the most readable statements, see Erich Fromm, *Escape from Freedom* (New York: Holt, Rinehart, and Winston, 1961).

[14] A number of sources point to the divergent theoretical and operational treatments of alienation. The following define the scope of the concept and provide comprehensive references: Melvin Seeman, "On the Meaning of Alienation," *American Sociological Review*

of operational definitions of it that greatly complicates comparing the results of relevant studies.[15]

In general, most studies have defined the alienated individual as one who feels either detached or at least extremely distant from the center of his community. He feels "powerless and estranged in a world of powerful forces."[16] Alienated individuals normally feel they cannot affect important community decisions. Others—"them," the powerful—make important and normally "wrong" community decisions. This point of view leads to discontent, frustration, cynicism, and a generally negative view of the political process. According to alienation theory, the normal result of this set of attitudes is disinterest in or avoidance of the community decision-making process. On occasion, however, political situations that appear more directly susceptible to the influence of the "powerless" arise. Referendums are excellent vehicles for this occasional participation. Voting usually takes a negative form to protest the "wrong," "unfair," and generally "stupid" decisions that "they" have made.

Literature testing the relationship between alienation and voting in school financial elections supports the proposition that VOTERS WHO ARE ALIENATED ARE MORE LIKELY TO OPPOSE SCHOOL FINANCIAL ISSUES THAN THOSE WHO ARE NOT (Horton and Thompson, 1960 and 1962; Gold, 1962; Templeton, 1966; Agger and Goldstein, 1965 and 1971).[17]

---

24 (December 1959):780-90; and Lewis S. Feuer, "What Is Alienation: The Career of a Concept," *New Politics* 1 (Spring 1962):116-34.

Recent and thorough reviews of applications of the concept to explanations of voting behavior are included in Joel D. Aberbach, "Alienation and Political Behavior," *American Political Science Review* 63 (March 1969): 86-99; and Frederic Templeton, "Alienation and Political Participation: Some Research Findings," *Public Opinion Quarterly* 30 (Summer 1966): 249-61. For a provocative essay on the future of alienation, see Robert E. Lane, "Allienation, Protest, and Rootless Politics in the Seventies," in Ray Hiebert et al. (eds.), *The Political Image Merchants: Strategies in the New Politics* (Washington, D.C.: Acropolis Books Ltd., 1971): pp. 273-300.

[15]This point—referring to the muddled or conflicting nature of the concept—has been made in most critiques. An excellent critique providing thorough references to others is contained in Robert L. Crain, Elihu Katz, and Donald B. Rosenthal, *The Politics of Community Conflict: The Fluoridation Decision* (Indianapolis: The Bobbs-Merrill Co., 1969), pp. 31-70. For a defense of alienation based on secularization of the concept, see Melvin Seeman, "The Alienation Hypothesis," *Psychiatry and Social Science Review* 3 (April 1969): 2-6.

[16]John E. Horton and Wayne E. Thompson, "Powerlessness and Political Negativism: A Study of Defeated Local Referendums," *The American Journal of Sociology* 67 (March 1962): 485-93.

[17]Several studies of voting in other local situations, particularly fluoridation referenda, have found relationships between negative voting and variants of alienation (factors generally lumped under the alienation umbrella, depending on one's point of view). Among these variants are the associations reported in the following: Arnold Simmel, "A Signpost for Research on Fluoridation Conflicts: The Concept of Relative Deprivation," *The Journal of Social Issues* 17,4 (1961): 34; William A Gamson, "The Fluoridation Dialogue: Is It an Ideological Conflict?" *Public Opinion Quarterly* 26 (Winter 1965); and Edward L. McDill and Jeanne Clare Ridley, "Status, Anomia, Political Alienation and Political Participation," *American Journal of Sociology* 68 (September 1962). For inferential evidence that detracts from the alienation hypothesis, see Crain, Katz, and Rosenthal, op. cit., and Clarence N.

Hence the individual's attitude toward, and perceived relationship to, his community, appears to be an important immediate stimulus to the direction of his vote. At least this appears to be the case for those individuals who can be clearly classified as at the center (elites) or on the periphery (alienates) of a community. The relationship between alienation and negative voting reported by Horton and Thompson (1962) is strong and holds up under certain controls, but it is clearly not perfect. Left unexplained, for example, is the behavior of individuals not easily classified as either elites or alienates. Gold (1962) reexamined the Horton and Thompson data and found that voters who are *both* alienated and lower class are more likely to oppose school bond issues than voters who do not share this combination of characteristics. Thus, the use of multivariate techniques allowed Gold to explain a much larger proportion of the variance in school financial election voting than Horton and Thompson could explain in their original analysis.

Templeton has also attempted to specify the relative importance of alienation, independent of social class status, in voting for both local and national elections. He found that alienation and negative voting were strongly associated on each of three local issues (fluoridation, school bond, and tax rate). Importantly, the relationship was most pronounced for the upper class portion of his sample. Agger and Goldstein (1971) also found that, to a degree, the effects of alienation on voting are independent of social class.

On the other hand, voting patterns in the presidential elections of 1956 and 1960 were not found to be significantly divergent for individuals classified as alienated or nonalienated. This finding led Templeton to conclude that local elections, by maximizing "both the access and the potential impact of interested individual citizens" (p. 261), provide better electoral vehicles for expression of alienation.

It is apparent from these studies that the effect of a voter's feeling of powerlessness in a world ruled by the powerful is often negative for local issues. It is also apparent that these feelings of powerlessness are not limited to individuals who might appear, on the basis of objective criteria such as class status or group affiliation, most justified in feeling this way. As a result it would seem useful to heed Seeman's advice[18] to probe further via refinement and secularization of the concept.

**Attitudes toward Governments and Governors:**
**Schools and School Officials**

An important part of refining and secularizing the concept of alienation involves

---

Stone, "Local Referendums: An Alternative to the Alienated Voter Model," *Public Opinion Quarterly* 29 (Summer 1965): 213-22.

[18] Seeman, op. cit.

specifying its object. As we have noted, general definitions of alienation usually refer to "society" or, slightly more specifically, to "community." Most surveys concerned with voting behavior—as opposed to other kinds of behavior—have been designed to tap feelings of alienation from government and government officials. At the same time, as one of the Survey Research Center scholars has noted the general public's evaluations of government are largely undifferentiated, combining ethical issues, the competence of public officials, the soundness of policy, and other evaluative criteria in a single judgment.[19] Because these evaluations of government and government officials have been successfully used to assess alienated voting behavior in general, it follows that public attitudes toward school governance and school officials would be useful in diagnosing the relationship between alienation and voting in school financial elections.

If some of the negative voting in school financial elections is a protest based on negative evaluations of government, it is obviously important to specify the object of those negative evaluations. School officials may be able to reverse some negative attitudes toward the schools but they are limited in their ability to reverse negative evaluations of public agencies and officials in general. Although little direct evidence is available, existing research emphasizes the importance of voter attitudes toward the schools.

Two researchers have considered the meaning of a voter's general attitude toward school officials. Their findings support the proposition that *voters who display cynical attitudes toward school officials are more likely to vote against school financial issues than those who trust school officials* (Agger and Goldstein, 1965 and 1971; Milstein and Jennings, 1970).[20] Agger and Goldstein's research not only directly relates cynical attitudes to negative voting but also provides indirect but strongly supportive evidence: citizens who feel that public school policy is best decided by the superintendent and his staff are more likely to vote in favor of a school budget proposal that those who feel such policy should be decided by a school board or citizen vote. In this regard, it is important to note that a study of voter participation (Parnell, 1964) based on the Agger and Goldstein data found that citizens who strongly favor *voter* decision-making are *less* likely than their more trusting counterparts to participate in a school budget election.

Milstein and Jennings tapped a subtly different kind of cynicism. They found that voters who have voted in successful school bond elections are more likely to agree that school officials have provided the "true facts" concerning the need for

---

[19] Donald Stokes, "Popular Evaluations of Government: An Empirical Assessment," in Harlen Cleveland and Harold Lasswell (eds.), *Ethics and Bigness* (New York: Harper and Row, 1962), pp. 61-72.

[20] For excellent, focused discussions of correlates to political cynicism, see Robert E. Agger, Marshall N. Goldstein, and Stanley A. Pearl, "Political Cynicism: Measurement and Meaning," *The Journal of Politics* 23 (August 1961): 477-506; and Edgar Litt, "Political Cynicism and Political Futility," *The Journal of Politics* 25 (May 1963): 312-23.

proposed facilities than voters who have voted in unsuccessful school bond elections.

The importance of attitudes toward the schools is also suggested by several findings regarding the relationship between attitudes toward the schools or education in general, and voting. These findings lead to the proposition that A VOTER WHO HAS FAVORABLE ATTITUDES TOWARD THE SCHOOLS OR EDUCATION IN GENERAL, AND TOWARD EDUCATIONAL PROGRAMS, IS MORE LIKELY TO VOTE IN FAVOR OF A SCHOOL FINANCIAL ISSUE THAN A VOTER WITH NEGATIVE ATTITUDES (Carter, 1960; Agger and Goldstein, 1965 and 1971; McKelvey, 1966; Fish, 1964; Mahan, 1968). A number of different questionnaire approaches have been used to elicit the expected finding that voters who agree that the schools are generally "doing a good job" are more likely to support school issues than the small proportion of voters who disagree.

Importantly, favorable attitudes toward specific components of an educational program have also been found to be positively related to positive voting in school financial elections. Fish found that voters with favorable opinions of programs and services included in a budget proposal are more likely to vote in favor of that proposal than voters with unfavorable opinions. Mahan reports that voters who oppose expansion of a school curriculum are somewhat more likely (the relationship is positive but modest) to cast votes against a bond issue than voters who favor expansion. Moreover, voters who oppose the extension and elaboration of educational facilities are more likely to vote against a school bond issue than voters who favor elaboration of facilities.

Agger and Goldstein found that citizens who approve of innovative teaching techniques in a district are more likely than those who do not to indicate that they would vote in favor of a property tax increase to pay for a larger school budget. We should emphasize that this finding holds while controlling for the effects of such important variables as social class and parental status. Finally, voters who exhibit favorable attitudes toward school financial management practices are also more likely to vote in favor of school financial elections than are those who hold unfavorable attitudes (Carter, 1960; Fish, 1964).

Obviously, a voter's evaluation of the schools plays an important part in his decisions to support or not support the educational system. This suggests (but in no way proves) that the object of a certain amount of the trust and cynicism that affect voting in school elections is the school. Hence, the concerned school official may be able to encourage the former and discourage the latter to the extent that he can bring about attitude change. How attitude change can be stimulated, and among what groups of citizens, are important questions that require new research attuned to existing theory and research surrounding attitude change.[21] Stone has suggested, as one interpretation of his data (which

---

[21] For an overview see the excellent reader edited by Marie Jahoda and Neil Warren, *Attitudes* (Baltimore: Penguin Books, 1966). An article in the reader is particularly relevant

show no significant relationship between turnout and voting in several elections,[22] that the attitudes of the "civic inactivists" are more malleable and susceptible to change than the attitudes of the civically active. One of the few direct tests of attitude change as it relates to voting in school financial elections is Agger and Goldstein's (1971) panel study. They found that citizens whose orientations toward the schools have improved or deteriorated over time are likely to be less supportive of a school budget than citizens whose attitudes have remained favorable over time, but more supportive than citizens whose attitudes have remained negative over time.

Finally, Milstein and Jennings (1970) report one exception to the general trend discussed here: there is no statistically significant relationship between a voter's attitude concerning "quality of education" available in his school district and his vote for or against a school bond issue. The populations sampled by these authors were largely satisfied with the quality of educaton.[23] Apparently, for many of these voters, other more salient attitudes and concerns played a more immediate role in determining the direction of their vote.

The irony of the Milstein and Jennings finding is reinforced by national opinion research. A national survey conducted in 1969 found that most individuals held schools and teachers in high esteem (Gallup, 1969). At the same time, a majority of respondents reacted negatively to a question about their willingness to support new taxes:

Suppose the local public schools said they needed much more money. As you feel at this time, would you vote to raise taxes for this purpose, or would you vote against raising taxes for this purpose? (Gallup, 1969, p. 78)

Thus, for many voters the decision concerning taxes is governed by attitudes other than their opinion of the quality of schools. Their favorable opinion of the

---

for voting behavior theories: C.I. Hovland, "Reconciling Conflicting Results Derived from Experimental and Survey Studies of Attitude Change," pp. 287-304. Our most reliable evidence on the effects of attitude change on voting comes from the Survey Research Center's studies of partisan voting for president. This evidence has been analyzed in a number of reports including Campbell et al., *The American Voter*. For a concise statement of these findings see Donald Stokes, "Some Dynamic Elements of Contests for the Presidency," *American Political Science Review* 60 (March 1966): 19-28. For an innovative study based on experimental research techniques, see David L. George, "An Experimental Study of Attitudinal Conflict and Political Involvement in a Voting Context," *Experimental Study of Politics* (December 1971), pp. 35-64.

[22]Clarence N. Stone, "Local Referendums: An Alternative to the Alienated Voter Model," *Public Opinion Quarterly* 29 (Summer 1965): 213-22.

[23]Other studies have found rather widespread general support for the schools despite increasing failure of school issues. One survey of Ohio voters—who have approved only 29 percent of requests for additional school funds during the last two years—found strong support for the schools. The survey concludes that "the schools are about as effective as people want them to be" and that levies are *not* failing because people are dissatisfied with the schools. See John R. Hoyle and Eldon L. Wiley, "What Are the People Telling Us?" *Phi Delta Kappan* 53 (September 1971): 50.

schools is outweighed by other considerations, making their decision the result of conflicting attitudes.

## Attitude Conflict

The possibility of attitude conflict reintroduces a variant of the cross-pressures phenomenon mentioned in Chapter 6. The cross-pressures hypothesis[24] holds that individuals whose political predispositions are *consistent* will make earlier and more predictable voting decisions and will evidence higher interest and information levels than voters with conflicting predispositions. The limited evidence available from partisan studies suggests a relationship between attitude conflict and "avoidance reactions" such as split ticket voting and late voting decisions.

What factors lead to attitude conflict? Borrowing from the discipline of sociology, we might assume that conflicting group affiliation will frequently lead to attitude and value conflict. Such an assumption was warranted by the early studies suggesting the importance of cross-pressures in partisan elections.

An analogy suggested by the group cross-pressures hypothesis can be drawn for school financial election voters by returning to the parental and homeownership affilations described earlier (Chapter 6). With the help of Figure 7-2, let us assume for a moment that these group affiliations are as potentially conflicting for the school election voter as occupational and religious statuses may be for partisan political choice.

Figure 7-2 suggests that consistent configurations lead to predictable voting behavior. An immediate criticism may be levied: the juxtaposed forces may be insignificant in comparison to more salient statuses or attitudes. The essence of the difficulty with the cross-pressures hypothesis, however, goes much deeper. Assume for the moment that we substitute the most salient forces affecting a given voter's choice in either kind of election (partisan or nonpartisan) for the two sets of forces in Figure 7-2. To predict the direction of his vote we must first evaluate the relative importance of the two forces to the individual. Among

---

[24] The effect of social cross-pressures on voting was an important concern of the research conducted by Columbia University scholars, as reported most fully in their second volume, Bernard R. Berleson, Paul F. Lazarsfeld, and William N. McPhee, *Voting: A Study of Opinion Formation in a Presidential Campaign* (Chicago: The University of Chicago Press, 1954), pp. 130-32 *et passim*. Corroborating findings linking psychological conflict and social cross-pressures are also presented by Angus Campbell et al., *The American Voter: An Abridgement* (New York: John Wiley & Sons, 1964), pp. 42-48.

For the best summary of cross-pressures research findings, see William H. Flanigan, *Political Behavior of the American Electorate* (Boston: Allyn and Bacon, Inc., 1968), pp. 64-68. Flanigan suggests that additional empirical work is needed to specify the nature and direction of the conflict/vote relationship. For an innovative multiple-method study attuned to this theory building task, see David L. George, "Attitudinal Conflict and Electoral Decision-Making," Ph.D. dissertation, University of Oregon, Eugene, Oregon, 1970.

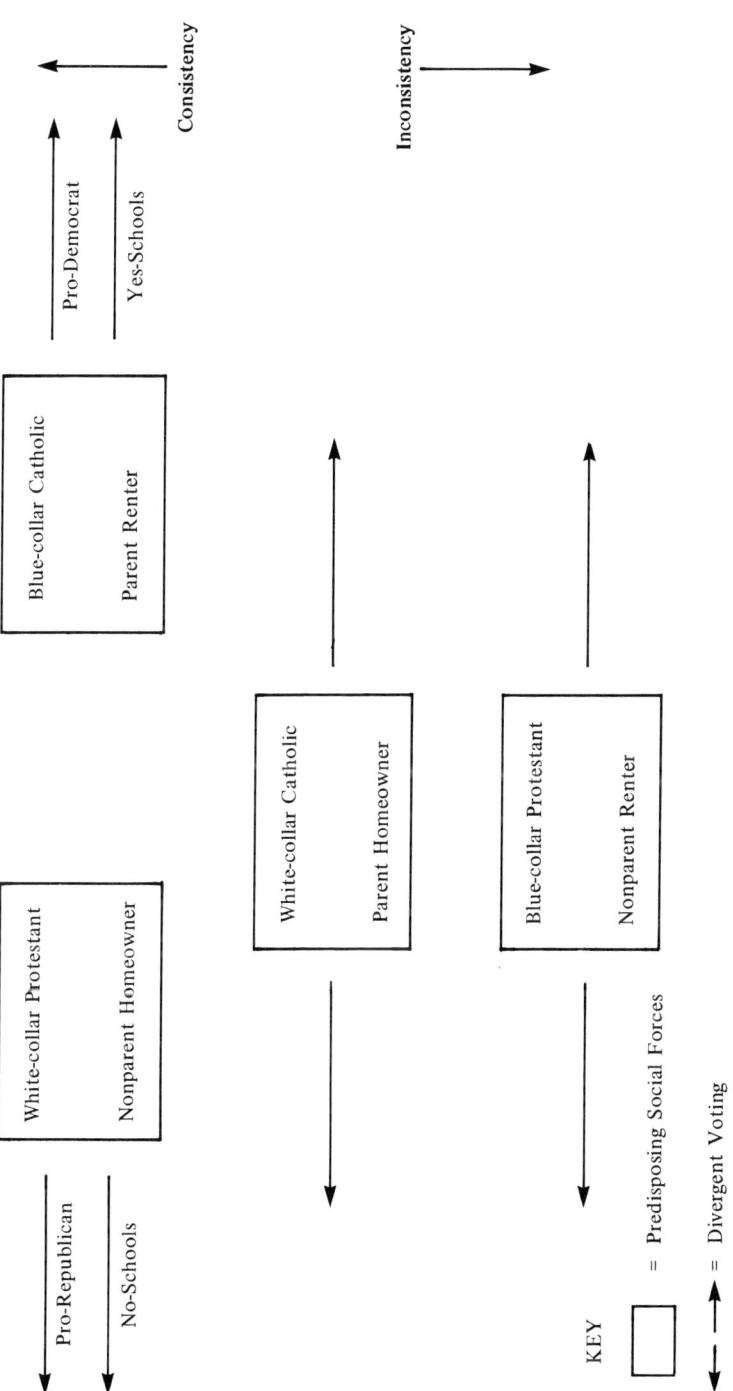

**Figure 7-2.** Examples of Cross Pressures in Voting in Local School and National Partisan Elections

Adapted from William H. Flanigan, *Political Behavior of the American Electorate* (Boston: Allyn and Bacon, Inc., 1968)p.64

the possible examples from Figure 7-2, we may note that a Republican vote may be entirely consistent with the world view of a white-collar Catholic if his religion is relatively unimportant to him. Finally, even if we make one more assumption to ensure conflict—that the two opposing forces are relatively equal and highly salient—our ability to predict the outcome of voting in either partisan settings or school financial elections is still uncertain. Seymour Martin Lipset has said that "individuals who are subject to pressures driving them in different political directions must either deviate or 'escape into apathy.'"[25] Although cross-pressures may indeed have an effect on a person's decision to vote or not to vote, they help us little in predicting the direction of his vote if he does choose to vote.

If attitude conflicts do exist, and the evidence concerning attitudes toward the schools strongly implies that they do, the question remains: What effect do they have on the voting act? Here speculation turns to the relationship between "cognitive inconsistency" (or consistency)[26] and voting in school financial elections. Only two of the studies reviewed (Agger and Goldstein, 1971; Carter and Chaffee, 1966) directly examined the voting behavior of individuals holding important conflicting attitudes. The results of those studies definitely indicate the need for further research.

Agger and Goldstein examined conflict between attitudes of cynicism toward school decisionmakers and attitudes toward taxes. They found that, "Contrary to expectation,... the cross-pressured voted almost as frequently as the nonconflicted" (p. 159). The cross-pressured, however, produced a slightly greater negative vote than did voters who evidenced consistent attitudes. That difference was enough to signal defeat for the particular elections studied.

Finally, one operational test of the cognitive consistency proposition from Figure 7-2 corroborates the suggestion that individuals holding mutually reinforcing (consistent) positive attitudes are more likely to cast positive ballots

---

[25] Seymour Martin Lipset, *Political Man: The Social Bases of Politics* (Garden City, New York: Anchor Books, Doubleday & Co., 1960), p. 13. This kind of conflict may well lead to a response of nonvoting amoung certain individuals, buttressing the "escape into apathy" explanation. Thus, if future research is supportive, we could add cognitive consistency to the list of correlates to participation in school financial elections presented in Chapter 3. But since this chapter is by definition a discussion of voting direction (rather than participation), the apathy argument is as irrelevant as the "deviation" explanation is circular. Obviously, 100 percent of those individuals in states of conflict between two or more opposing political predispositions, who do not withdraw but choose to participate via a vote, will deviate from one of those predispositions. To predict the vote we must predict the *direction* of the deviation.

[26] Cognitive consistency theory is the result of work by several social-psychologists. For the classic statement, see Leon Festinger, *A Theory of Cognitive Dissonance* (Stanford: Stanford University Press, 1957). One of Carter's earliest reports validates Festinger's dissonance reduction explanation by measuring attitude change of a sample of nonvoters who either expressed attitudes of support for the schools or for the value of voting. See Richard F. Carter, "Bandwagon and Sandbagging Effects: Some Measures of Dissonance Reduction," *Public Opinion Quarterly* 23 (Summer 1959): 279-87.

in school elections. Carter and Chaffee (1966) found that citizens who view the schools favorably and who do not perceive the general tax burden to be "too great" are more likely than those who view the schools unfavorabley and/or perceive the tax burden to be heavy to vote in favor of school financial issues.

## Synthesis

By now it is apparent that many attitudes and values are *potentially* important in affecting voter choice. The order or salience of specific attitudes varies greatly among individuals. For one individual the stimulus "school bond election" may evoke an image of college students rioting, whereas the same stimulus may cause his neighbor to picture future wealth and status for his offspring. These mental images, which may be directly tied to the ballot, are, to some degree, the predictable result of differing world views based on the differing combinations of attitudes and perspectives mentioned above. The interpretation suggested by much of the evidence reviewed in this chapter is that these sets of attitudes serve to anchor many voting decisions. Boskoff and Zeigler (1964) reach a similar conclusion following their study of voting in local elections:

In the case of voting, perhaps status position and exposure to influence patterns may be regarded as the 'transitory' component. *Style of life,* the complex of crucial attitudes and values by which resources and facilities are judged, may constitute the 'permanent' component that is more decisively connected with voting choice in some sequence of elections. (p. 141, emphasis added)

When a person holds to a set of attitudes consistently, he comes to have a world view that acts as a strong screen allowing only selectively consistent new pieces of information to enter into his vote decision. Obviously, this would seem to be the case with individuals located at the extremes on such continuums as cynicism/trust, center/periphery, and alienation/nonalienation. We need to know more about individuals between these extremes as well as about those whose attitude inconsistencies prevent a fixed world view.

# 8 Theory, Practice, and Future Research

Although all the research reports that formed the data base for this book examine voting behavior in school financial elections, subtle but important differences in point of view suggest that the research may be classified into two groups. Some investigations focus on determinants of voter behavior, others on the determinants of election outcome.[1]

## Differences in Focus

Research of the first kind examines the effect a number of potentially salient influencing factors (independent variables) have on a citizen's decision to participate and to vote yes or no (the dependent variable). These studies commonly employ survey methodology and are conducted in a limited geographical area and over a short period. Despite these limitations in methodology and scope, the results of these studies, on the whole, provide a fairly accurate profile of the consistent yes or no voter in normal school financial elections.

By focusing on election outcome, the second kind of study generally covers a much wider geographical area and time period. Hence, the results of these studies form the basis for more confident generalizations. Unfortunately, the comparison of aggregates as large as school districts or communities does not allow meaningful comparison of many important characteristics that make up a profile of the individual voter; the heterogeneity of most school districts or communities precludes analysis of many important factors.

The typology presented in Figure 8-1 illustrates the different focuses we have found in most election studies. The space encompassed by circle 1 on the left side of the unit of analysis continuum represents research designed to test specific correlates to voter choice. Studies that fit in the space encompassed by circle 3 on the right side of the continuum focus on election outcome.

Both kinds of studies are based on certain assumptions that may or may not

---

[1] This point is forcefully made by Peter B. Natchez in his excellent critical review of studies of voting in American presidential elections; "Images of Voting: The Social Psychologists," *Public Policy* 18 (Summer 1970): 553-88. We can assume that this difference in focus is at least partly responsible for the differing conclusions regarding voter rationality. For an up-to-date review that makes this distinction between voting studies, see Evron M. Kirkpatrick, "Toward a More Responsible Two-Party System," *American Political Science Review* 65 (December 1971): 971-74.

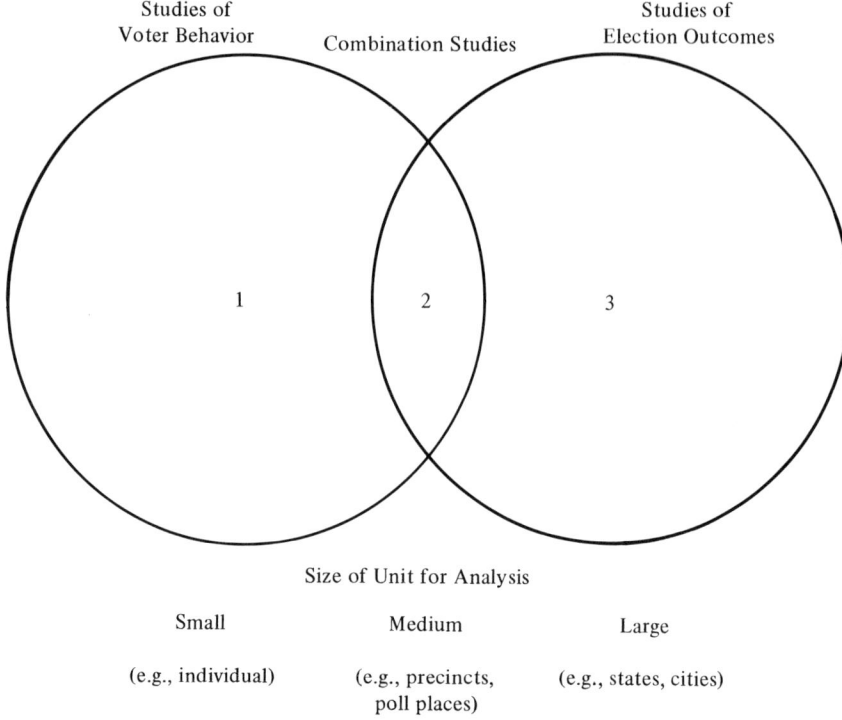

**Figure 8-1.** A Typology of Research Approaches to the Study of Voting Behavior in School Financial Elections

be explicit in the research reports. Studies of voting behavior agree with the partisan voting literature in assuming that an array of forces predetermine or shape the choice of most voters.[2] The reasoning arising from this assumption holds that the more that is known about the order and salience of these underlying forces, the more specific will be the description (profile) of the "normal" voter. The first task of studies applying this reasoning to partisan elections is to specify the "normal" Democratic, Republican, and Independent voter, and the strength of these partisan ties.[3] The second task is to trace and specify a profile of the malleable or inconsistent voter. This profile provides background for understanding voter deviations from expectations based on the norm.

[2] Angus Campbell et al., *The American Voter;* and Angus Campbell et al., *Elections and the Political Order.* "Array of forces" refers to the many variables considered by the SRC researchers to be of varying immediate causal importance to voter choice. For an excellent illustration and discussion of this "funnel of causality" concept, see Natchez, op. cit., pp. 562.

[3] Reference here is to the concept of individual psychological party identification as operationalized in the SRC studies.

It is at this point that the effect of situational factors (short-term forces) is finally brought into the analysis. Individuals with weak partisan ties can be expected to react to the economic situation, foreign policy issues, candidate appeal, and other similar short-term forces. This dimension, the "situation," is considered relatively insignificant in the decision-making process of most voters:

Current pressures arising outside the political order continue to affect the [voter's] evaluation process, and from time to time they may contribute to a critical margin of political victory. Yet for most of the people most of the time such contemporary forces turn out to be but minor terms in the decision equation.[4]

This "critical margin of political victory" is the overriding concern of studies encompassed by circle 3 of Figure 8-1. By both definition and design, most studies of election outcome begin by assessing the effect of situational influences on election results. Comparisons are made between elections at different times, and in different geographical areas.

Just as studies of voting behavior may eventually give cursory attention to the effect of situational variables (frequently treating them together under the heading "stimulants to participation") on election outcome, studies of election outcome may eventually assess the differential impact of situations on certain kinds of voters. The overlap between voting behavior and election outcome is occasionally present in a single empirical study.[5]

## Emerging Partial Theories

In addition to the basic conceptual differences mentioned above, the research literature we have reviewed explicates and tests (with varying degrees of precision) several distinct partial theories to explain the empirical relationships reported in the preceding chapters. Several of these partial theories are listed in Table 8-1. Like the findings and propositions that the theories apply to, the list is inductively based. That is, it is intended to cover the major explanations offered in the literature, which does not necessarily cover the potential range of explanations. The amount of additional explanation required to solve the problem is apparent from the obvious overlap and interrelationships that exist among the partial theories listed.[6]

[4]Campbell et al., *The American Voter* p. 66.

[5]For the best such synthesis see Gerald M. Pomper, *Elections in America: Control and Influence in Democratic Politics* (New York: Dodd, Mead & Co., 1970), particularly Chapters 4 and 5, pp. 68-125.

[6]The overlapping and interrelated nature of both variables and partial theories commonplace to social research reflects the complexity of most social problems worth inquiry. For an excellent introductory statement of this problem and some of the means for coping with it, see Hubert M. Blalock, Jr., *An Introduction to Social Research* (Englewood Cliffs, New Jersey: Prentice-Hall, Inc., 1970).

Table 8-1
**A List of Partial Theories Used to Explain Electoral Behavior in School Financial Elections**

| Partial Theory | Abbreviation | Useful References for Understanding the Theory* |
|---|---|---|
| Economic Self-Interest | ESI | Downs (1957 and 1962); Riker (1961); Wilson and Banfield (December 1964 and in Margolis 1965); and Frey and Kohn (1970) |
| Politicized Electorate | PE | Coleman (1957); Key (June 1953); Campbell et al. (1964); Salisbury and Black (1963); Jennings and Zeigler (1966); and Crain, Katz, and Rosenthal (1969) |
| Informed Democratic Electorate | IDE | Several articles in "observational" literature bibliography, and Carter et al. Summary (1966) |
| Socioeconomic Status | SES | Milbrath (1965); Lazarsfeld, Berelson, and Gaudet (1948); Campbell et al. (1964); and Lane (1959) |
| Community Responsibility Attitudes | CRA | Wood (1959); Hofstadter (1955); Downs (1962); Boskoff and Zeigler (1964); Wilson and Banfield (1964); and Agger and Goldstein (1971) |
| Social Distance Attitudes | SDA | Agger and Goldstein (1971); Horton and Thompson (1962); Aberbach (1969); *Journal of Social Issues* (Number 4, 1961); and Milbrath (1965) |
| Influence and Persuasion Channels | IPC | Klapper (1960); Lazarsfeld, Berelson, and Gaudet (1948); Berelson, Lazarsfeld, and McPhee (1954); and Carter et al. (1960 and 1966) |

*This list is not intended to be inclusive, but these works provide both a good understanding of the evolutionary nature of theory progression in each of these areas and a comprehensive list of citations to relevant literature. Full citations are contained in the bibliography.

The seven labels provided in this list are intended to summarize the array of partial theories that have been suggested to explain many of the research findings we have reviewed. In some cases, several smaller and slightly different theories have been combined under one classification; in other instances, segments of larger theories are reduced to this level. In both cases, the aim has been to arrive at summary theoretical statements that fairly reflect the substance and range of explanations that have occurred throughout the relevant research literature.

The propositions that we have presented in preceding chapters may be summarized by this partial theory scheme. The fact that several of the propositions can be explained by more than one partial theory underscores the danger of accepting such a classification as anything more than a baseline summary of the state-of-the-research. If we can draw one conclusion with total certainty following this exercise it is that much more exploration is needed. Many questions remain.

These questions are readily apparent from a perusal of the Appendix, which lists the evidence that led to the development of propositions stated in the text. This Appendix refers the reader to the relevant evidence for each proposition presented earlier by listing the findings that served as our data base by type of variable. Although this classification of "variable type" frequently suggests partial theory, the two concepts are not synonymous. This is apparent when we examine the cross-reference of each finding in the Appendix to partial theories presented in Table 8-1. More than one entry is required for almost every variable, meaning that a similar table contructed to reflect the knowledge applicable to each partial theory would be several times as lengthy. The message suggested by this overlap is clear: the "researcher/theoretician" should give some thought to future research designs more directly attuned to a dynamic research/theory relationship.

At this point, it should prove worthwhile to review partial theories that have been introduced in previous chapters in light of the evidence discussed throughout and referenced by variable in the Appendix. Of course, to a large extent the previous chapters have accomplished this task, but the following review summarizes related theories and evidence without the interruption of somewhat artificial chapter boundaries.

*Economic Self-Interest*

Several researchers have assumed that the probability of school issue defeat will increase with the cost of the issue (citations are provided in Chapter 5). Certainly, if a sizeable number of voters are motivated by economic self-interest concerns, then the assumption is reasonable. Although a few studies report strong correlations between indicators of cost and negative votes, by far the largest portion of evidence suggests there is no significant relationship between relative issue cost and election outcome. It is only when tax rate increases are used to operationally define cost that a majority of relevant studies report the expected strong negative correlations with positive election outcomes.

One plausible interpretation of this apparently inconsistent body of evidence is that many voters are uncertain of the relative cost of school issues, especially as it compares with the cost of similar issues in other communities and in their community at different times. Under this interpretation, costs and attendant economic self-interest concerns may serve as important determinants of the vote only if they are dramatized. The combination of a significant increase in the tax rate and the increasingly more watchful eye of the local media and taxpayer's associations appears likely to achieve the degree of visability needed for prompting greater cost consciousness on the part of most voters.

Research indicating that cost variables are of little or no use in separating successful from unsuccessful districts complicates but does not invalidate theories that stress the importance of the economic impact of issues. To clarify this issue, future research needs are as follows: (1) to assess the voter's understanding of the relative and absolute cost of school financial issues and (2) to examine the relationship between objective/subjective measures of cost and ability to pay and their influence on economic self-interest determinations.

Economic-based explanations of individual voting behavior receive significant support from findings that treat the relationship between two demographic factors—age and parental status—and voter choice. Relevant studies unanimously agree that increasing age is strongly correlated with negative voting in school financial elections and that parental status (having school age children) is strongly related to positive voting in those elections.

The schools provide parents with obvious economic advantages. Parents cannot purchase schools' short-run "baby sitting" functions for an equivalent price on the open market, to say nothing of the long-run employment and salary benefits that are expected to accrue to the children. Clearly parents of school age children have a measurable stake in the schools.

Although school costs are absorbed by citizens of all ages, the direct benefits of education—even when measured by standards of the "public good"—appear to diminish with age. Particularly among the retired, economic self-interest considerations would seem destined to prompt negative voting. In school elections, a retired person is asked to evaluate positively a proposal that may benefit the race, the public, or perhaps a family member of another generation, but that will take a portion of what is normally a reduced and fixed income.

The data from numerous studies (reviewed in Chapter 6) strongly suggest that the parents of school age children (the trend is most pronounced among parents of children in the lower grades) and the elderly react to school financial proposals in a manner that is predictable given obvious economic motivations.

The utility of the economic self-interest explanation diminishes greatly, however, when it is applied to other classifications of voters. Although renters pay at least a portion of the property tax on dwellings, tax costs are clearly more visable to homeowners. It would seem reasonable, then, to assume that renters would be more likely to vote positively than would homeowners. The bulk of available evidence, however, strongly suggests that there is no appreciable difference in the voting patterns of homeowners and renters.

The economic self-interest model does not seem to apply to the wealthy either. Property taxes increase with the value of property, which is, of course, highly correlated with income and other measures of wealth. Nevertheless, higher income individuals frequently provide the greatest proportion of support for school financial issues. At the same time, there is no reason to assume that educational benefits within a school district differ greatly on the basis of individual wealth. Indeed a case could be made for an inverse relationship between income and educational benefits: the unit cost for educational benefits may increase in relation to an individual's income.

Part of the apparently anomalous behavior of the wealthy can be explained by the theory of the marginal utility of income: as dollars increase, their value decreases. Indeed, an important future research need would be met by research that specifies the relationship among marginal utility of income, perceived educational benefits, and voting in school financial elections. Regardless of the outcome of such research, however, available data and a logical interpretation of them suggest that an explanation beyond that of economic self-interest is needed to account for the support high-income individuals give school tax issues while receiving little or no personal benefits from the schools.

*Socioeconomic Status*

An explanation of voting behavior that goes beyond economic self-interest focuses on persons who have acquired a relatively greater amount of commodities—not only goods but respect, deference, etc.—that are valued highly in a society. According to several theories, these people are most likely to favor public issues. Simply stated, these theories assume that individuals who have received most from society are most likely to want to reciprocate. Since social benefits have been translated into private dividends that are already "in the bank," it is not illogical to suggest that these individuals feel closer to the "center" of their community and thus tend to be more aware of, concerned about, and interested in community projects and needs.

It is assumed that "higher class" individuals' long-range view of the "public interest" overshadows the narrow concerns of personal costs increases (within reasonable limits). Frequently, this view will result in support for the public issue at hand. Gaps in the relationship between this theory and relevant research however, are signified by the phrase "within reasonable limits." If an issue demands a sufficiently large portion of personal resources, this private concern will override perceived public benefits, no matter how desirable the long-range effects. A future research need is a specification of the relationship, as perceived by the individual, between public benefits and private costs and of the point at which private costs supplant public benefits as the dominant concern. If carried out with appropriate controls for social class status, this research would be a step toward an improved theory of the effect of social and economic influences on school election voting behavior.

In the meantime, we can note that the studies reviewed in Chapter 6 provide overwhelming evidence of a strong positive relationship between two common objective indicators of an individual's socioeconomic status—income and educational attainment—and positive voting in school financial elections. Substantially less evidence exists for assessing the relationship between other indicators of class and voting in these elections: moreover, there is less unanimity in that evidence.

A careful perusal of the findings arrayed in the Appendix suggests a number of future research needs that must be met by any attempt to refine partial theories of class and voting. For example, should the proposition that describes a strong positive relationship between class and positive voting in school elections be restated to reflect the potential curvilinearity of the relationship between class and voting. Such curvilinearity has been suggested by several findings from Jordan's (1966) quartile analysis of voting in Los Angeles school elections and by the unanimous finding that blacks are more likely than whites to vote in favor of school financial elections, despite the fact that blacks are disproportionately represented in the lower SES category (Wilson and Banfield, 1964; Jordan, 1966; Smith, 1968; Hahn and Almy, 1971).

*Community Responsibility and Social Distance Attitudes*

It was noted above that the economic self-interest theory of voting behavior is incomplete without a consideration of the apparently anomalous behavior of the upper class and income segment of the population. Researchers who correlate social and economic class with social behavior posit that each class promotes a set of attitudes or beliefs that directly affects behavior. The most important factor explaining the disproportionate positive voting in most school financial elections by individuals with incomes in excess of $20,000 may well be that they all see the world through a similar perceptual screen that is inherent in their class. However, a simpler explanation—that higher incomes improve the capacity to pay taxes—must hold for at least some of the cases.

It is important to determine if certain attitudes or attitude indexes such as "world view" or "life styles" are inherent in classes or are different from and more powerful than class and economic background as predictors of voting behavior. If so, then their roots must obviously be traced to other sources—e.g., personality factors, physiological needs and drives, etc. Boskoff and Zeigler's suggestion, which has received substantial support from attitude research, may represent the key departure point for reducing future research needs:

In the case of voting, perhaps status position and exposure to influence patterns may be regarded as the "transitory" component. Style of life, the complex of crucial attitudes and values by which resources and facilities are judged, may constitute the "permanent" component that is more decisively connected with voting choice in some sequence of elections.[7]

---

[7]Boskoff and Zeigler, *Voting Patterns in a Local Election*. These authors suggest and define the concept of "style of life" in addition to noting difficulties inherent in its operationalization, p. 141.

Because attitude configurations and class status are probably related but not perfectly overlapping, the relationship between attitude structures and behavior (in this case, voting behavior) deserves special attention. Two closely related attitudinal dimensions that have been the subject of a few high quality studies are community responsibility attitudes and social distance attitudes. A number of strong correlations between these attitudes and voting in local elections have been reported by studies that used differing operational procedures. Virtually unanimously, the studies agree that individuals who have relatively strong community ties and who feel that they in some way contribute to and are affected by community and educational decision-making are likely to support school issues (Agger and Goldstein, 1965 and 1971; Boskoff and Zeigler, 1964; Carter, 1960; Fish, 1964; Mahan, 1968; McKelvey, 1966; Wilson and Banfield, 1964 and 1971).

Exceptions to this general proposition occur only when attempts are made to infer community responsibility attitudes from indirect but objective data such as "length of residence" or age. These two qualities are frequently found to be unrelated or negatively related to positive voting in school elections.

Corroboration of the general proposition is available from evidence suggesting that individuals who feel extremely distant from community power centers, powerless to affect community decisions, and distrustful of perceived decision-makers, are much more likely to oppose school financial and other public issues than those with a less pessimistic view of the world (Horton and Thompson, 1960 and 1962; Gold, 1962; Templeton, 1966; Agger and Goldstein, 1965 and 1971; Milstein and Jennings, 1970).

These findings suggest that support for or opposition to school issues is frequently a function of an individual's perception of his relationship to his community. A voter's attitude toward the community decision-making (political) process is an important indicator of the direction of his vote in school financial elections. However, broad ideological loyalties (conservative/liberal) are not good indicators of voting direction in the same elections (Mahan, 1968; Jordan, 1964; Boskoff and Zeigler 1964; Fish, 1964).

Any assessment of the stability of attitudinal determinants must consider the fairly even division between studies that do and studies that do not report a significant relationship between partisan national and nonpartisan local voting patterns of individuals and groups exhibiting varying social and partisan predispositions. As we reported in Chapter 7, several studies have found no significant relationship between voting patterns in the two kinds of elections (Boskoff and Zeigler, 1964; Templeton, 1966; Jordan, 1966; Hahn and Almy, 1971; Key, 1953; Salisbury and Black, 1963). These studies detract from the hypothesis that relatively permanent attitudinal configurations flow from status and underly predictable patterns of voter choice regardless of the type of election. Such findings, of course, do not reflect on hypotheses positing a relationship between a particular attitudinal configuration and voting in a particular election. Nor do they serve to devalue the relationship between attitudes and voting if objective indicators of such concepts as class do not tap the attitude syndrome that most directly affects the voting decision. A future research need is to specify the best possible attitudinal syndrome for each type of election, controlling for variables such as class and partisan affiliation.

*Stimulating Voter Participation: The Informed Democratic Versus the Politicized Electorate*

The theory and research summarized in the preceding sections provide a basis for understanding "normal" voter behavior in school financial elections. The concept of "normalcy" is based on an assumption behind most school voting research—research that asks why some voters make positive choices while others make negative ones. The assumption is that voting behavior is something other than random or unexplainable individual behavior. Apparently, the assumption is correct since evidence from Chapters 6 and 7 suggests that when all other things are equal, the direction in which many individuals vote can be predicted on the basis of other, nonpolitical information. Indeed, some facts about a voter's background characteristics and his voting in past school elections not only help predict his future vote but are also useful in explaining why voting in these elections is a stable (over time) act for many individuals.

Frequently, of course, in the real world "all other things" are not equal, which diminishes the accuracy of predictions based on the "normal" voter. Those who would like to effect basic change in voting patterns should note the evidence presented in Chapter 5 from studies concerned with the following basic questions: To what extent do certain environmental and political forces affect school financial election outcomes? Or, when does a school election situation become "abnormal" and what are the consequences?

Answers to the above questions provide the basis for assessing two general theories of voter behavior. Both theories recognize that the "normal electorate" in these elections is smaller than the voting population in many other elections and much smaller than the eligible voting population. This recognition has prompted some school supporters to plead for greater voter turnout. The observational literature [8] indicates that many school officials would probably second the following motion offered by one school superintendent on the eve of a recent budget election:

We want bodies to come in and vote. I can't really say that it isn't important to me whether they vote yes or not, but it's very important that we do have a large vote so the board has a clear mandate from the people of the district.[9]

---

[8] We formed this opinion on the basis of a survey of educational journal articles, which conforms to the report in Beal et al. (1966, p. 8) that "numerous articles are devoted to the topic of encouraging all eligible voters to register and vote."

[9] "Junction Chief Wants Large Vote," *Eugene Register Guard*, August 1, 1971.

This desire for greater voter participation in school elections is based on a strong faith in the democratic process. So are the frequent admonitions for bigger and better multiple media campaigns. The assumption inherent in campaigns that stress greater public participation in school financial decision-making is that the schools have an ongoing broad base of popular support. Such an assumption leads one to believe that issue success is simply a matter of (1) informing voters of a need and (2) reminding them to vote. This theory is explicit in at least one "how-to-win" article:

... We realized that a successful bond issue depended upon the voters having enough information on which to base a decision. Informed citizens will vote for school bonds—9 out of 10 times.[10]

Empirical underpinnings for this faith in the informed democratic electorate are almost nonexistent. It appears valid to assert the existence of widespread, basically favorable attitudes toward education (Carter, 1960; Agger and Goldstein, 1965 and 1971; McKelvey, 1966; Fish, 1964; Mahan, 1968). However, these attitudes appear to be relatively unimportant determinants of school election voting patterns.

A more directly relevant correlation is the persistently strong relationship between turnout increases and negative voting (at least in first time elections). When coupled with the frequent lack of association between many "campaign techniques" and election success, this evidence strongly suggests that trust in the democratic electorate is seldom anything more than an act of faith.

The likely explanation for the strong relationship between high turnout and negative voting is school-related conflict that in turn leads to a politicized electorate. Theory and research from different kinds of community studies,[11] together with evidence from studies that assessed the relationship between levels of community conflict interest group activity, and school financial election outcome provide strong grounds for adopting the interpretation that the turnout factor simply intervenes between conflict (the independent or "causal" variable) and election outcome (the dependent variable). If a given conflict stimulates both greater negativism toward the schools and an abnormal high turnout for a school election, then it is difficult to assign direct "causes" to the effect.

A causal model—admittedly an oversimplification—of this explanation is provided in Figure 8-2. As the arrows in the diagram indicate, this explanation assumes that conflict stimulates a relatively high negative response from the electorate in addition to a high turnout for the election in question. This model emphasizes the impact of conflict on outcome regardless of the size of the voter

---

[10] Robert R. Denny, "Selling Bonds," *American School Board Journal* 134,5 (1949), as cited in Beal et al., p. 13.

[11] Reference here is to the community conflict literature that has been cited in both Chapters 4 and 5. Particularly useful works are those by Coleman, Coser, and Mack cited in full in footnote 19, Chapter 4.

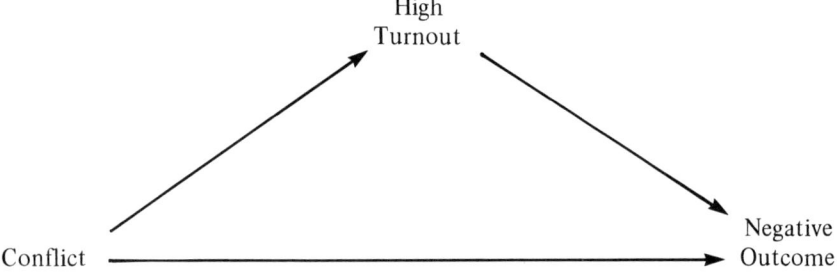

**Figure 8-2.** One Causal Map of the Relationship between Community Conflict, Voter Turnout, and Outcome in School Financial Elections

turnout. To the extent that this explanation holds true, it renders irrelevant debates concerning the impact of voter turnout, democratic versus elite decision-making in school affairs, and other hypotheses concerning the effect of changing participation rates.

Additional evidence suggests the need for a subtle but important modification that will enable the model to reflect the centrality of the participation variable in explaining probable election outcomes. Figure 8-3 meets this need.

The explanation of election outcomes suggested by the evidence listed in Table 8-2 is reflected more accurately by the model in Figure 8-3. This model suggests that a number of highly changeable forces—some controllable by schools, others not—directly affect participation increases, which in turn, affect the probability of election defeat.

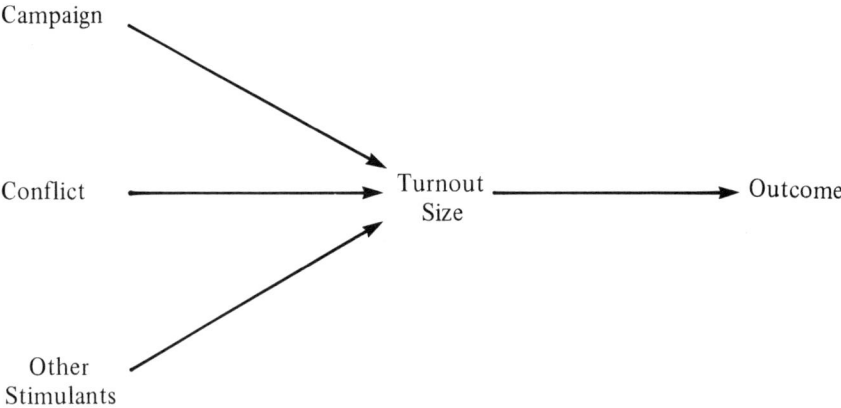

**Figure 8-3.** The Causal Relationship between Turnout Stimulants, Turnout, and Outcome in School Financial Elections

Table 8-2
Characteristics of Individuals Most Likely to Participate In and Vote in Favor of School Financial Elections

| Most Likely Participants | Most Likely Yes Voter |
|---|---|
| parents of school age children | parents of school age children |
| high income | high income |
| high education | high education |
| middle-aged | younger |
| whites | blacks |
| homeowners | NSD |
| high interest in schools | high interest in schools, community |
| trusting (opposites from the alienation syndrome) | trusting (opposites from the alienation syndrome) |

As the figure indicates, community conflict is only one contributor to the high correlation between size of turnout and issue defeat.

Profiles of the person most likely to vote and the person most likely to vote yes provide another explanation. These profiles are based on background factors that appear most strongly associated with voter participation, choice, and attitudes. Table 8-2 presents these voter profiles.

The most striking feature of Table 8-2 is the similarity between the two profiles. The column "Most Likely Participants" provides a starting point for analyzing school elections by describing the normal electorate. If the second column, which describes the most likely yes voter, differed significantly from the first, then the answer to the school's financial problems would lie in implementing the democratic solution; that is, increasing voter turnout. The columns are, however, remarkable similar, which means that in most instances the voter who is most favorably predisposed toward the schools is already well represented in school financial elections. As a result, a general increase in turnout will produce a relatively greater representation of those less likely to favor school financial elections. This result is directly explainable by Tingsten's Law of Dispersion—an increase in participation yields a more representative sample of the total eligible population.

A second major branch of knowledge corroborates the suggestion that traditional campaigns designed to increase voter participation in school financial elections may not meet their intended objective. Communications research has established that mass media campaigns are more likely to affect the behavior of certain subpopulations (selective audiences) within the general population. In almost every case, those identifiable subpopulations affected are groups possessing characteristics far different from those listed in the "Most Likely Yes Voters" column of Table 8-2.

The law of dispersion and the results of communications research both support the following conclusion, which is apparent from other evidence touching on the relative importance of voter predispositions, attitudes, and backgrounds: a very large number of voters and potential voters in school financial elections have made a "standing" decision about the direction of their vote. Unfortunately for the schools, the standing decision of a great number of people in the voting pool appears to have changed from a majority in support to a majority in opposition.

Recent survey data suggest that the "law of dispersion" remains in effect. Table 8-3 compares the actual voting behavior of people who voted with the intended voting behavior of those who did not vote. The table reports data from two surveys—one by Gallup (1969) of a national sample and one by Milstein and Jennings (1970) of New York State. Clearly, from the schools' point of view there is nothing to be gained by expanding the electorate from those who voted in school elections (column 1) to those who were eligible to vote but did not (column 2).

**Table 8-3**
**Actual and Intended Voting Behavior for School Financial Elections: 1969**

|  | 1 VOTERS | | 2 NONVOTERS | |
|---|---|---|---|---|
|  | N.Y. | National | N.Y. | National* |
| FOR | 56% | 47% | 51% | 45% |
| AGAINST | 44 | 47 | 49 | 49 |
| Undecided | NA | 6 | NA | 6 |
| Total | 100% | 100% | 100% | 100% |

*The Gallup survey actually compared voters with the total sample of voters and nonvoters. This column therefore gives the voting preferences of the entire sample.

**Theory of the Normal Vote: Promise and Problems**

Both the research findings and the partial theories reviewed have presented a strong case for basing predictions of school election outcomes on a baseline profile of a community's "normal vote." Despite the widespread use of the normal vote, all normal vote theories are limited because they are static. Whether one is attempting to explain a presidential election outcome on the basis of the normal partisan division of the electorate[12] or to explain the outcome of a

---

[12] See the discussion in the concluding section of Chapter 4 and the citations listed in footnote 27 of that chapter.

nonpartisan election on the basis of social, economic, or psychological criteria, the "norm" or baseline data must be subject to constant reevaluation. This need is stressed by time-line data that served to introduce this book (Table 1-1). These data suggest a fundamental and widespread change in the nation's school election voting patterns. Beginning sometime in the late 1960s, the proportion of defeated school financial issues has increased annually. Corroborative data taken from recent annual Gallup (1969, 1970, 1971, and 1972) surveys of citizen attitudes suggest that the nationwide trend toward greater negative voting in school elections is continuing. Table 8-4 combines the Gallup data from four nationwide samples of the responses adults gave to an identical question designed to tap their probable vote in a school financial election.

The first column of Table 8-4 indicates that an increasing number of individuals are negatively predisposed toward school financial elections. The remaining columns point to an important change in one major component—parental status—of the normal vote model suggested in Table 8-2 and the ensuing discussion. In 1969, a majority of adults with children attending public schools would have voted in favor of a school financial proposal while a majority of individuals without children in the public schools or with children in

**Table 8-4**
**Response of National Sample to Gallup Poll of Public Attitudes Toward Education 1969-1972***

|  | National Totals | No Children In Schools | Public School Parents | Private School Parents |
|---|---|---|---|---|
| **1972** | | | | |
| For | 36% | 35% | 37% | 38% |
| Against | 56 | 56 | 56 | 55 |
| No Opinion | 8 | 9 | 7 | 7 |
| **1971** | | | | |
| For | 40 | 37 | 44 | 37 |
| Against | 52 | 53 | 49 | 59 |
| No Opinion | 8 | 10 | 7 | 4 |
| **1970** | | | | |
| For | 37 | 35 | 43 | 37 |
| Against | 56 | 57 | 53 | 58 |
| No Opinion | 7 | 8 | 4 | 5 |
| **1969** | | | | |
| For | 45 | 41 | 51 | 40 |
| Against | 49 | 53 | 44 | 56 |
| No Opinion | 6 | 6 | 5 | 4 |

Source: Gallup, 1969, 1970, 1971, 1972.

*The same question was used each year: "Suppose the local public schools said they needed much more money. As you feel at this time, would you vote to raise taxes for this purpose, or would you vote against raising taxes for this purpose."

private schools would have voted against such a proposal. By 1972, however, parental status for all practical purposes had become useless as a predictor of voter predisposition toward school financial elections. Fifty-six percent of the parents of children in the public schools as well as of nonparents and the total sample would oppose a school financial issue that required additional tax support.

The implications of this change in the distribution of public opinion are obvious. The four annual Gallup surveys reflect a trend toward a greater unanimity of opinion among individuals of divergent income, age, and other important demographic categories as well as of differing parental status. Thus, to the extent that the survey is valid (that the question accurately taps actual voting behavior) and to the extent that the national sample represents actual community populations, turnout fluctuations along a number of seemingly important dimensions would have little effect on reversing the contemporary trend toward increasing defeat of school financial elections. A nationwide school financial election held in April 1972 would have lost by almost exactly the same margin (56 percent opposed) *even if* the electorate could have been controlled to include *only* parents of public school children, or *only* parents of private school children, or *only* nonparents!

Of course, we cannot conclude on the basis of this evidence that the composition of the turnout would make no difference in 1972 or in future elections. As Table 8-5 indicates, the increase in proportion of negative responses in not as dramatic in such categories as income and age as it is for parental status.

The picture presented in Table 8-5 is not a pleasant one for school supporters even though it provides some basis for expecting election results to vary if voters from the various categories sampled are disproportionately represented. If voter preferences in an average school district conformed to the percentages in the table, a school financial election success in 1972 could be guaranteed only if a very select group—a highly "abnormal" electorate—were allowed to vote: nonwhite college graduates under thirty who are making between ten and fifteen thousand dollars in clerical or sales occupations. Even with these absurd constraints on participation, however, the 1972 election would be close! At a minimum, over 40 percent of the voters in this "ideal" electorate would vote no. Even with participation and these demographic categories as the only variables, election success is simply more difficult to accomplish in 1972 than it was in 1969, and much more difficult than it was in years prior to that date.

The data arrayed in Tables 8-4 and 8-5 do not call for wholesale revision of earlier propositions that attempted to explain which groups of voters are most likely to support school issues and why support from these groups can be expected. Such revision is not required because, in the first place, these surveys may point to, but do not necessarily represent, a trend. Second, the surveys simple represent the nation's adult population, not the likely participants in school elections and certainly not the voting pool of particular communities. Finally other data classifications within these categories could make a significant difference in apparent trends. For instance, in the income category of Table 8-5, the net change of 13 percent may not apply to all income levels above $15,000. Additional breakdowns of this classification may yield different results. Clearly, further longitudianl research is needed both at the national level to validate these trends and to test for change in other important variables, and at the local level

Table 8-5
**Percentage of Adults That Would Vote Against School Tax Increases by Selected Background Characteristics: Gallup Surveys of 1969 and 1972**

|  | Percentage Opposed | | Net Change |
|---|---|---|---|
| Category | 1969 | 1972 | |
| Total Sample | 49% | 56% | + 7% |
| *Age* | | | |
| Under 21 | NA | 42 | NA |
| 21-29 yrs. | 39 | 49 | +10 |
| 30-49 yrs. | 48 | 57 | + 9 |
| 50 yrs.+ | 55 | 61 | + 6 |
| *Income* | | | |
| $15,000+ | 41 | 54 | +13 |
| 10,000-14,999 | 47 | 52 | + 5 |
| 7,000- 9,999 | 48 | 59 | +11 |
| 5,000- 6,999 | 50 | 58 | + 8 |
| 3,000- 4,999 | 50* | 64 | +14 |
| Under 3,000 | 57* | 58 | + 1 |
| *Education* | | | |
| Elementary Grades | 60 | 64 | + 4 |
| High School Incomplete | 54 | 61 | + 7 |
| High School Complete | 50 | 60 | +10 |
| Technical, Trade, or Business School | 47 | 59 | +12 |
| College Incomplete | 43 | 45 | + 2 |
| College Graduate | 34 | 41 | + 7 |
| *Occupation* | | | |
| Business and Professional | 40 | 50 | +10 |
| Clerical and Sales | 52 | 47 | − 5 |
| Farm | 62 | 65 | + 3 |
| Skilled Labor | 47 | 60 | +13 |
| Unskilled Labor | 56 | 61 | + 5 |
| Nonlabor Force | 53 | 62 | + 9 |
| *Race* | | | |
| White | 49 | 57 | + 8 |
| Nonwhite | 47 | 48 | + 1 |

Source: Gallup 1969 (pp. 79-80) and 1972 (p. 42).

*Approximate percentages obtained by collapsing two more discrete categories.

to avoid the error of "personification"—treating micro units as analogues of macro units and extending findings accordingly.[13]

Even if it is assumed for the moment that the Gallup data represent valid trends that could be found in many communities, the demographic profile of the voters most likely to make positive and negative choices appears to have changed very little over time. The "best bets" for positive votes in school elections are still young, highly educated, relatively wealthy, white collar workers. The problem for the schools is not that the model represented in Table 8-2 is correct but that there are simply fewer yes votes available.

This does not mean that the future longitudinal research called for above should ignore potential deviations suggested by some of the highest net changes listed in Table 8-5. A particularly intriguing subject for hypothesis regarding the impact of national economic conditions on personal cost-benefit determinations, which may in turn affect voting in school elections, are the dramatic increases in negative voting among those with incomes exceeding $15,000 and with jobs in business and professional occupations. Perhaps most intriguing for future research is what appears to be the beginning of a divergence in the trend lines charting the relationship between two seminal indicators of SES—income and education—and voting intentions. These recent data suggest marked disturbances at the extremes of the income scale—areas that were formerly among the most reliable vote predictors. The education scale, on the other hand, has remained relatively stable at the extremes with the only major changes occurring among trade and business students and high school graduates. If these data hold true, the high correlation between income and education levels as predictors of voter behavior may be subject to change.

## Linking Research to Theory and Practice

The major objective of this book is to provide a summary statement concerning what may be inferred about voter behavior in school financial elections. Our data base consists of such relatively isolated outcroppings of empirical research as Ph.D. dissertations, journal articles, and published and unpublished research reports. We hope that in the preceding pages we have made some progress toward that goal, which includes improving out ability to understand, explain, and predict voting patterns in school financial elections.

A project such as this is only as valuable as it is useful. We have intended that a central contribution of the book should be to stimulate and guide future research. The hope is that this book will prove useful as a tool for improving the link between past, present, and future research, as well as for inproving the link between research undertaken at different levels and with different disciplinary

---

[13] Heinz Eulau, *The Behavioral Persuasion in Politics* (New York: Random House, 1963), pp. 126-27.

and theoretic perspectives. Throughout the book, and particularly in this chapter, we have attempted to highlight those points in the existing array of research and theory most in need of further research clarification. Inevitably there are many instances where important future research needs are implied but not fully explained.

Second, we have assumed that the evidence presented in this book may be used by individuals attempting to affect the outcome of school financial elections, thereby serving to improve the link between research and practice. Both supporters and opponents of school financial issues will be able to garner insights from many of the propositions developed in the preceding pages to help their election strategies. We reemphasize, however, that we have not intended to write a "how to win a school election" manual.[14] Indeed, an obvious and major conclusion from many of the propositions developed in the preceding pages is that many important determinants of school election voting behavior prohibit manipulation or control of election outcomes by anyone—friend or foe of the schools—employing traditional campaign techniques.

However, a certain element of control remains available. Initially, the school official who wants to achieve success in financial elections must test the extent to which his election situation and community demographic and attitudinal profile match the generalizations developed here. The clear message from this evidence is that school districts attempting to influence election outcomes should, at the outset, spend more resources on analyzing their constituency and less on blatant attempts to influence the direction of the vote over a six-week campaign period. To a certain extent, officials may base their analysis on intuition; but aggregate voting and census records are cheap and easily obtainable and should be used to identify pockets of support and resistance within particular communities.

A most useful data source that can provide the school official with his own positive/negative voter profile, which will be more accurate than the one developed here, is survey research.[15] Although useful survey research is somewhat more costly than aggregate data collection, these costs should be relatively low compared to common costs associated with campaigns, repeated elections, and so forth.

---

[14] A number of reports that provide such prescriptions exist and are cited in the "Observational Case Studies" section of the bibliography. Most of these observations are not based on empirical research and are frequently valid only for the election and point of time at hand. Exceptions that offer sound and specific tactical advice in light of what we know from empirical research can be found in William J. Banach and Lawrence Westley, "Public Relations, Computers, and Election Success," paper presented to the Association for Educational Data Systems, May 19, 1972, St. Paul Minnesota; and C. Montgomery Johnson, *Public Opinion, Voter Behavior, and School Support* (Olympia, Washington: S.C.O.R.E., 1971).

[15] For excellent technical advice along with some of the supporting rationale developed here, see Michael Y. Nunnery and Ralph B. Kimbrough, *Politics, Power, Polls, and School Elections* (Berkeley: McCutchan Publishing Co., 1971).

Once he is armed with some knowledge of how his community matches the generalizations developed here, the school official may take some strategic steps. At this point, value questions become preeminent. Each school official must make these kinds of choices based on his values and knowledge of the total situation. Often this choice will evoke a significant dilemma. The following very plausible situation serves as an example: Assume that a school district conducts research and identifies a relatively stable, small block of voters who regularly vote in school elections, that this block is well described by our model participant profile (Table 8-2), and that there has been a gradual shift in that block's vote in the direction of greater negative voting in all subcategories of the voting pool. The campaign can take one of five possible directions:

1. Attempt to increase general participation, assuming the larger voting pool will be more favorable
2. Attempt to discourage participation, assuming the smaller group of participants will be more favorable
3. Attempt to selectively recruit more yes voters, assuming the no vote will remain constant
4. Attempt to selectively discourage participation of no voters, assuming yes vote remains constant
5. Attempt to change the net distribution of the normal vote division from less no to more yes choices

The evidence reviewed here strongly suggests that, philosophical arguments aside, greater participation is seldom the road to success. On the other hand, attempts to discourage participation, on either a selective or mass basis, involve obvious value dilemmas within the democratic framework. The long-run solution that many would opt for is to create a more favorable distribution of voters (number 5), but we doubt that any single group of school supporters can accomplish that except over the long run.

The tactical direction that is suggested by the evidence presented in this book and that is also congruent with politics as practiced in a democracy is alternative number 3: many districts will be forced to take advantage of normal low turnouts by selectively recruiting more voters who are likely to favor the issue at hand while assuming that the negative votes will remain constant. At least for the short run and from a pragmatic perspective, school finance in many areas may depend on vigorous political campaigns designed to stimulate maximum participation of likely school supporters.

# Appendix
## Synthesis of Empirical Research on Voting in School Financial Elections: Correlates to "Yes Voting" and Election Success

Appendix
Synthesis of Empirical Research on Voting in School Financial Elections: Correlates to "Yes Voting" and Election Success*

| Variable** | DIRECTION OF CORRELATION*** | | | Partial Theory**** |
|---|---|---|---|---|
| | Sig. + | Sig. − | Nsr | |

FACTOR I. SCHOOL DISTRICT CHARACTERISTICS: WEALTH AND ORGANIZATION

| Variable** | Sig. + | Sig. − | Nsr | Partial Theory**** |
|---|---|---|---|---|
| PROPERTY ASSESSMENT RATE (ASSESSED VALUATION) | Jordan 1966<br>Davidson 1967 | Barbour 1966<br>Davidson 1967 | Fish 1964<br>Murphy 1966<br>Beal et al. 1966<br>Crider 1967<br>Hicks 1967<br>Tebbutt 1968 | ESI, SES |
| REAL DOLLAR SIZE OF ISSUE | | Barbour 1966<br>Cooper 1967<br>Varden 1973 | Hicks 1967<br>Dykstra 1964 | ESI |
| MILLAGE SIZE (TAX RATE) | Davidson 1967 | Saalfeld 1972<br>Goettel 1971 | Beal et al. 1966<br>Dykstra 1964<br>Barbour 1966<br>Marlowe 1970<br>Wirt & Kirst 1972 | ESI |
| TAX RATE INCREASES (different time periods) | Wentzel 1964<br>Varden 1973 | N. Y. State Ed. Dept. 1970<br>Fish 1964<br>Saalfeld 1972 | | ESI |
| TAXABLE WEALTH (operational variation includes per pupil and proportion of local taxes) | Marlowe 1970<br>Dykstra 1964 | Goettel 1971 | N. Y. State Ed. Dept. 1970<br>Dykstra 1964<br>Saalfeld 1972 | SES, ESI |

| Variable | References | Codes |
|---|---|---|
| PER PUPIL EXPENDITURE | Davidson 1967 | SES, ESI, PE |
| | Smith et al. 1968 | |
| | N.Y. State Ed. Dept. 1970 | |
| | Marlowe 1970 | |
| | Hicks 1967 | |
| SCHOOL OWNERSHIP (proportion of nonpublic schools in district) | Barbour 1966 | ESI |
| | Dykstra 1964 (in high school districts) | |
| BOARD CONTROL (index including: length of term, select procedures, etc.) | Carter & Sutthoff 1960 (bond elections) | IPC, IDE, PE |
| | Carter & Ruggels 1966 (medium sized districts) | |
| | Carter & Sutthoff 1960 (tax elections) | |
| | Carter & Ruggels 1966 (large & small) | |
| SCHOOL DISTRICT TYPE (elementary, H.S., consolidated, etc.) | Davidson 1967 | ESI, IPC |
| | Beal et al. 1966 | |
| | Barbour 1966 | |
| SCHOOL DISTRICT SIZE (number of students) | Barbour 1966 | IPC, SDA |
| | Beal et al. 1966 | |
| | Carter & Sutthoff 1960 | |
| | Davidson 1967 | |
| | Saalfeld 1972 | |
| | Beal et al. 1966 | |
| | Minar 1966 | |
| | Dykstra 1964 | |
| | Hicks 1967 | |
| | N.Y. State Ed. Dept. 1970 | |
| | Wentzel 1964 | |
| | Crider 1967 | |
| BOARD SOLIDARITY (agreement over necessity of board proposal) | Crider 1967 | IPC |
| | Carter & Ruggels 1966 | |

\*Dependent variables  
\*\*Independent variables  
\*\*\*The variable in question was positively (Sig. +) or negatively (Sig. −) associated with election success or yes voting, or found to be not statistically related (Nsr) to those dependent variables.  
\*\*\*\*Refers to the partial theories listed in Table 8-1

## DIRECTION OF CORRELATION***

| Variable** | Sig. + | Sig. − | Nsr | Partial Theory***** |
|---|---|---|---|---|
| BOARD SELECTION PROCEDURES (elected vs. appointed) | Carter & Sutthoff 1960 (bond: appointing districts more likely to succeed) | | Carter & Sutthoff 1960 (tax) | IPC, IDE, PE |
| BOARD STATUS (socioeconomic) | Minar 1966 | | | IPC, SES, PE, IDE |
| BOARD LONGEVITY (terms more or less than 2 years) | Carter & Sutthoff 1960 (in medium sized districts for tax elections; in large districts for bond elections) | | Carter & Sutthoff 1960 (medium, small size-bond; large and small-tax) | IPC, PE |
| SUPERINTENDENT EXPERIENCE | Carter & Ruggels 1966 | | Barbour 1966 | IPC |
| BOARD ATTITUDE (toward various "goals" for their schools) | Carter & Ruggels 1966 | | | IPC |
| TEACHER-PUPIL RATIO | | | N.Y. State Ed. Dept. 1970 | ESI |
| USE OF BUSSING | | | Dykstra 1964 | PE |
| TEACHER SALARY INCREASES | | | Goettel 1971; Carter & Ruggels 1966 | PE |
| DISTRICT INDEBTEDNESS | | Davidson 1967 | Hicks 1967; Goettel 1971 | ESI, SES |

FACTOR II: ELECTION CHARACTERISTICS

| | | | |
|---|---|---|---|
| CONCURRENT ELECTIONS (school bond or tax issues appearing on ballot with state or national candidates or issues) | Marlowe 1970 | Kean 1964<br>Murphy 1966<br>(1st time elect.) | Crider 1967<br>Murphy 1966<br>(subsequent elect.) | PE, IDE |
| STATED PURPOSE OF ISSUE | Crider 1967<br>Barbour 1966<br>Kear 1964 | | Beal et al. 1966 | IPC, IDE |
| TIME OF YEAR (operationalized according to season, months, quarter, etc.) | | | Murphy 1966<br>Kean 1964<br>Beal et al. 1966<br>Barbour 1966<br>Crider 1967 | PE, IDE |
| PAST VOTING PATTERNS— SCHOOL FINANCIAL ELECTIONS | Willis (winter 1967-68) (Areas with records of either extremely high or low support for SFE are less likely than med. support areas to change) Peal et al. 1966<br>Saalfeld 1972<br>Nelson 1968<br>Varden 1973 | | | PE, IPC |

\*Dependent variables
\*\*Independent variables
\*\*\*The variable in question was positively (Sig. +) or negatively (Sig. −) associated with election success or yes voting, or found to be not statistically related (Nsr) to those dependent variables.
\*\*\*\*Refers to the partial theories listed in Table 8-1

## DIRECTION OF CORRELATION***

| Variable** | Sig. + | Sig. − | Nsr | Partial Theory.***** |
|---|---|---|---|---|
| PAST VOTING PATTERNS–OTHER ELECTIONS (the relationship between voting in local nonpartisan elections and national partisan contests) | Jennings & Zeigler 1966<br>Williams & Adrian 1959<br>Salisbury & Black 1963 (voting for elective office; local nonpartisan and national partisan) | | Boskoff & Zeigler 1964<br>Templeton 1966<br>Jordan 1966<br>Hahn & Almy 1971<br>Key 1953<br>Salisbury & Black 1963 (referenda and partisan office) | PE, IPC, IDE, SES |
| TURNOUT | Spinner 1967 (other than first time elections)<br>Marlowe 1970 (urban areas)<br>Willis (winter 1967-68) (suburban areas) | Carter et al. 1960, 1961, 1966<br>Lieber 1967<br>Wentzel 1964<br>Spinner 1967 (first time elections)<br>Barbour 1966<br>Willis (winter 1967-68)<br>Goettel 1971<br>Marlowe 1970<br>Crider 1967<br>Minar 1966<br>Jordan 1966<br>Dykstra 1964 | Stone 1965<br>Beal et al. 1966<br>Turner 1968<br>Murphy 1966<br>Boskoff & Zeigler 1964<br>Hahn Dec. 1968 | PE, IDE, IPC |
| ELECTION FREQUENCY (number of elections held over a five-year period) | Minar 1966 | Beal et al. 1966 | | PE |
| ELECTION TYPE | Carter & Savard 1961 (Voter dissent is likely to be higher for tax rate than for bond or miscellaneous issues.) | | | PE, ESI |

FACTOR III: VOTER DEMOGRAPHIC CHARACTERISTICS

| | | | |
|---|---|---|---|
| INCOME | Boskoff & Zeigler 1964<br>Milstein & Jennings 1970<br>Smith et al. 1968<br>Fish 1964<br>Hahn & Almy 1971<br>Gallup 1969<br>Schoonhoven & Patterson 1966<br>Hatley 1970<br>Wilson & Banfield 1971<br>Davidson 1967 | McMahon 1966 | Tebutt 1968<br>Hicks 1967<br>Jordan 1966 | SES, ESI |
| EDUCATION | McKelvey 1966<br>Tebbutt 1968<br>Schoonhoven & Patterson 1966<br>Jordan 1966<br>Gallup 1969<br>Hatley 1971<br>Hahn & Almy 1971<br>Wilson & Banfield 1971 | McMahon 1966<br>Davidson 1967<br>Jordan 1966 | | SES, CRA, SDA,<br>IPC, ESI |
| OCCUPATION | Carter & Ruggels 1966 | McMahon 1966 | | SES, ESI |
| SES (INDEX) | Boskoff & Zeigler 1964<br>Minar 1966<br>Willis (winter 1967-68) | Turner 1968<br>Jordan 1966 | Tebbutt 1968<br>Boskoff & Zeigler 1964 | SES, ESI |

\*Dependent variables
\*\*Independent variables
\*\*\*The variable in question was positively (Sig. +) or negatively (Sig. —) associated with election success or yes voting, or found to be not statistically related (Nsr) to those dependent variables.
\*\*\*\*Refers to the partial theories listed in Table 8-1

| Variable** | DIRECTION OF CORRELATION*** | | | Partial Theory**** |
|---|---|---|---|---|
| | Sig. + | Sig. − | Nsr | |
| HOME OWNERSHIP | Jordan 1966 | McKelvey 1966<br>Smith et al. 1968 | Wentzel 1964<br>Cooper 1967<br>Hicks 1967<br>Tebbutt 1968 | SES, ESI |
| AGE | | McKelvey 1966<br>Carter & Ruggels 1966<br>King 1963<br>Tebbutt 1968<br>Smith et al. 1968<br>McMahon 1966<br>Jordan 1966<br>Boskoff & Zeigler 1964 | | ESI, CRA |
| CHILD STATUS | King et al. 1963<br>Fish 1964<br>Smith 1964<br>Schoonhoven & Patterson 1966<br>Tebbutt 1968<br>Gallup 1969<br>Hatley 1970<br>Carter & Ruggels 1966 | | | ESI, IPC |
| SEX | Smith et al. 1964 (men=more likely)<br>Boskoff & Zeigler 1964 (women=more likely) | | Mahan 1968<br>Tebbutt 1968 | ESI |
| AREA OF RESIDENCE | King et al. 1963<br>Jordan 1966<br>Boskoff & Zeigler (urban/suburban) | | Smith et al. 1964<br>Boskoff & Zeigler 1964 (previous residential background) | SES, ESI, CRA |

| | | | |
|---|---|---|---|
| LENGTH OF RESIDENCE | | Smith et al. 1964<br>Milstein & Jennings 1970 | Tebbutt 1968<br>Jordan 1966<br>Boskoff & Zeigler 1964 | CRA |
| RACE<br>(operationally,<br>blacks=more likely<br>than whites) | Smith et al. 1968<br>Jordan 1966<br>Hahn & Almy 1971<br>Wilson & Banfield 1964<br>Wirt & Kirst 1972 | | | SES, ESI |
| MARITAL STATUS | Smith et al. 1968 | | | ESI |
| PARTY AFFILIATION | Carter & Ruggels 1966<br>(greater Democratic %<br>of district's regular<br>voters = greater yes vote) | | | PE |
| RELIGIOUS AFFILIATION<br>(Catholics=less likely) | Smith et al. 1968<br>Carter & Ruggels 1966<br>Gans 1967 | | Tebbutt 1968 | ESI |

FACTOR IV: VOTER PSYCHOLOGICAL CHARACTERISTICS

| | | | |
|---|---|---|---|
| CYNICISM<br>(toward school officials) | Agger & Goldstein<br>1965, 1971<br>Parnell 1964<br>Milstein & Jennings 1970 | | | SDA |

\*Dependent variables
\*\*Independent variables
\*\*\*The variable in question was positively (Sig, +) or negatively (Sig, −) associated with election success or yes voting, or found to be not statistically related (Nsr) to those dependent variables.
\*\*\*\*Refers to the partial theories listed in Table 8-1

| | *DIRECTION OF CORRELATION*** | | | Partial |
| Variable** | Sig. + | Sig. − | Nsr | Theory**** |
| --- | --- | --- | --- | --- |
| EDUCATIONAL ATTITUDES | Carter & Sutthoff 1960<br>Agger & Goldstein 1965, 1971<br>McKelvey 1966<br>Fish 1964<br>Mahan 1968 | | Milstein & Jennings 1970 | SDA, CRA<br>IDE |
| CIVIC IMPROVEMENT ORIENTATION | Agger & Goldstein 1965, 1971<br>Boskoff & Zeigler 1964<br>Wilson & Banfield 1964, 1971 | | | CRA |
| IDEOLOGICAL ORIENTATION | Carter & Ruggels 1966 | | Mahan 1968<br>Jordan 1964<br>Boskoff & Zeigler 1964 | PE |
| TAX ORIENTATION | Agger & Goldstein 1965, 1971<br>Carter & Ruggels 1966<br>Milstein & Jennings 1970 | | | ESI, CRA |
| ALIENATION | | Horton & Thompson 1962<br>Gold 1962<br>Templeton 1966<br>Agger & Goldstein 1965, 1971 | | SDA, CRA |
| ECONOMIC ORIENTATION | | | Mahan 1968<br>Fish 1964 | SES |
| COGNITIVE CONSISTENCY | Carter & Chaffee 1966 | | Agger & Goldstein 1971 | IPC |

FACTOR V: INFORMATION FACTORS, SOURCE AND CONTENT

| | | | CRA |
|---|---|---|---|
| INFORMATION SOURCE | Fish 1964<br>Carter & Sutthoff 1960<br>Tebbutt 1968<br>Boskoff & Zeigler 1964 | | |
| VOTER PARTICIPATION STIMULANTS | | Beal et al. 1966<br>Carter & Ruggels 1966 | IDE, PE, IPC |
| USE OF CITIZEN ADVISORY COMMITTEE | Davidson 1967 | Barbour 1966 | IDE, IPC |
| USE OF CONSULTANTS | | Barbour 1966 | IDE, IPC |
| CAMPAIGN TECHNIQUE EFFORT | | Carter & Ruggels 1966<br>Beal et al. 1966 | IDE, IPC |
| | | Turner 1968<br>Whisler 1965<br>Beal et al. 1966<br>Boskoff & Zeigler 1964<br>Berner 1969 | |
| LENGTH OF CAMPAIGN | Beal et al. 1966<br>Barbour 1966<br>Crider 1967 | Murphy 1966 | IDE, IPC |
| PARTICIPATION IN SCHOOL AFFAIRS (direct and indirect) | Carter & Sutthoff 1960 | Boskoff & Zeigler 1964<br>Tebbutt 1968 | IPC, IDE, ESI |

*Dependent variables
**Independent variables
***The variable in question was positively (Sig. +) or negatively (Sig. —) associated with election success or yes voting, or found to be not statistically related (Nsr) to those dependent variables.
****Refers to the partial theories listed in Table 8-1.

| | *DIRECTION OF CORRELATION*** | | | |
|---|---|---|---|---|
| *Variable*** | *Sig. +* | *Sig. −* | *Nsr* | *Partial Theory*****|
| NEWSPAPER SUPPORT | | | Beal et al. 1966<br>Barbour 1966 | IPC |
| **FACTOR VI: POLITICAL CHARACTERISTICS (CROSS–REFERENCE WITH FACTOR II: ELECTION CHARACTERISTICS)** | | | | |
| INTEREST GROUP ACTIVITY | | Jennings & Zeigler 1970<br>Crider 1967<br>Carter & Ruggels 1966<br>Berner 1969<br>Meyers 1964 | Beal et al. 1966 | PE, IDE, IPC |
| COMMUNITY CONFLICT (as assessed via a variety of observational techniques) | | Carter & Ruggels 1966<br>Minar 1966<br>King et al. 1963<br>Gans 1967<br>Masotti 1967<br>Goldhammer & Pellegrin 1968 | | CRA, PE |
| SCHOOL-COMMUNITY RELATIONS | | Carter & Ruggels 1966 | | IPC, IDE |

*Dependent variables
**Independent variables
***The variable in question was positively (Sig. +) or negatively (Sig. −) associated with election success or yes voting, or found to be not statistically related (Nsr) to those dependent variables.
****Refers to the partial theories listed in Table 8-1

# Bibliography

This bibliography is organized in four parts. Part I, "Basic Empirical Research," cites reports, journal articles, dissertations, and books that report the results of research on voting behavior in school financial elections conducted during the last ten years. This literature provides the basic data for the book. The citations that were used in the inventory are annotated to allow the reader to evaluate the research along several dimensions: time period (the time during which data were collected, not the publication date), geographic setting, type of election coverage, unit-of-analysis, and type of data. In addition, a brief statement gives the general highlights of the research.

The second part, "Theory," provides citations to studies of voting behavior in partisan elections and in nonpartisan local elections (other that school elections); to important literature treating characteristics, attitudes, and situations that may influence voting behavior; and to other relevant references that provide theoretical directions.

Part III, "Observational Literature," cites anecdotal literature that describes voting behavior in school elections from the viewpoint of the "interested observer."

The final part, Methodological Literature," cites literature that describes the problems encountered in attempts to retrieve, synthesize, and utilize research information; to methodological suggestions for improving the foregoing; and to literature that provides useful models of the propositional inventory technique.

## Part I: Basic Empirical Research

Advisory Commission on Intergovernmental Relations. *Public Opinion and Taxes.* Washington, D.C..: ACIR, May 1972.

Agger, Robert E. "The Politics of Local Education—A Comparative Study of Community Decision-Making," *Bulletin of the Oregon School Study Council,* University of Oregon, 1961.

Agger, Robert E., and Goldstein, Marshall N. *Educational Innovations in the Community.* Cooperative Research Project # OE 3-10-039. Eugene: University of Oregon, 1965.

    For an expanded and more accessible treatment of the research reported here, see the following citation.

———. *Who will Rule the Schools: A Cultural Class Crisis.* Belmont, California: Wadsworth Publishing Co., 1971.

    1959-1967; Eugene, Springfield, Junction City, and Portland, Oregon; budget elections; individuals; survey data. The panel technique allows explicit treatment of change and cause in this excellent examination of "citizen orientation toward the schools" and the relationship of these orientations to voting in school budget elections over time.

Banach, William J., and Westley, Lawrence. "Public Relations, Computers, and Election Success." An unpublished paper presented to the Association for Educational Data Systems, May 19, 1972, St. Paul, Minnesota.

1965-1971; Oakland County, Michigan; all school financial elections held during above time period; individuals and precincts; aggregate and survey. This is a "cook-book" approach to winning school financial elections and a good one since it stresses the importance of systematic analysis of community support patterns leading to a selective campaign.

Barbour, Edwin Lyle, "Effects of Socio-Economic Factors on School Bond Elections in Iowa." Ph.D. dissertation, Iowa State University, 1966.

This study is based on data described in the annotation to Beal and others, below.

Barr, Richard H., and King, Irene A. *Bond Sales for Public School Purposes: 1967-68* (Updated each year to the present time; Irene A. King is cited as the sole author of the most recent addition). Washington, D.C.: Department of Health, Education and Welfare, 1969, 1970, 1971, 1972, and 1973.

Best source of summary data regarding school bond election outcomes in both numbers and dollar amounts for the entire nation.

Barr, W. Monfort, and Lindley, A.T. "Bond Issue Election Defeats: Selected Western States, 1966-67," In Committee on Educational Finance, National Education Association, *Fiscal Planning for Schools in Transition.* Proceedings of the Twelfth National Conference on School Finance, March 23, 24, 25, 1969, Jung Hotel, New Orleans, Louisiana. pp. 197-211.

Beal, George M., and others. *Iowa School Bond Issues Data Book.* Ames Iowa: Iowa State University, Department of Sociology and Anthropology, 1966.

1960-1965; Iowa; bond elections held throughout the state during the five-year period; individuals (school superintendents); survey (mail). The authors propose and use a "social action model" for this investigation that attempts to assess the effects of a wide range of variables on the outcome of school bond elections in Iowa. All findings are based on perceptions and reports of school superintendents.

_____ . *Vocational School Bond Issues in Iowa.* Ames, Iowa: Department of Sociology and Anthropology, Iowa State University, 1967.

Based on the same data described in Beal and others, above.

_____ . *Iowa School Bond Issues: Summary Report.* Ames, Iowa: Department of Sociology and Anthropology, Iowa State University, 1966.

Summarizes project findings, based on the same data described above.

_____ . Hartman, John J.; and Lagomarcino, Virgil. "An Analysis of Factors Associated with School Bond Elections." *Rural Sociology* 33 (September 1968): 313-27.

Best, James, and Besag, Frank. "1970 School Levy Survey: A Survey of 18 School Districts Where the School Levy Was Defeated Twice in 1969-70," An unpublished survey conducted for the School Levy Study Commission, 1970.

1969-1970; Washington; school tax levy elections of that year; individuals; survey (mail and telephone). We examined an early draft of this study that lacked a methodological appendix mentioned in the text. Those interested in the report should contact the authors.

Boozer, Raymond L. "A Study of the Voting Publics in Grand Rapids, Michigan, to Provide the Basis for Planning and Conducting Millage Elections in That District." Ph.D. dissertation, Michigan State University, 1969.

1964-1968; Grand Rapids, Michigan; six school millage elections—three passed and three failed; individuals (sampled from five major "voting publics"); survey (mail). Assesses the effect of parental and religious status on voting in these elections. Asserts that the major purpose of the study is to provide Grand Rapids Board of Education with a "workable plan which may be used by them in conducting future school millage campaigns" (p. 9).

Bureau of Governmental Research and Service. "Record of Vote on Proposed School District Special Tax Levies to Exceed the Six Per Cent Constitutional Limitation." Unpublished. Eugene: University of Oregon, 1971.

Cahill, Robert S., and Hencley, Stephen P. (eds.). *The Politics of Education in the Local Community.* Danville, Ill.: The Interstate Printers and Publishers, Inc., 1964.

Carlson, John William Jr. "The Relationship of School Board Contests to Budget Defeats in Selected School Districts in New Jersey." Ed. D. dissertation, Temple University, 1969.

Carter, Richard F. "Bandwagon and Sandbagging Effects: Some Measures of Dissonance Reduction." *Public Opinion Quarterly* 23 (Summer 1959): 279-87.

_____. *Voters and Their Schools.* Stanford, California: Institute for Communication Research, Stanford University, 1960.

1958; three urban areas, one each from the southeast, midwest, and pacific coast; school bond elections; individuals; survey (personal interviews). Much of this analysis is devoted to assessing citizen's attitudes toward the schools. One voter sample was interviewed before and after a bond election. Provides the basis for more comprehensive material on voter behavior in school elections, contained in volumes III and IV of the 1966 report cited below.

Carter, Richard F., and Savard, William G. *Influence of Voter Turnout on School Bond and Tax Elections.* Cooperative Research Monograph, No. 5. Washington, D.C.: Government Printing Office, 1961.

Based on the data described in Carter and Sutthoff (below), this succinct summary of the relationship between turnout and election outcome is perhaps the most well known of publications from the Carter project.

_____. "Study of Voter Turnout." *The Education Digest* 27 (January 1962): 16-18.

Carter, Richard F., and Sutthoff, John. *Communities and Their Schools.* Stanford, California: School of Education, Stanford University, 1960.

1948-1959; United States; school tax and school bond elections; individuals and school districts; survey (personal interviews and mail) and aggregate. In an attempt to assess the degree of congruence of perception—"understanding"—among school and community leaders, parents, voters, mass media representatives, and other important community groups, these researchers conducted personal interviews with national samples of school and community leaders in eighty-two school districts and with 5,000 registered voters. In addition, a national sample of 1,054 school districts was represented by a mail survey of superintendents. "Understanding" (and indicators of the concept) is then correlated with the vote in school financial elections while controlling for a number of potentially important factors such as district size, geographic location, and so forth.

Carter, Richard F., and Sweigert, Ray L., Jr. "Rehearsal Dissonance and Selective Informations Seeking," in Wayne Danielson (ed.), *Paul J. Deutschmann Memorial Papers in Mass Communications Research.* Cincinnati: Scripps Howard, 1963.

Carter, Richard F.; Greenberg, Bradley S.; and Haimson, Alvin. *The Structure and Process of School Community Relations. Volume I. Informal Communications about the Schools.* Stanford, California: Institute for Communications Research, Stanford University, 1966.

This volume serves as background material for their analysis of voting in school financial elections (volumes III and IV below) by measuring flows of information and influence between school and community.

Carter, Richard F., and Chaffee, Steven H. *The Structure and Process of School Community Relations. Volume II. Between Citizens and Schools.* Stanford, California: Institute for Communications Research, Stanford University, 1966.

1964; United States; school bond and tax elections; individuals; survey (personal interviews). This volume also serves as background to the analysis of voting conducted in Volumes III and IV by examining the relationship between different "consumer roles"—parental status, utility, and educational attainment—and citizen participation in the schools.

Carter, Richard F., and others, *The Structure and Process of School-Community Relations, Volume III. The Structure of School-Community Relations.* Stanford, California: School of Education, Stanford University, 1966.

1950-1964; United States; school tax and bond elections; individuals and school districts; survey (personal interviews and mail).

Examines the effect of 860 variables grouped into twenty-six divisions on the following four dependent variables: (1) Acquiescence: percentage of yes voters on issues studied; (2) participation: percentage of eligible voters who turned out for elections studied; (3) understanding: amount of common perception among ten "informed observers" from each community regarding the impact of and inventory of factors that may affect school-community relations; and (4) quiescence: the degree to which controversy and conflict are lacking in districts, measured also by factor perception of the ten informed observers from each community. This volume lists each of the 860 variables and includes the N, mean, median, standard deviation, skewness, and correlation with each of the four dependent variables. This volume is indispensible for the analysis presented in the next volume and is an excellent source for research ideas.

Carter, Richard F., and Ruggels, W. Lee. *The Structure and Process of School-Community Relations, Volume IV. The Process of School-Community Relations.* Stanford, California: School of Education, Stanford University, 1966.

This report presents an analysis of the raw data presented in Carter and others, volume III (above). The results of factor and multiple regression analysis that served to refine the analysis are reported along with extended treatment of the interrelationship between the four dependent variables.

Carter, Richard F., and Oddell, William R. *The Structure and Process of School Community Relations. Volume V. A Summary.* Stanford, California: Institute for Communications Research, Stanford University, 1966.

Condenses the four technical studies (volumes I through IV) to provide an outline of primary factors affecting school community relations.

Cooper, John R. "Institutional Factors Affecting the Outcome of School Bond Referenda." Ph.D dissertation, University of Virginia, 1967.

1961; United States; school bond issues; school districts; aggregage data. Examines the effect of "alternative rules of choice" (majority vs. greater than a majority, for passage, and all registered voters vs. property owners as participants) on the outcome of school bond elections. Used a table of random numbers to sample U.S. school district files containing success/failure records at the Investment Bankers Association. Contains state-by-state summary of voting rules.

Cowan, Oliven T. "An Investigation of the Impact of Certain Factors on School Tax Issues as Perceived by Selected Groups in North Carolina." Ed.D. dissertation, University of North Carolina, 1968.

1965-1967; North Carolina; school tax issues; individuals; survey (mail).

Asked a sample of "informed observers"—board members, superintendents, county commissioners, newspaper editors, and legislators—to rank the importance of a number of factors that may affect the outcome of school financial elections. Data are analyzed via analysis of variance.

Crider, Russel J. "Identification of Factors Which Influence the Passage or Failure of School Bond Issues in Selected Counties of Mississippi." Ed.D. dissertation, University of Southern Mississippi, 1967.

1959-1965; Mississippi; school bond elections; school districts; survey (mail). This research assessed the impact of orginizational factors, which are apparently unique to Mississippi, on voting in bond elections.

Crosswait, Billy N. "Factors Related to the Success and Failure of Bond Issues in the Independent School Districts of South Dakota." Ed.D. dissertation, University of South Dakota, 1967.

1956-1965; South Dakota; school bond elections; school districts; survey (mail). Employs a comparative analysis of successful and unsuccessful school districts to determine the effect of factors such as newspaper attitude toward the proposal, time of year of election, use of outside consultants, and so forth.

Davidson, George W. "The Relationship of Selected Factors to the Success or Failure of School Tax Referenda." Ed.D. dissertation, University of Illinois, 1967.

1963-1964; Illinois; tax and bond elections; school districts; aggregate. Tests the total impact and interrelationships among nineteen independent variables suggested by previous research to play an important part in the outcome of school financial elections. The linear discriminant function allows the author to build a multivariate model for predicting probable election outcomes.

Dillingham, Harry C. *A Study of the Response of Cincinnati Voters to a Reduction in Elementary and Secondary Services.* Cincinnati: University of Cincinnati, 1969.

1966-1967; Cincinnati, Ohio; budget elections; individuals; survey (pre- and post-election interviews).

Compares the intended and actual votes of a stratified sample of registered voters before and after an announced reduction in school services. Provides direct tests of the "cross pressures hypothesis" in a school financial election setting.

Dykstra, Sidney. "A Study of the Relationships of Nonpublic School Enrollment to the Approval of School Millage and Bond Proposals." Ph.D. dissertation, University of Michigan, 1964.

1958-1963; Michigan; school millage and bond elections; school districts; survey (mail). Although the researcher's initial concern is the relationship between nonpublic school enrollment and voter support for school issues, he tests a number of other plausible hypothesis suggested by the literature.

Fish, Lawrence Dean. "An Analysis of Factors Associated with Voter Behavior in School Budget Elections." Ed.D. dissertation, Washington State University, 1964.

1960-1961; Lake Oswego, Oregon; school budget elections; individuals (voters); survey (personal interview).

This is a case study of voting behavior in a series of five school budget elections held in one Oregon school district. This unique survey design uses a sample population of school election voters (as opposed to a random sample of the community or eligible voter population). Assesses the determinants of consistency (voting in the same direction) and conflict (divergent voting) among individuals who participated in more than one of the five elections.

Fisher, R. "Voting in 1970: Some Facts and Figures." *Today's Education* 59 (September 1970): 64-65.

Frost, Philip Charles, "Selected Referenda Campaigns in Evanston Township High School: A Case Study." Ph.D. dissertation, Northwestern University, 1970.

1969-1970; Evanston, Illinois; school tax referenda; individuals (voters and participants in campaign); survey (mail and personal interviews).

Focuses on the organizational structure, methods, and tactics of school election campaigns. Good analysis of selective campaigning techniques.

Gallup, George, *How the Nation Views the Public Schools.* Princeton, New Jersey: CFK/Ltd., Gallup International, 1969.

1969; United States; hypothetical school tax elections; individuals; surveys (personal interviews).

This is the first of four annual modified probability samples (N = 1,505) of the nation's adult population designed to assess citizen attitudes toward the schools on a variety of issues. Importantly, key questions regarding probable voting behavior in school financial elections are repeated (worded identically) each year.

_____ . "Second Annual Survey of the Public's Attitude toward the Public Schools." *Phi Delta Kappan,* 52 (October 1970): 99-112. Second of four annual surveys, same research design as described above.

_____ . "The Third Annual Survey of the Public's Attitude toward the Public Schools, 1971," *Phi Delta Kappan* 53 (September 1971): 33-48.

Third of four annual surveys, same research design as described above.

_____ . "Fourth Annual Gallup Poll of Attitudes toward Education." *Phi Delta Kappan* 54 (September 1972): 33-46.

Most recent annual survey, same research design as described above.

Goettel, Robert J. "The Relationship between Selected Fiscal and Economic Factors and Voting Behavior in School Budget Elections in New York State," A paper presented at the American Educational Research Association, Annual Conference, New York City, February 4, 1971.

1969; New York State; school budget elections; school districts; aggregate.

Assesses the effect of several economic factors on participation and dissent in school budget elections. The researcher is unsatisfied with the amount of variance explained by his multivariate analysis; therefore he presents an excellent section on future research needs.

――――. "Voter Behavior and School Budget Elections." *APSS Know How* 23 (September 1971): 1-4.

Condensation of research described in preceding citation.

Gold, David. "Independent Causation in Multivariate Analysis; The Case of Political Alienation and Attitudes towards a School Bond Issue." *American Sociological Review* 27 (February 1962): 85-87.

Reexamines the Horton and Thompson data (described below) using multivariate analysis. Presents a convincing argument that SES and alienation *together* provide a strong predictor of voting in school bond elections.

Goldhammer, Keith, and Pellegrin, Ronald J. *Jackson County Revisited: A Case Study in the Politics of Education.* Eugene: University of Oregon, 1968.

1962-1966; Jackson County, Oregon; school budget and board elections; community; aggregate.

Traces the effect of community conflict over both educational and noneducational issues on the educational program and voting for educational issues in a large suburban school district.

Gott, Prentice L. "Selected Factors Associated with Success and Failure of School Bond Issue Campaigns in Kentucky." Ed. D. dissertation, George Peabody College of Teachers, 1962.

Hahn, Harlan. "Voting in Canadian Communities: A Taxonomy of Referendum Issues." *Canadian Journal of Political Science* 1(December 1968): 462-69.

1955-1965; Canada; referendums for different purposes (including school finance); cities; aggregate.

Examines the turnout/vote relationship for the following types of issues: (1) flouridation; (2) Sunday entertainment; (3) sports facilities; (4) schools or libraries; (5) water, street, or sewer improvements; (6) city government reform issues; (7) hospitals. His data provide unique scope of election coverage and precision in the measure of turnout since Canadian communities are periodically canvassed for an official *potential* voter list.

――――. "Ethos and Social Class: Referenda in Canadian Cities." *Polity* 2 (December 1969): 395-415.

See above annotation for data description.

Hahn, Harlan, and Almy, Timothy A. "Ethnic Politics and Racial Issues: Voting in Los Angeles." *The Western Political Qualterly* 24 (December 1971): 719-730.

1969; Los Angeles, Calif.; Mayorality (Yorty & Bradley) and school (1 bond, 2 tax, and 1 board) elections; precincts and census tracts, aggregate.

Examines ethnic and racial voting patterns in Los Angeles. Compares degrees of political assimilation in elections for different issues and personalities.

———. "Voters and the Schools: Revolt in Los Angeles." *CTA Journal* (January 1970).

Harper, Joe W. "A Study of Community Power Structure in Certain School Districts in the State of Texas and its Influence on Bond Elections." Ed.D. dissertation, North Texas State University, 1965.

1960-1964; four Texas school districts; school bond elections; individuals (influentials); survey (personal interview).

Uses reputational method to identify community power structures and their influence on school bond election outcomes in four communities.

Hartman, John J., and Beal, George M. *Role Performance of Selected Individuals and Groups in School Bond Elections.* Ames, Iowa: Iowa State University, 1968.

Based on the same data described in Beal et al. below, this paper traces the impact of campaign involvement on election outcome.

Hatley, Richard V. "Family Income, Voting Behavior, and Financial Referendums: Educational Finance and Politics in Albuquerque, 1968-1969." Ed.D. dissertation, University of New Mexico, 1970.

1968-1969; Albuquerque, New Mexico; school tax and income surtax referendums; precincts and individuals; aggregate and survey (mail).

Examines the effect of a number of important variables on voting in school financial elections. Hypotheses are tested using different units for analysis (precincts and individuals) and analysis techniques. Makes important methodological as well as substantive contribution.

———. "School District Financial Referendum Campaign Strategies and Voting Behavior of District Residents." *Kansas Studies in Education* 21 (Spring/Summer 1971): 37-44.

Henningsen, Allan C. "Analysis of Factors Affecting the Outcome of Bond Issues in the Public Schools of Missouri." Ed.D. dissertation, University of Missouri, 1970.

1968-1969; Missouri; school bond elections; school districts; survey (mail, to district superintendents).

Focuses on the effect of election setting variables such as time of year, location of polling places, and so forth.

Hicks, Robert E. "An Analysis of the Influence of Certain Fiscal Variables on the Success of Proposed School Tax Levies and Bond Issues for Public School Support in Ohio." Ph.D. dissertation, Ohio State University, 1967.

1962-1966; Ohio; school tax and bond issues; school districts; aggregate.

Uses a variety of fiscal variables in a stepwise multiple regression program in an attempt to predict the outcome of school financial elections. Since these variables, taken together, explain only 13 percent of the variance in election outcome over time, the author concludes that the primary determinants of success or failure rest with variables not analyzed in his study.

Horton, John E. "The Angry Voter: A Study in Political Alienation." Ph.D. dissertation, Cornell University, 1960.

The more refined treatment of these data may be found in Horton and Thompson (1962) described below.

Horton, John E., and Thompson, Wayne E. "Powerlessness and Political Negativism: A Study of Defeated Local Referendums." *The American Journal of Sociology* 67 (March 1962): 485-493.

March 1957 and March 1958; two upstate New York communities; school bond elections; individuals (registered voters); personal interviews.

This classic study tests the hypothesis that referenda may serve as institutional outlets for protest and that voting against local issues may be an expression of political protest on the part of powerless and ordinarily apathetic members of the community. Gold (cited above) should be read with this.

Hukill, William. *Winning Bond Elections.* Cedar Rapids, Iowa: Design Associates, 1973.

1960-1972; Iowa; school bond issues; school districts; aggregate.

This short (24 page) report does a good job of pinpointing the tactical relevance of a number of research findings. Provides good timeline data.

Jennings, M. Kent, and Zeigler, Harmon. "Interest Representation in School Governance." Unpublished paper presented at the 1970 annual meeting of the American Political Science Association, September 11, 1970, Los Angeles, California.

1965-1968; United States; school financial elections; school boards; survey (personal interviews).

Within the framework of previous interest group theory, the authors examine plausible antecedents to the growth and intensity of interest groups in education and assess the impact of interest group activity on educational decision-making. Tests the relationship between interest group activity and election outcome. Rigorous, controlled data analysis lend authority to the research.

Johnson, C. Montgomery. *Public Opinion, Voter Behavior, and School Support.* Olympia, Washington: S.C.O.R.E., 1971.

1965-1970; Washington; school tax levies; individuals; survey (personal interview).

Underscores the tactical importance of survey research findings from a number of sources. The data description above refers to information from several private surveys of public opinion in the state of Washington.

Jones, Jack James, "Effectiveness of School Bond Election Campaign Strategies." Ph.D. dissertation, University of Southern California, 1970.

November 1966 and March 1968; Alhambra, California; school bond elections; precincts; aggregate.

Designed to compare the effectiveness of two types of campaigns for school bond issues—one selective, the other general—on determining election outcome.

Jordan, Wilson K. "An Analysis of the Relationship between Social Characteristics and Educational Voting Patterns." Ed.D. dissertation, University of California at Los Angeles, 1966.

1963; Los Angeles, California; one school bond election; census tracts; aggregate.

Examines the association between eleven demographic variables and the percent voting for a school bond issue by census tract (709 at that time). Quartile analysis is applied to independent variables (tracts are dichotomized on a yes/no basis yielding a series of two-by-four contingency tables), which makes the analysis sensitive to curvilinear relationships.

_____ . "An Analysis of the Relationship between Social Characteristics and Educational Voting Patterns." In Committee on Educational Finance, National Education Association, *Fiscal Planning for Schools in Transition.* Proceedings of the Twelfth National Conference on School Finance, March 23, 24, 25, 1969, Jung Hotel, New Orleans, Louisana, pp. 239-45.

Kean, Gordon Ross. "Selected Variables in the Success of Tax Override Elections in California School Districts." Ed.D. dissertation, University of Southern California, 1964.

1957-1962; California; school tax override elections; school districts; survey (mail, to superintendents).

Tests a number of hypotheses suggested by the literature. Survey conducted in conjunction with Murphy (below). An unusual feature is a detailed state-by-state listing of legal provisions relating to all types of school elections.

Keating, Thomas N. "The Effectiveness of Procedures Used in School Building Programs in Nebraska." Ed.D. dissertation, University of Nebraska, 1963.

Kenney, Donald F. "A Functional Analysis of Citizens' Committees During School Financial Elections." Ph.D. dissertation, Stanford University, 1962.

King, Gary W., and others. *Conflict over the Schools: Sociological Analysis of a Suburban School Bond Election.* East Lansing, Michigan: Institute for Community Development and Services, Michigan State University, 1963.

1957-1958; Meridian Township, Okemoos School District (near East Lansing), Michigan; school bond elections; individuals; survey (personal interviews).

Assesses the voting behavior of suburban residents in school bond elections, while controlling for variations in SES, neighborhood, and so forth.

King, Irene A. *Bond Sales for Public School Purposes 1970-1971.* Washington, D.C.: Office of Education, Department of Health, Education and Welfare, 1972.

1970-1971; United States; school bond elections; elections; aggregate.

Continues the annual report of number and dollar amount of the nation's bond elections that succeeded during the year. For earlier reports see the Richard A. Barr citations, above.

Lawrence, Harry Archibald Jr. "The Relationship of Certain Financial Factors to School Budget Approval in New Jersey." Ed.D. dissertation, Rutgers–The State University, 1966.

1960-1964; New Jersey; school budget elections; school districts; aggregate.

Assesses the impact of a number of financial variables on election outcome in New Jersey school districts and uses multiple-discriminant technique to predict membership in one of three groups of school districts: (1) successful in all elections for four years preceding 1964; (2) unsuccessful in 1964 and two or more times previously; and (3) unsuccessful in 1964 and less than two defeats during the previous four years.

Lee, Frank Loren. "A Rating Scale for the Prediction of the Outcome of School Bond Elections in Nebraska." Ph.D. dissertation, University of Nebraska, 1964.

Levitt, Morris, and Feldbaum, Eleanor. "Taxpayer Resistance to Adequate School Support." Proceedings of the 14th National Conference on School Finance, March 28-30, 1971. Committee on Educational Finance, National Education Association, Washington, D.C., 1972.

Lieber, Ralph H. "An Analysis of the Relationship of Weekly Community Suburban Papers to the Outcome of School Voting Issues." Ph.D. dissertation, Northwestern University, 1967.

1960-1966; Cook County, Illinois; school bond and budget elections; school districts; aggregate for voting, content analysis for newspaper articles.

Uses rigorous methodology to quantify newspaper "support" of a given election and correlates such support with success or failure in the school elections sampled.

Lindbloom, Ray Leander. "Public Voting Behavior in School Budget and Bond Issues and Its Realtionship to Local School Property Tax Incidence." Ed.D. dissertation, Teachers College, Columbia University, 1960.

Linn, Frank J. "Voting Dates and Their Implications for School Elections in Arkansas." Ed.D. dissertation, University of Arkansas, 1967.

Maguire, John W. "Changing Voter Profile and School Elections: The Younger

Voters' Impact on School and Community." *Intellect* 101 (November 1972): 113.

A short summary of recent data from different sources that helps specify the impact of young voters on school financial elections.

Mahan, James M. "An Investigation of the Relationship between Overt Voting Behavior and Expressed Personal Attitudes." Ed.D. dissertation, Syracuse University, 1968.

1967; "Suburbenville" (pseudonym), New York; school bond election; individuals (sample of citizens who participated in the bond election); survey (mail).

In this survey of school bond election voters, the author uses the following measurement devices to assess the relationship between expressed value orientation and overt voting behavior: (1) traditional vs. emergent value orientations as measured by the Differential Value Inventory (DVI); (2) conservative vs. liberal politico-economic beliefs as measured by the Economic Liberalism Conservativism Scale (ELC); (3) expansionist vs. non-expansionist school facilities views as measured by the Facilities Scale (FS); and broad vs. narrow curriculum views as measured by the Curriculum Scale (CS).

_____. "Relationships of Economic, Social, and Educational Attitudes to the Outcome of a School Bond Issue: An Investigation of Voter Values and Voting Action." Unpublished paper presented to the annual meeting of the American Educational Research Association, New Orleans, Louisiana, February 25 to March 1, 1973.

Summary of dissertation described above.

Marlowe, Byron H. "An Explanation of Voter Behavior in School District Tax Elections." Unpublished paper presented at the annual meeting of the American Educational Research Association, Los Angeles, California, February 5-8, 1969.

Similar to the analysis present in Marlowe, 1970 (below).

_____. "Voter Behavior in School Bond and Tax Elections in Ohio," in Committee on Educational Finance, National Education Associations, *A Time for Priorities: Financing the Schools for the 70's.* Washington, D.C.: NEA, 1970, pp. 158-67.

1946-1969; Ohio; school bond and tax elections; school districts; aggregate.

Offers correlates to election outcome based on a comprehensive data set: all school tax and bond elections held from 1946 to 1970.

Masotti, Louis M. *Education and Politics in Suburbia: The New Trier Experience.* Cleveland: Press of Western Reserve University, 1967.

Excellent case study of community controversy, organized around the North et al. proposition that "social conflict often performs integrative as well as disintegrative functions."

Masse, Bernard, "A Comparison of the Relationship of Influentials to Schools in High and Low Support Communities." Ph.D. dissertation, University of Michigan, 1964.

McDaniel, Charles Pope, Jr. "A Study of Factors Affecting the Outcome of School Bond Issues in Selected Georgia School Districts." Ed.D. dissertation, University of Georgia, 1967.

1960-1965; three counties in Georgia; school bond elections; "civic elites," survey (personal interviews) and observational.

Attempts to identify common factors affecting outcome of school financial elections as perceived by community elites.

McKelvey, Troy V. "A Cooperative Study of Voting Behavior in Two Coterminous Systems of Local Government." Ph.D. dissertation, University of California at Berkeley, 1966.

1965; Albany, California (San Francisco Bay Area); one municipal and one city bond election; individuals (voters and nonvoters); survey (mail questionnaire).

Assesses the relationship among voter attitudes, their social characteristics, and their voting behavior in two types of bond elections (school and municipal). Theoretical concern is with the effect of the voter's image of the educational or municipal government system on his voting behavior. Findings are presented with careful controls.

McMahon, Stephen T. "Demographic Characteristics and Voting Behavior in a Junior College Creation, Tax Levy and Bond Issue Election." Ph.D. dissertation, University of Texas, 1966.

November 1963; Austin, Texas; three measures relating to the establishment of a new Junior College; precincts; aggregates.

Tests a series of hypotheses based on the assumption that "supporters of the public schools are those who view the schools as vehicles for advancement in the social hierarchy." Uses multiple regression and multiple-discriminant analysis to derive a model that is then subjected to split-half reliability test.

Meyers, Alfred Victor. "The Financial Crisis in Urban Schools: Patterns among Organized Groups in an Urban Community." Ed.D. dissertation, Wayne State University, 1964.

1957-1963; Detroit, Michigan; school financial elections; interest group leaders; personal interviews and observations.

Uses derivations of community power study techniques to select panels of opposition and support leaders, then interviews these individuals and draws appropriate conclusions regarding the structure of opposition and support toward school financial elections.

Milstein, Mike M., and Jennings, Robert E. *Factors Underlying Bond Referendum Successes and Failures in Selected Western New York School Districts: 1968-1969.* Buffalo, New York: Department of Educational Administration, State University of New York at Buffalo, 1970.

1968-1969; western New York; school bond elections; individuals (voters and nonvoters); survey (personal interviews).

Compares the attitudes and behaviors of voters and nonvoters in recent New York bond elections. Sample of voters is drawn from four suburban school districts, each of which had a recent bond issue. Two of the districts succeeded in passing a bond issue while two failed in passing their bond issues.

Mitchell, Holly W. "Identification and Evaluation of Factors Affecting School Bond Issues in Missouri Public Schools," Ph.D. dissertation, University of Missouri, 1962.

Minar, David W. "The Community Bases of Conflict in School System Politics." *American Sociological Review* 31 (December 1966): 822-35.

1958-1962; Cook County, Illinois; school board and school financial elections; school districts; aggregate.

Focuses on the "social routes and institutional consequences of conflict in school district politics." Assesses the relationship between several important community level variables and: (1) participation, operationalized as the sum of votes cast in all board elections and referenda during the five-year period as a proportion of total eligible votes, and (2) dissent, operationalized as the sum of no votes as a proportion of the sum of all votes cast in a five-year period.

Morrissey, Ann Elizabeth. "A Study of Selected School Building Referenda in Nassau County, Long Island, New York: With the View of Suggesting Principles for the Promotion of Referenda." Ed.D. dissertation, New York University, 1963.

1956-1961; Nassau County, Long Island, New York; school bond elections; school districts; survey (interviews with superintendents and other community leaders).

Reports the reasons for school election success or failure as perceived by school superintendent and other "community leaders." Formulates strategic guides on the basis of this and other research.

Murphy, Edward V. "Selected Variables in the Success of Bond Elections in California School Districts." Ed.D. dissertation, University of Southern California, 1966.

This study is a companion study to the Kean dissertation reported earlier. The only basic difference is that the Kean study focused on tax override elections while the Murphy study looked at school *bond* elections. The same questionnaire was the data source for both studies.

Nelson, Carl M., Jr. "A Prediction Model for Determining the Outcome of School Bond Elections," Ed.D. dissertation, University of Arkansas, 1968.

September 1966 and September 1967; Arkansas; school bond elections; school districts; survey (mail questionnaires to superintendents).

Uses multiple regression analysis and other intercorrelation techniques to derive a regression model of thirteen factors from an original list of seventy-three independent variables that explain 72 percent of the variance in school bond elections.

New York State Education Department. *Studies of Public School Support: 1968 Series.* Albany, New York: State Education Department, 1969.

_____ . *Studies of Public School Support: 1969 Series.* Albany, New York: State Education Department, 1970.

1964-1969; New York State; school budget elections; counties; aggregate.

Primarily a presentation of descriptive data concerning school district budget defeats in New York State. A brief analysis section tests nine hypotheses with aggregate data from a sample of New York counties.

Overbeck, Wayne E. "Junior College Bond Elections: Why Do They Fail (Or Pass)?" Unpublished seminar paper, December 1969.

_____ . "Junior College Bond Elections: Longitudinal Case Studies in Five New Districts That Lost at Least One Election before Winning." Ph.D. dissertation, University of California at Los Angeles, 1970.

1960-1969; Southern California; junior college bond elections; junior college districts; survey (open-ended interviews with positional and opposition leaders identified by reputational methods) and content analysis of newspapers.

Attempts to specify changes that occurred between unsuccessful and successful bond elections in each of the districts studied.

_____ . "Winning a Junior College Bond Election: How to Change the Voters' Minds." Unpublished seminar paper, August 1969.

Parnell, Dale Paul, "Voter Participation Patterns in Three Oregon School Districts," Ed.D. dissertation, University of Oregon, 1964.

1960-1963; Oakridge, Eugene, and Junction City, Oregon; school budget elections; individuals (voters and nonvoters); survey (personal interviews with a panel).

Compares the attitudes and voting behaviors of voters and nonvoters in school budget elections. Data are from the Agger and Goldstein (1965) study described above.

Roper Research Associates, Inc. "A Study of Community Attitudes toward Education and West Valley Junior College." A report of research conducted for the West Valley Junior College District, August 1968.

1968; San Francisco Bay Area, California; one junior college bond issue;

individuals; survey (personal interviews with a cross-section sample of the district's adult population).

Reports the questions used, the sampling method, and the findings of a public opinion poll conducted for the junior college.

Saalfeld, Bernard Francis. "Taxpayers and Voters: Collective Choice in Public Education." Ph.D. dissertation, University of Oregon, 1972.

1968-1969; Oregon; school budget elections; school districts; aggregate.

Uses multivariate analysis to test the hypothesis that "as educational demands increase disproportionately to the rise in wealth, the amount remaining for alternative goods diminishes accordingly which eventually leads the voter to balk at further increases in his educational tax bill" (p. 17). Provides intriguing suggestions for future research that applies the concept of the "normal vote" to school financial elections.

Schoonhoven, John van, and Patterson, Wade N. *A Comparative Study of Inconsistent Voter Behavior in School Budget Elections.* Eugene, Oregon: Oregon School Study Council, School of Education, University of Oregon, 1966

1964; Lane County, Oregon; school budget elections; individuals (a sample of eligible voters who did not vote in the first election but did vote in the second [successful] budget election of that year); survey (mail).

Assesses correlates of "inconsistent voting"—as operationalized above—in two school districts. Suggests, as an important future research need, comparison of inconsistent with consistent voters within school districts.

Seeker, William A. "Power Structure and School Bond Elections." Ph.D. dissertation, Texas A & M, 1969.

1967-1968; two Texas communities (less than 10,000 population); school bond elections; individuals (the "power elite" of the communities); survey (personal interviews) and observation.

Attempts to "investigate the relationship of community to the results of school bond elections." Provides detailed observation of the school-community relationship in these two areas, and interesting discussion of power structure identification techniques.

Smith, Ralph V., and others. *Community Organization and Support of the Schools.* Cooperative Research Project No. 1828. Ypsilanti, Michigan: Field Services Division, Eastern Michigan University, 1964.

Forerunner of the report cited directly below.

_____ . *Community Support for the Public Schools in a Large Metropolitan Area.* Ypsilanti, Michigan: Eastern Michigan University, 1968.

1965; Detroit SMSA; school millage elections; individuals (adult population); survey (personal interviews with sample (N=1,175) stratified by ecological zone.

A multidisciplinary study by scholars from the fields of sociology, geography, and public health. Organizing questions relate to the effects of a high rate of deconcentration of the population in a large metropolitan area on the central city school district and suburban school districts. The authors argue that support for the public schools varies in relation to the distribution of social characteristics over urban space. To test this hypothesis they ask respondents to indicate their voting behavior in a recent election and also to indicate their latent support by answering hypothetical questions regarding how they would vote in certain school financial election situations.

Spinner, Arnold. "The Effects of Voter Participation upon Election Outcomes in School Budget Elections in New York State, 1957-1966." Ph.D. dissertation, New York University, 1967.

1957-1966; New York State; all school financial elections held during the period; school districts; survey (mail, to superintendents).

Provides important specification of the relationship of turnout to election outcome in election sequences. Although the data are incomplete and may present validity problems in some instances, the size of his sample—2,600 elections across the state and over a nine-year time span—lends authority to his findings.

Staley, David. *An Analysis of Tax Levy Defeats in Six Oregon School Districts.* Eugene, Oregon: Oregon School Study Council, University of Oregon, 1964.

Stollar, Dewey H., and others. *Analysis and Interpretation of Research for School Board Members.* Final Report. Knoxville: Department of Educational Administration and Supervision, University of Tennessee, 1969. Chapter 2, "Community Support for Education Elections Involving School Issues."

Short review of relevant literature.

Stone, Clarence N. "Local Referendums: An Alternative to the Alienated Voter Model." *Public Opinion Quarterly* 29 (Summer 1965): 213-22.

1953-1962; "Littletown" (pseudonym for "a small town"); eighteen different types of local school issues including four school bond elections; one city; aggregate.

Classic critique of alienation theory as applied to explanations of local nonpartisan election outcomes.

Sutthoff, John. "Local-Cosmopolitan Orientation and Participation in School Affairs." *Administrator Notebook* 9 (November 1960)

Tebbutt, Arthur V. "Voting Behavior and Selected Communications in a Bond and Rate Referenda for a Suburban School District.:" Ph.D. dissertation, Northwestern University, 1968.

1967; Wilmette, Illinois; one school bond and one school tax issue held concurrently; individuals (sample of voters and population at large); survey (personal interviews).

Templeton, Frederic. "Alienation and Political Participation: Some Research Findings." *Public Opinion Quarterly* 30 (Summer 1966): 249-61.

1960; Berkeley, California; voting for president in 1956 and 1960, and in three local issues concerning fluoridation, school bonds, and property tax rate; individuals (adult population); survey (personal interviews).

Examines the relationship between alienation and voting in both local and national elections. A version of Srole's Anomie Scale is used to operationalize alienation.

Thompson, Wayne E., and Horton, John E. "Political Alienation as a Force in Political Action." *Social Forces* 38 (Spring 1960): 190-95.

Earlier version of the work reported in Horton and Thompson (above).

Turner, Pat E. "An Analysis of School Bond Campaign Techniques and Their Voting Patterns." Ed.D. dissertation, University of California at Los Angeles, 1968.

1966; one school bond election; Los Angeles, California; attendance areas of Los Angeles schools; aggregate.

This unique research design tests—in a natural experimental situation—the effectiveness of two campaign techniques (small community meetings and house canvassing) in securing a favorable vote in a school bond election.

Varden, Stuart Allan, "A Longitudinal Study of the Relationship between Selected Fiscal Factors, Past Voting Behavior, and the Outcomes of School Budget Elections in New York State." Ed.D. dissertation, Teachers College, Columbia University, 1973.

1972; New York State; school budget elections; school districts; aggregate.

Uses multiple regression analysis to assess the effect of a number of variables on school budget election outcomes in New York. The variables are organized into the following three components: (1) fiscal and economic variables, (2) community climate variables, and (3) past school election voting behavior.

Wentzel, Jacob Noecker, "A Study of Factors Perceived to Influence the Outcome of School Budget Elections in New Jersey." Ed.D. dissertation, Temple University, 1964.

1958-1962; New Jersey; school budget elections; school districts; survey (professional educators and lay community leaders) and aggregate.

Uses responses from educators and community elites to derive a list of factors considered of greatest import in determining negative outcomes in school elections. Then tests the validity of these factors by examining the differences between a sample of "rejecting districts" (districts having two or more rejections on the first ballot during the preceding five years) and a sample of "non-rejecting districts" (districts that approved the five first ballot budgets during the period).

Whisler, Norman Leroy. "Public Relations Activities and Voter Support of

Public Schools." Ph.D. dissertation, Ohio State University, 1965.

1960-1964; Michigan; school bond and school tax elections; school districts; survey (mail to superintendents) and aggregate.

To assess the effects of major public relations practices of school districts on voting behavior in school financial elections, the author compares the public relations activities of two types of districts: (1) strong support (two or more issues passed during the time period without any defeats) and (2) weak support (two or more issues defeated without more than one passing). Uses a pretested instrument (Walton instrument) for evaluating district PR effort and uses the t-test to test the significance of differences between the means of the two groups of districts. The effect of district public relations efforts has been the subject of a good amount of speculation and some research. By using a reliable instrument and employing rigorous control measures, this study represents an important advance.

Willis, Charles L. "Analysis of Voter Response to School Financial Proposals." *Public Opinion Quarterly* 31 (Winter 1967-68): 648-51.

1955-1962; Akron, Ohio; school bond and tax elections; census tracts; aggregate.

Examines the relationship between distance, location, social characteristics, and so forth of the city's "subareas" and voter reaction to school financial proposals. Provides a specific, controlled profile of model support/non-support areas.

_____ . "Voter Response to School Financial Proposals in Sub-Areas of Akron, Ohio, 1955-1962, and Selected Characteristics of the Population in the Sub-Areas." Ed.D. dissertation, Indiana University, 1964

Summarized in Willis (Winter 1967-68) above.

Wilson, James Q., and Banfield, Edward C. "Political Ethos Revisited." *American Political Science Review* 65 (December 1971): 1048-62.

1966-1967; Boston, Massachusetts; hypothetical "vote" on various public expenditure issues including school issues; individuals (homeowners); survey (personal interviews, over-sampled for certain ethnic groups).

The authors reexamine their earlier (below) "ethos" theory using survey data. They begin by redefining "public and private regarding" as "unitary" and "individualist" "ethos." They argue that the following three attitude configurations are components of this dimension, though they find that the configurations are not strongly related: (1) "holist v. localist," (2) "community v. people," (3) "good government v. self-benefit." They test the relationship between these attitude components and voting on local fiscal issues, as well as tracing the roots of the attitude components by assessing their association with various individual characteristics, including income, education, ethnicity, religion, and immigrant generation.

_____. "Public-Regardingness as a Value Premise in Voting Behavior." *American Political Science Review* 58 (December 1964): 876-87.

1955-1962; Cleveland, Chicago, Detroit, Kansas City, Los Angeles, Miami, and St. Louis; different types of local financial measures including school tax issues; precincts; aggregate.

Presents the provocative "public-regardingness" hypothesis that holds ethnic or cultural attributes to be the most important—controlling for income—determinants of "public-regarding" attitudes, which lead to support for local financial issues. These concepts are refined in Wilson and Banfield (December 1971) above. Readers interested in the public-regarding hypothesis should also review Wolfinger and Field (1966), cited in part II of this bibliography.

Wirt, Frederick M., and Kirst, Michael W. *The Political Web of American Schools.* Boston: Little, Brown & Co., 1972.

Witt, Irving M., and Pearce, Frank C. *A Study of Voter Reaction to a Combination Bond-Tax Election on March 26, 1968.* San Mateo, California: San Mateo College, 1968.


**Part II: Theory**

Abelson, Robert P., and Bernstein Alex. "A Computer Simulation Model of Community Referendum Controversies." *Public Opinion Quarterly* 27 (Spring 1963): 93-122.

Aberbach, Joel D. "Alienation and Political Behavior." *American Political Science Review* 63 (March 1969): 86-99.

Adrian, Charles R. *Governing Urban America.* 2nd. Ed. New York: McGraw-Hill, 1961.

Advisory Commission on Intergovernmental Relations. *Public Opinion and Taxes.* Washington, D.C.: 1972.

Agger, Robert E.; Goldrich, Daniel; and Swanson, Bert E. *The Rulers and the Ruled: Political Power and Impotence in American Communities.* New York: John Wiley and Sons, 1964.

Agger, Robert E.; Goldstein, Marshall N.; and Pearl, Stanley A. "Political Cynicism: Measurement and Meaning." *Journal of Politics* 23 (August 1961): 477-506.

Alford, Robert R. *Party and Society: The Anglo-American Democracies.* Chicago: Rand McNally and Company, 1963.

_____. "The Comparative Study of Urban Politics." In Leo F. Schnore and Henry Fagin (eds.), *Urban Research and Policy Planning.* Beverly Hills, California: Sage Publications 1967.

_____. "The Role of Social Class in American Voting Behavior." *Western Political Quarterly* 16 (March 1963): 180-94.

_____. and Lee, Eugene C. "Voting Turnout in American Cities." *American Political Science Review* 62 (September 1968): 796-813.

Ayres, Richard E., and Bowen, William G. "Registration and Voting: Putting First Things First." *American Political Science Review* 61 (June 1967): 359-79.

Bachrach, Peter. *The Theory of Democratic Elitism.* Boston: Little Brown and Company, 1967.

Bachrach, Peter, and Baretz, Morton S. "Two Faces of Power," *American Political Science Review* 56 (December 1962): 947-52.

Banfield, Edward C., and Wilson, James Q. *City Politics.* New York: Vintage Books, 1963.

Banfield, Edward C.; Wilson, James Q.; Wolfinger, Raymond; and Field, John ["Exchange of Letters"], *American Political Science Review* 60 (December 1966): 998-1000.

Beck, Henry. "Minimal Requirements for a Biobehavioral Paradigm." *Behavioral Science* 16 (September 1971): 442-54.

Berelson, Bernard R.; Lazarsfeld, Paul F.; and McPhee, William N. *Voting: A Study of Opinion Formation in a Presidential Campaign.* Chicago: University of Chicago Press, 1954.

Berner, William S. "Campaign Conduct and the Outcome of Library Bond Referendums." In Guy Garrison (ed.), *Studies in Public Library Government, Organization, and Support.* Urbana, Illinois: University of Illinois, 1969.

Boskoff, Alvin, and Zeigler, Harmon. *Voting Patterns in a Local Election.* Philadelphia: J.B. Lippincott Company, 1964.

Boulding, K.E. "The Economics and Financing of Technology in Education: Some Observations." In E.L. Morphet and D.L. Jesser (eds.), *Planning for Effective Utilization of Technology in Education.* Denver: Designing Education for the Future, 1968.

Buchanan, James M., and Flowers, Marilyn,. "An Analytical Setting for a 'Taxpayer's Revolution." *Western Economic Review* 7 (December 1969): 349-59.

Burke, Arvid J. "Finance–Public Schools," In Chester W. Harris (ed.), *Encyclopedia of Educational Research, Third Edition.* New York: MacMillan Company, 1960 pp. 553-65.

Burns, James MacGregor, and Peltason, Jack Walter. *Government by the People: The Dynamics of American National, State, and Local Government.* Englewood Cliffs, New Jersey: Prentice-Hall, Inc., 1957.

Campbell, Angus, and others, *Elections and the Political Order.* New York: John Wiley and Sons, 1964.

_____. *The American Voter.* Abridged edition. New York: John Wiley and Sons, 1964.

Carter, Richard F. "Bandwagon and Sandbagging Effects: Some Measures of Dissonance Reduction." *Public Opinion Quarterly* 23 (Summer 1959): 279-87.

Cartwright, Dorwin, editor. *Field Theory in Social Science: Selected Theoretical Papers by Kurt Lewin.* London: Tavistock Publications Ltd., 1952.

Centers, Richard. *The Psychology of Social Classes.* Princeton, New Jersey: Princeton University Press, 1949.

Clark, Kenneth B., and Clark, Mamie P. "Racial Identification and Preference in Negro Children." In Eleanor E. Maccoby, Theodore M. Newcomb, and Eugene L. Hartley (eds.), *Readings in Social Psychology: Third Edition.* New York: Holt, Rinehart and Winston, 1958, pp. 602-611.

Coleman, James S. *Community Conflict.* New York: The Free Press, 1957.

Collingnon, Frederick C. "Public Regardingness in the Behavior of Voters in the Baltimore Metropolitan Areas," Unpublished paper. Cambridge, Massachusetts, Harvard-MIT Joint Center for Urban Studies, 1971.

Converse, Philip E. "Information Flow and the Stability of Partisan Attitudes." In Angus Campbell and others *Elections and the Political Order.* New York: John Wiley and Sons, 1966, pp. 136-58.

_____. "The Concept of the Normal Vote." In Angus Campbell and others, *Elections and the Political Order.* New York: John Wiley and Sons, 1966.

Converse, Philip E., and others. "Continuity and Change in American Politics." *American Political Science Review* 63 (December 1969): 1083-1105.

_____. "Stability and Change in 1960: A Reinstating Election." *American Political Science Review* 55 (June 1961): 269-80.

Conway, M.M. "Voter Information Sources in a Nonpartisan Local Election." *Western Political Science Quarterly* 21 (March 1968): 69-77.

Coser, Lewis A. *Continuities in the Study of Social Conflict.* New York: The Free Press, 1967.

_____. *The Functions of Social Conflict.* New York: The Free Press, 1954.

Crain, Robert L.; Katz, Elihu; and Rosenthal, Donald B. *The Politics of Community Conflict: The Fluoridation Decision.* Indianapolis: Bobbs-Merrill Company, 1969.

Crespi, Irving. "What Kinds of Attitude Measures are Predictive of Behavior?" *Public Opinion Quarterly* 35 (Fall 1971): 329.

Daudt, H. *The Floating Voter and the Floating Vote: A Critical Analysis of American and English Election Studies.* Leiden, The Netherlands: H.E. Stenfert Kroese, 1961.

Davis, James A. "Structural Balance, Mechanical Solidarity, and Interpersonal Relations." *American Journal of Sociology* 68 (January 1963): 444-61.

DeVries, Walter, and Tarrance, Lance, Jr. *The Ticket-Splitter: A New Force in American Politics.* Grand Rapids, Michigan: William B. Eerdmans Publishing Company, 1972.

Downs, Anthony. *An Economic Theory of Democracy.* New York: Harper and Row, 1957.

_____. "The Public Interest: Its Meaning in a Democracy." *Social Research* 29 (April 1962): 1-36.

Dreyer, Edward C. "Media Use and Electoral Choices: Some Political Consequences of Information Exposure." *Public Opinion Quarterly* 35 (Winter 1971-1972): 544-53.

Duncan, Hugh Dalziel. *Communication and the Social Order.* New York: The Bedminster Press, 1962.

Durand, Roger. "Ethnicity, Public-Regardingness, and Referenda Voting," *Midwest Journal of Political Science* 16 (May 1972): 259-68.

Dye, Thomas R., and Zeigler, L. Harmon. *The Irony of Democracy: An Uncommon Introduction to American Politics.* Belmont, California: Wadsworth Publishing Company, 1970.

Eitzen, D. Stanley. "Status Inconsistency and Wallace Supporters in a Mid-western City." *Social Forces* 48 (June 1970): 493-98.

_____. "Status Inconsistency and the Cross-Pressures Hypothesis," *Midwest Journal of Political Science* 16 (May 1972): 287-94.

Eldersveld, Samuel J. "Theory and Method in Voting Behavior Research." *Journal of Politics* 13 (February 1951): 70-87.

Eulau, Heinz. *Behavioral Persuasion in Politics.* New York: Random House, 1963.

Farquharson, Robin. *Theory of Voting.* New Haven: Yale University Press, 1969.

Festinger, Leon. *A Theory of Cognitive Dissonance.* California: Stanford University Press, 1957.

Feuer, Lewis S. "What is Alienation: The Career of a Concept." *New Politics* 1 (Spring 1962): 116-34.

Flanigan, William H. *Political Behavior of the American Electorate.* Boston: Allyn and Bacon, Inc., 1968.

Frey, Rene L., and Kohn, Leopold. "An Economic Interpretation of Voting Behavior on Public Finance Issues." *Kyklos* 23 (Fasc. 4, 1970). 792-805.

Fromm, Erich. *Escape from Freedom.* New York: Holt, Rinehart, and Winston, 1961.

Gamson, William A. "The Fluoridation Dialogue: Is It an Ideological Conflict?" *Public Opinion Quarterly* 26 (Winter 1965): 526-37.

Gamson, William A., and Lindberg, C.G. *An Analytic Summary of Fluoridation Research: With an Annotated Bibliography.* Cambridge, Massachusetts: Social Science Program, Harvard School of Public Health, 1960.

Gans, Herbert J. *The Levittowners: Way of Life and Politics in a New Suburban Community.* New York: Pantheon Books, 1967.

George, David L. "Attitudinal Conflict and Electoral Decision-Making," Ph.D dissertation. Eugene: University of Oregon, 1970.

_____. "An Experimental Study of Attitudinal Conflict and Political Involvement in a Voting Context." *Experimental Study of Politics* (December 1971): 35-64.

Glaser, William A. "Television and Voting Turnout." *Public Opinion Quarterly* 29 (Spring 1965): 71-86.

Goldstein, Marshall, and Cahill, Robert S. "Mass Media and Community Politics." In Robert S. Cahill and Stephen P. Hencley (eds.). *The Politics of Education in the Local Community.* Danville, Illinois: Interstate Printers and Publishers, Inc., 1964.

Gould, Julius, and Kolb, William L. (eds.). *A Dictionary of the Social Sciences.* New York: The Free Press, 1964.

Greenbery, B.S. "Voting Intentions, Election Expectations and Exposure to Campaign Information." *The Journal of Communication* 15 (September 1965): 149-60.

Gulley, William H., and Newton, Charles H. "Methods of Measuring the Distribution of Socio-Economic Conditions." *Socio-Economic Planning Sciences* 6 (April 1972): 187-96.

Gurr, Ted Robert. *Why Men Rebel.* New Jersey: Princeton University Press, 1970.

Gurr, Ted Robert, and Panofsky, Hans (eds.). *American Behavioral Scientist* (June 1964).

Hall, John S. "Voting Behavior in Two Divergent Social Areas of San Diego." Master's thesis, San Diego State College, 1970.

Hamelman, Paul W., and Mazze, Edward M. "Toward a Cost/Utility Model for Social Science Periodicals." *Socio-Economic Planning Sciences* 6 (October 1972): 465-76.

Hamilton, Howard D. "The Municipal Voter: Voting and Nonvoting in City Elections." *American Political Science Review* 65 (December 1971): 1135-40.

Hiebert, Ray, and others. *The Political Image Merchants: Strategies in the New Politics.* Washington, D.C.: Acropolis Books, Ltd., 1971.

Hofferbert, Richard I., and Sharkansky, Ira. *State and Urban Politics: Readings in Comparative Public Policy.* Boston: Little, Brown and Company, 1971.

Hofstadter, Richard. *The Age of Reform* New York: Alfred A. Knopf, 1955.

Horton, John E., and Thompson, Wayne E. "Powerlessness and Political Negativism: A Study of Defeated Local Referendums." *American Journal of Sociology* 67 (March 1962): 485-93.

Jackson, Raymond. "A Taxpayer's Revolution and Economic Rationality.' *Public Choice* 10 (Spring 1971): 93-96.

Jennings, M. Kent, and Zeigler, Harmon. "Class, Party, and Race in Four Types of Elections: The Case of Atlanta." *Journal of Politics* 28 (May 1966): 391-407.

Johnson, Claudius O., and others. *American National Government.* New York: Thomas Y. Crowell Company, 1960.

Johnson, Gerald W. "Research Note on Political Correlates of Voter Participation: A Deviant Case Analysis." *American Political Science Review* 65 (September 1971): 768-76.

Kornhauser, William, *The Politics of Mass Society.* Glencoe, Illinois: The Free Press, 1959.

Katz, Daniel, "Psychological Studies of Communication and Persuasion." In Leslie W. Kindred (ed.), *Communications Research and School-Community Relations.* Philadelphia: College of Education, Temple University, 1965, pp. 58-79.

Kaufman, Walter O., and Greer, Scott. "Voting in a Metropolitan Community: An Application of Social Area Analysis." *Social Forces* 38 (March 1960): 196-204.

Keech, William R. *The Impact of Negro Voting: The Role of the Vote in the Quest for Equality.* Chicago: Rand McNally and Company, 1968.

Key, V.O., Jr. "Partisanship and the County Office: The Case of Ohio." *American Political Science Review* 47 (June 1953): 525-32.

_____. *American State Politics: An Introduction.* New York: Alfred A. Knopf, 1956.

_____. *Politics, Parties, and Pressure Groups. Fifth Edition.* New York: Thomas Y. Crowell, 1964.

_____. *The Responsible Electorate.* Cambridge, Mass.: Harvard University Press, 1966.

Key, V.O., Jr., and Munger, Frank. "Social Determinism and Electoral Decision: The Case of Indiana." In Eugene Burdick and Arthur Brodbeck (eds.), *American Voting Behavior.* Glencoe, Illinois: The Free Press, 1959.

Kindred, Leslie W. (ed.). *Communications Research and School-Community Relations.* Philadelphia: College of Education, Temple University, 1965.

Kirkpatrick, Evron M. "Toward a More Responsible Two-Party System." *American Political Science Review* 65 (December 1971): 971-74.

Klapper, Joseph T. *The Effects of Mass Communications.* Glencoe, Illinois: The Free Press, 1960.

Klecka, William, "Applying Political Generations to the Study of Political Behavior: A Cohort Analysis," *Public Opinion Quarterly* 35 (Fall 1971): 358-73.

Koepp, Don. "Nonpartisan Elections in the San Francisco Bay Area." *Public Affairs Report* 3 (August 1962): 1-4.

Lane, Robert E. *Political Life: Why and How People Get Involved in Politics.* New York: The Free Press, 1959.

_____ . "Alienation, Protest, and Rootless Politics in the Seventies," In Ray Hiebert and others, *The Political Image Merchants: Strategies in the New Politics.* Washington, D.C.: Acropolis Books Ltd., 1971, pp. 273-300.

Lazarsfeld, Paul F.; Berelson, Bernard R.; and Gaudet, Hazel. *The Poeple's Choice.* Second edition. New York: Columbia University Press, 1948.

Levy, Marion J., Jr. "Does It Matter If He's Naked? Bawled the Child." In Klaus Knorr and James Rosenan (eds.), *Contending Approaches to International Politics.* Princeton University Press, 1969.

Lewin, Kurt. *A Dynamic Theory of Personality.* New York: McGraw-Hill Books, 1935.

_____ . *Field Theory in Social Science: Selected Theoretical Papers,* London: Tavistock Publications Ltd., 1952.

Lindahl, Ruth G., and Berner, William S. *Financing Public Library Expansion: Case Studies of Three Defeated Bond Issue Referendums.* Springfield: Illinois State Library, 1968..

Lippman, Walter, *The Public Philosophy.* New York: Mentor Books, 1955.

Lipset, Seymour Martin. *Political Man: The Social Bases of Politics.* Garden City, New York: Anchor Books, 1963.

Litt, Edgar. "Political Cynicism and Political Futility," *Journal of Politics* 25 (May 1963): 312-23.

Lucier, Richard L. "The Oregon Tax Substitution Referendum: The Predictors of Voting Behavior." *National Tax Journal* 24 (March 1971): 87-90.

Mack, Raymond W. "The Components of Social Conflict." *Social Problems* 22 (Spring 1965): 388-97.

Martin, Roscoe C. *Grass Roots.* University of Alabama Press, 1957.

Masotti, Louis H. *Education and Politics in Suburbia: The New Trier Experience.* Cleveland: The Press of Western Reserve University, 1967.

Mayer, Kurt, "The Theory of Social Classes." *Harvard Educational Review* 23 (Summer 1953): 149-57.

McCleskey, Clifton, and Nimmo, Dan. "Differences between Potential, Registered and Actual Voters: The Houston Metropolitan Area in 1964." *Social Science Quarterly* 49 (June 1968): 103-114.

McClosky, Herbert. "Consensus and Ideology in American Politics," *American Political Science Review* 58 (June 1964): 361-82.

McDill, Edward L., and Ridley, Jeanne Clare. "Status, Anomia, Political Alienation and Political Participation." *American Journal of Sociology* 68 (September 1962): 205-13.

McNeil, Elton B. (ed.). *The Nature of Human Conflict.* Englewood Cliffs, New Jersey: Prentice-Hall, Inc., 1965.

Meier, Dorothy, and Bell, Wendell. "Anomie and Differential Access to the Achievement of Life Goals," *American Sociological Review* 24 (1959): 189-201.

Mendelsohn, Harold, and Crespi, Irving. *Polls, Television, and the New Politics.* Scranton; Chandler Publishing Company, 1970.

Meranto, Philip J. *School Politics in the Metropolis.* Columbus, Ohio: Charles E. Merrill, 1970.

Merriam, Charles E., and Gosnell, Harold F. *Nonvoting, Causes and Methods of Control.* Illinois: University of Chicago Press, 1924.

Mills, C. Wright. *The Power Elite.* London: Oxford University Press, 1956.

Miner, Jerry. *Social and Economic Factors in Spending for Public Education.* Syracuse: Syracuse University Press, 1963.

Natchez, Peter B. "Images of Voting: The Social Psychologists." *Public Policy* 18 (Summer 1970): 553-88.

National Education Association. *Evaluation of Teacher Salary Schedules.* 1966-67, 1967-68, and 1968-69. Washington, D.C.: Research Division, 1968.

Netzer, Dick. *Economics of the Property Tax.* Washington: Brookings Institute, 1966.

Norton, J.A. "Referenda Voting in a Metropolitan Area." *Western Political Science Quarterly* 16 (March 1963): 195-212.

Nunnery, Michael Y., and Kimbrough, Ralph B. *Politics, Power, Polls, and School Elections.* Berkeley, California: McCutchan Publishing Company, 1971.

Page, Benjamin I., and Brody, Richard A. "Policy Voting and the Electoral Process: The Vietnam War Issue." *American Political Science Review.* 66 (September 1972), 979-995.

Pettigrew, Thomas; Riley, Robert T.; and Vannemann, Reeve D. "George Wallace's Constituents," *Psychology Today* 5 (February 1972): 47-49.

Pinard, Maurice. "Structural Attachments and Political Support in Urban

Politics: The Case of Fluoridation Referendums." *American Journal of Sociology* 68 (March 1963): 518.

Plaut, Thomas A.F. "Analysis of Voter Behavior on a Fluoridation Referendum." *Public Opinion Quarterly* 23 (Summer 1959-1960): 213-22.

Pomper, Gerald M. *Elections in America: Control and Influence in Democratic Politics.* New York: Dodd, Mead, and Company, 1968.

_____. "Ethnic and Group Voting in Nonpartisan Municipal Elections." *Public Opinion Quarterly* 30 (Spring 1966): 79-97.

Pool, Ithiel DeSola, "Mass Communication and Political Science." in Leslie W. Kindred (ed.), *Communications Research and School-Community Relations.* Philadelphia: College of Education, Temple University, 1965, pp. 133-50.

Quayle, Oliver A., III. "Charting the Volatile and Shifting Electorate." In Ray Hiebert and others. *The Political Image Merchants: Strategies in the New Politics.* Washington, D.C.: Acropolis Books Ltd., 1971, pp. 131-33.

Reese, Matthew, "Locating the 'Switch-Split' Vote." In Ray Hiebert and others, *The Political Image Merchants: Strategies in the New Politics.* Washington, D.C.: Acropolis Books Ltd., 1971, pp. 162-64.

Reich, Charles A. *The Greening of America.* New York: Bantam Books, 1971.

Riker, William H. "Voting and the Summation of Preferences: An Interpretative Bibliographical Review of Selected Developments During the Last Decade." *American Political Science Review* 55 (December 1961): 900-911.

Robinson, James A., and Standing, William H. "Some Correlates of Voter Participation: The Case of Indiana." *Journal of Politics* 22 (February 1960): 96-111.

Rosenberg, Morris. "Some Determinants of Political Apathy." *Public Opinion Quarterly* 18 (Winter 1954-55): 349-65.

Salisbury, Robert H., and Black, Gordon. "Class and Party in Partisan and Non-Partisan Elections: The Case of Des Moines." *American Political Science Review* 57 (September 1963): 584-92.

Schafer, Walter, "Rural and Small-Town Delinquency: New Understanding and Approaches." Paper presented at National Outlook Conference on Rural Youth, Washington, D.C., October 1967.

Schafer, Walter, and Olexa, Carol. *Tracking and Opportunity: The Locking Out Process and Beyond.* San Francisco: Chandler Publishing Company, 1971.

Schattschneider, E.E. *The Semisovereign People: A Realist's View of Democracy in America.* New York: Holt, Rinehart and Winston, 1960.

Schlesinger, Joseph A. *Ambition and Politics: Political Careers in the United States.* Chicago: Rand McNally and Company, 1966.

Seeman, Melvin, "On the Meaning of Alienation," *American Sociological Review* 24 (December 1959): 780-90.

_____. "The Alienation Hypothesis." *Psychiatry and Social Science Review* 3 (April 1969): 2-6.

Segal, David R. "Status Inconsistency, Cross Pressures, and American Political Behavior." *American Sociological Review* 34 (June 1969): 352-58.

Shermer, Matt. *The Sense of the People, or the Next Development in American Democracy.* New York: American Referendum Association, 1969.

Simmel, Arnold, "A Signpost for Research on Fluoridation Conflicts: The Concept of Relative Deprivation." *Journal of Social Issues* 17,4 (1961): 26-36.

Stokes, Donald, "Popular Evaluations of Government: An Emprical Assessment." In Harlen Cleveland and Harold Lasswell (eds.), *Ethics and Bigness: Scientific, Academic, Religious, Political, and Military.* New York: Harper and Row, 1962, pp. 61-72.

_____. "Some Dynamic Elements of Contests for the Presidency." *American Political Science Review* 60 (March 1966): 19-28.

Stollar, Dewey H., and others. *Analysis and Interpretation of Research for School Board Members. Final Report.* Knoxville: Department of Educational Administration and Supervision, University of Tennessee, 1969.

Stone, Clarence N. "Local Referendums: An Alternative to the Alienated Voter Model." *Public Opinion Quarterly* 20 (Summer 1965): 222.

Stouffer, Samuel A. *Communism, Conformity, and Civil Liberties.* Garden City, New York: Doubleday, 1955.

Swisher, Carl Brent. *The Theory and Practice of American National Government.* New York: Houghton Mifflin Company, 1951.

Templeton, Frederic. "Alienation and Political Participation: Some Research Findings." *Public Opinion Quarterly* 30 (Summer 1966): 249-61.

Thomas, Norman C. "The Electorate and State Constitutional Revision: An Analysis of Four Michigan Referenda." *Midwest Journal of Political Science* 12 (February 1968): 115-29.

_____. "The Electorate and State Constitutional Revision: An Analysis of Four Michigan Referenda." In Richard I. Hofferbert and Ira Sharkansky (eds.), *State and Urban Politics: Readings in Comparative Public Policy.* Boston: Little, Brown and Company, 1971, pp. 149-62.

Tingsten, Herbert, *Political Behavior: Studies in Election Statistics.* London: P.S. King and Son, Ltd., 1937.

_____. *Political Behavior.* Totowa, New Jersey: Bedminister Press, 1963.

Uyeki, Eugene S. "Patterns of Voting in a Metropolitan Area, 1938-1962." *Urban Affairs Quarterly* 1 (June 1966): 65-77.

Verba, Sidney. *Small Groups and Political Behavior: A Study of Leadership.* Princeton University Press, 1961.

Vines, Kenneth N., and Glick, Henry Robert. "The Impact of Universal Suffrage: A Comparison of Popular and Property Voting." *American Political Science Review* 61 (December 1967): 1078-87.

Williams, Oliver P., and Adrian, Charles R. "The Insulation of Local Politics Under the Non-Partisan Ballot." *American Political Science Review* 53 (December 1959): 1052-63.

Wilson, James Q., and Banfield, Edward C. "Public-Regardingness as a Value Premise in Voting Behavior." *American Political Science Review* 58 (December 1964): 876-87.

\_\_\_\_\_. "Voting Behavior in Municipal Public Expenditures: A Study in Rationality and Self-Interest." In Julius Margolis (ed.), *The Public Economy of Urban Communities.* Washington, D.C.: Resources for the Future, Inc., 1965, pp. 74-91.

\_\_\_\_\_. "Political Ethos Revisited." *American Political Science Review* 65 (December 1971): 1048-62.

\_\_\_\_\_. "Public-Regardingness as a Value Premise in Voting Behavior." In Richard I. Hofferbert and Ira Sharkansky (eds.), *State and Urban Politics: Readings in Comparative Public Policy.* Boston: Little, Brown and Company, 1971, pp. 112-13.

Wirt, Frederick M. "Suburban Patterns in American Politics." Speech presented at American Political Science Association annual meeting, New York, September 1960.

Wolfinger, Raymond E. "The Influence of Precinct Work on Voting Behavior." *Public Opinion Quarterly* 27 (Fall 1963): 387-98.

Wolfinger, Raymond E., and Field, John Osgood. "Political Ethos and the Structure of City Government." *American Political Science Review* 60 (June 1966): 306-26.

\_\_\_\_\_. "Political Ethos and the Structure of City Government." In Richard I. Hofferbert and Ira Sharkansky (eds.), *State and Urban Politics: Reading in Comparative Public Policy.* Boston: Little, Brown and Company, 1971, pp. 194-231.

Wood, Robert C. *Suburbia,.* Boston: Houghton-Mifflin 1959.

World Publishing Company. *Webster's New World Dictionary of the American Language: College Edition.* Cleveland, 1960.

**Part III Observations**

Allen, W.W. "School Bond Issues and Tax Referenda." *Illinois Education* 56 (February 1968): 257-59.

American Association of School Administrators and National School Public

Relations Association. *Winning Ways: How to Conduct Successful Election Campaigns for Public School Tax and Bond Proposals.* Washington, D.C. 1960.

Anderson, Helen H. "How to Launch a Community College: College of DuPage, DuPage County, Illinois." *American School Board Journal* 155 (December 1967): 22-24.

Banach, William J., and Westley, Lawrence. "Public Relations, Computers, and Election Success." Paper presented to Association for Educational Data Systems, St. Paul, Minnesota, May 1972.

Bishop, R.E. "How Watermelons Won a Millage Campaign." *School Management* 9 (May 1965): 88-90.

Blome, A.C. "Can We Stem the Tide in Our School Bond Elections?" *American School Board Journal* 150 (March 1965): 62-63.

"Bond Issues Across the Nation." *American School & University* 42 (July 1970): 38-40.

Bowman, J. Aaron. "Resolve: Win That Next Referendum." *American School Board Journal* 156 (April 1969): 29-30.

_____. "How to Lose Your Next Referendum," *American School Board Journal* 157 (March 1970): 47.

"Building Campaign Literature: The Urgency is Gone," *School Management* 13 (May 1969): 74-76.

Bylin, James, "Bond-Vote Battle: Los Angeles Campaign to Pass a School Issue Uses Political Tactics." *Wall Street Journal* 173 (March 31, 1969): 1.

Carter, B., and DeVries, T. "Ten Commandments of Successful School Tax Campaign." *Clearing House* 42 (December 1967): 210-12.

Cognetta, R. "Demand for Education: Report of a School Bond Election." *California Journal of Educational Research* 17 (September 1966): 193-99.

Cooper, L.G. "No Communication: Bond Bid Fails," *American School Board Journal* 155 (July 1967): 18-20.

Crosby, Otis A. 'How to Make Bonds a Winning Issue," *Nation's Schools* 72 (July 1963): 27-28.

_____. "Today's Pocketbook Public: The Symptoms and Their Counterpart." *Association of School Business Officials of the United States and Canada. Proceedings* 49 (1963): 233-39.

_____. "Reinforce and Update for a Yes Vote." *American School Board Journal* 151 (July 1965): 43

_____. "To Get a Yes Vote: Let's Take Know for an Answer." *Michigan Education Journal* 43 (March 1966): 20-22.

_____. "How to Prepare Winning Bond Issues." *Nation's Schools* 81 (April 1968): 81-82.

Denny, Robert R. "Selling Bonds" *American School Board Journal* 139 (November 1959): 24.

Denny, Robert R., and Harris, John H. "Active Citizens' Committee Wins School-Bond Election." *American School Board Journal* 149 (September 1964): 21-22.

Educational Research Service. "School Bond and Budget or Tax Rate Referendums, 1970." *ERS Information Aid Number 10* (August 1971).

Flanigan, J.M. "Is There a Taxpayer's Revolt?" *Phi Delta Kappan* 49 (October 1967): 88-91.

Flukiger, W. Lynn, and others. "The Art and Science of School Money (Symposium)." *Overview* 3 (October 1962): 25-43.

"Fresh New Way to Win a School Bond Election." *School Management* 3 (January 1964): 50-51.

Garber, Lee O. "School Bond Elections Should be Publicized Fully and Fairly, Displayed Conspicuously." *Nation's Schools,* 69, 2 (1962): 82-104.

Gipe, M.W. "Results and Trends in California School District Bond Elections." *California Education* 2 (October 1964): 23-27.

Grieder, Calvin. "Much Can Be Learned When a Bond Election Fails." *Nation's Schools* 70 (August 1962): 6.

Hall, J.F. "How Evanston Passed Its Bond Issue." *NEA Journal* 54 (December 1965): 67-69.

Hanson, Carrol B. "How to Pass a Bond Issue." *School Management* 13 (July 1969): 67-69.

Hanson, E.M. "Bond Issue Brochure Wins an Election and Schoolmen's Applause," *Nation's Schools* 76 (July 1965): 28-29.

Harrington, John H. "Blueprint for a Successful Bond or Tax Election." *Nation's Schools* 63 (October 1959): 54-57.

Harrison, C.H. "Getting Public Support for Bond Issues and Budgets." *Nation's Schools* 86 (October 1970): 91-92.

Hernandez, D.E. "Politics and Education: Teachers and Administrators in Tampa Campaign for Adequate School Budgets." *Clearing House* 40 (November 1965): 174-77.

Hinckley, J.F., and Sommi, J. "How to Win a Lost Bond Vote." *School Management* 8 (November 1964); 72-74.

"How a Professional Public Relations Man Handles a Bond Vote." *School Management* 4 (June 1960): 57-60, 88-89.

"How Not to Lose a Bond Issue," *School Management* 10 (October 1966): 80-82.

"How One District Reversed a Bond Defeat," *School Management* 6 (March 1962): 93-95.

"How to Bounce Back from a Bond Issue Defeat." *School Management* 7 (November 1963): 57-62.

"How to Introduce a New Idea to Your Taxpayers." *School Management* 5 (February 1961): 48-50, 78.

Hoyle, John R., and Wiley, Eldon L. "What Are the People Telling Us?" *Phi Delta Kappan* 53 (September 1971): 50.

Jenkins, Jo. "Senior Citizens: How to Perk Their Interest in Schools." *American School Board Journal* 156 (August 1968): 15.

Jennings, Robert E., and Milstein, Michael M. "The School Budget: Achieving Public Support for Education." *Clearing House* 43 (April 1969): 458-462.

Johnson, Y.O. "Improving School Elections." *Social Education* 30 (March 1966): 178-79.

Jordan, W.C. "And They Vote No." *Clearing House* 38 (February 1964): 351-53.

"Junction Chief Wants Large Vote," *Eugene Register-Guard* (August 1, 1971).

Kelly, R.E. "The Diminishing Vote." *Ohio Schools* (May 1963): 16.

_____. "Dispelling the Myth." *Ohio Schools* (December 1963): 20-21.

Kingsley, W. Harold. "How to Campaign Effectively for School Bonds and Taxes." *NEA Journal* 49 (February 1960): 27-28.

Lieber, Ralph H. "How to Tell It a Yes Vote Is in the Cards." *American School Board Journal* 156 (April 1969): 31.

Lyman, W., and Piel, W.J. "How Laymen Helped to Put Over a Budget Vote" *School Management* 6 (October 1962): 95-96.

Manning, William R., and Olsen, Lionel R. "Winning a Bond Election." *Educational Executive's Overview* 3 (October 1962): 27-29.

Mayer, F.C. "How to Find Out Why the Voters Said No." *School Management* 11 (October 1967): 78-79.

McCloskey, Gordon. "How to Boost Your Chances for a Bond Issue Victory." *American School Board Journal* 157 (November 1969): 44.

McGirr, Clinton J. "Those Who Don't Know Vote No." *Overview* 1 (February 1960) 96-97.

National School Public Relations Association, *Workbook to Win Votes in School Campaigns.* Washington, D.C. 1963.

Nolte, M.C. "Elections of Necessity Must be Held in All Kinds of Weather." *American School Board Journal* 148 (February 1964): 11-12.

_____. "Count Votes Carefully Before Starting Reorganization Battle." *American School Board Journal* 155 (February 1968): 14-15.

Ogletree, Earl. "Plight of the Chicago Schools." *Phi Delta Kappan* 50 (February 1969); 324-26.

O'Leary, E.J. "Garden City Reports Successful Bond and School Millage Elections." *American School Board Journal* 148 (March 1964): 17-18.

Olson, L.C. "Two Approaches Help Schools Get the Financing They Need: Second Effort Turned a Losing Bond Issue Around." *Nation's Schools* 78 (September 1966): 62-64.

Osborn, D.K. "Anatomy of a Millage Vote." *Grade Teacher* 81 (March 1964): 128.

Overbeck, Wayne. "Junior College Bond Elections: Why Do They Fail (Or Pass)?" Unpublished seminar paper.

Ovsiew, Leon, and Castetter, W.B. *Budgeting for Better Schools.* Englewood Cliffs, New Jersey: Prentice-Hall, 1960.

Panas, Jerold. "But Some Districts Still *Do* Win School Referendums." *American School Board Journal* 158 (March 1971): 40-42.

Panas, Jerold, and Stabile, R. "Districts Win Bond Elections the Hard Way." *Nation's Schools* 79 (May 1967): 75-78.

"Press Investigation." *School Management* 11 (April 1967): 156.

Rushing, Joe B. "Involving the Community in School Planning." *American School Board Journal* 141 (July 1960): 18-19.

Shields, Hannah. "San Mateo Reverses Nine Years of Bond Defeats." *Nation's Schools* 81 (May 1968): 77.

Simpson, R.J. "Does PR Breed False Security? School Districts in the Metropolitan Detroit Area." *Michigan Education Journal* 41 (January 1964): 5-8.

Smith, Everett, and Muns, Arthur C. "Developing a Favorable Climate for Tax Referenda." *Illinois Education* 52 (February 1964): 236-37.

"Teachers Tackle Problem of Low Voter Turnout." *School and Community* 52 (January 1966): 14-15.

Westie, C.M. "Voter Opinion Survey." *Michigan Education Journal.* 43 (March 1966): 22-24.

Whinnery, John C. "Eighty-Four Percent Voted Yes." *Phi Delta Kappan* 42 (October 1960); 14-15.

Wilcox, William H., and O'Brien, James J. "How to Win Campaigns: Critical Path Method Adapted to Referenda Could Save Civic Leaders from Doing Too Little Too Late." *National Civic Review* 56 (May 1967): 265-69.

Williams, J.R. "School Bond and Tax Referenda Can Be Won." *Illinois Education* 57 (April 1969): 341-42.

## Part IV Methodology

*American Behavioral Scientist,* June 1964, special issue edited by Ted Gurr and Hans Panhofsky; and *Americal Behavioral Scientist,* January-February 1967.

Berelson, Bernard R., and Steiner, Gary A. *Human Behavior: An Inventory of Scientific Findings.* New York: Harcourt, Brace, and World, Inc., 1964.

Bisco, Ralph L. "Social Science Data Archives: Progress and Prospects." *Social Science Information* (February 1967): 39-74.

Blalock, Hubert M. *Social Statistics.* New York: McGraw-Hill Book Company, 1960.

_____. "Correlated Independent Variables: The Problem of Multi-colinearity." *Social Forces* 42 (December 1963): 233-37.

_____. *An Introduction to Social Research.* Englewood Cliffs, New Jersey Prentice-Hall, 1970.

Brittain, J.M. *Information and Its Users: A Review with Special Reference to the Social Sciences.* New York: Wiley-Intersciences, 1971.

Brock, Clifton. *The Literature of Political Science: A Guide for Students, Librarians, and Teachers.* New York: R.R. Bower Co., 1969.

Cohen, Morris, and Nagel, Ernest. *An Introduction to Logic and Scientific Method.* New York: Harcourt, Brace, and World Inc., 1934.

Cort, David. "Book Review: Human Behavior: An Inventory of Scientific Findings." *New York Times* (April 5, 1964), 230.

de Grazia, Alfred. "Continuity and Innovation in Reference Retrieval in the Social Sciences: Illustrations from the Universal Reference System." *American Behavioral Scientist* (February 1967).

Dennis, Jack. "Book Reviews: Political Participation: How and Why Do People Get Involved in Politics?" *The American Political Science Review* 59 (December 1965): 1027.

Deutsch, Karl W.; Platt, John; and Senghaas, Dieter. "Analysis of 62 Advances Since 1900 Shows that Most Come from a Few Centers and Have Rapid Effects." *Science* 171 (February 1971): 450-59.

Duncan, Otis Dudley, and Davis, Beverly. "An Alternative to Ecological Correlation." *American Sociological Review* 18 (1953): 665-66.

Farrar, D.E., and Glauber, R.R. "Multicolinearity in Regression Analysis: The Problems Revisited." *Review of Economics and Statistics* (February 1967): 92-107.

Garrison, Lloyd W. *American Politics and Elections: Selected Abstracts of Periodical Literature.* Santa Barbara, California: American Bibliographical Center, CLIO Press, 1968.

Gold, David. "Some Problems in Generalizing Aggregate Associations." *American Behavioral Scientist* 8 (December 1964): 16-18.

Goodman, L.A. "Ecological Regressions and the Behavior of Individuals." *American Sociological Review* 18 (1953): 663-64.

_____. "Some Alternatives to Ecological Correlations." *American Journal of Sociology* 44 (May 1959): 610-25.

Hamelman, Paul W., and Mazze, Edward M. "Toward a Cost/Utility Model for Social Science Periodicals." *Socio-Economic Planning Sciences* 6 (October 8, 1972): 465-76.

Hadmon, Robert B. *Political Science; A Bibliographical Guide to the Literature.* Metuchen, New Jersey: Scarecrow Press, 1965.

Hoel, Paul G. *Introduction to Mathematical Statistics.* New York: John Wiley and Sons, 1947.

Holsti, Ole R. "Content Analysis." In Gardner Lindzey and Elliot Aronson (eds.), *The Handbook of Social Psychology. Second Edition.* Reading, Massachusetts: Addison–Wesley, 1968, pp. 596-692.

Hovland, C.I. "Reconciling Conflicting Results Derived from Experimental and Survey Studies of Attitude Change." In Marie Jahoda and Neil Warren (eds.), *Attitudes.* Baltimore: Penguin Books, 1966, pp. 287-304.

Jackson, Elton F., and Curtis, Richard F. "Conceptualization and Measurement in the Study of Social Stratification." In Hubert M. Blalock and Ann B. Blalock (eds.), *Methodology in Social Research.* New York: McGraw-Hill Book Company, 1968, pp. 112-49.

Jahoda, Marie, and Warren, Neil (eds.), *Attitudes.* Baltimore: Penguin Books, 1966.

Janda, Kenneth. *Data Processing: Applications to Political Research.* Evanston, Illinois: Northwestern University Press, 1965.

_____ . *Information Retrieval: Applications to Political Science.* Indianapolis: The Bobbs-Merrill Company, 1968.

Kaplan, Abraham. *The Conduct of Inquiry: Methodology for Behavioral Science.* San Francisco: Chandler Publishing Company, 1964.

Landauer, Carl. "Toward a Unified Social Science." *Political Science Quarterly* 86 (December 1971): 563-85.

Lasswell, Harold D., and Kaplan, Abraham. *Power and Society: A Framework for Political Inquiry.* New Haven: Yale University Press, 1950.

Lohman, Maurice A., and Sayres, William C. *"Why People Vote No": Case Study Observations.* New York: State Education Department, University of the State of New York, 1960.

Menzel, Herbert. "Comment on Robinson's 'Ecological Correlations and the Behavior of Individuals.'" *American Sociological Review* 15 (October 1950): 674.

Merton, Robert K. *Social Theory and Social Structure: Revised and Enlarged Edition.* Glencoe, Illinois: The Free Press, 1957.

Milbrath, Lester W. *Political Participation: How and Why Do People Get Involved in Politics?* Chicago: Rand McNally and Company, 1965.

Nagel, Ernest. "Methodological Problems of the Social Sciences." In *The Structure of Science: Problems in the Logic of Scientific Explanation.* Harcourt, Brace and World, 1961.

Naroll, Frada; Naroll, Raoul; and Howard, Forrest. "Position of Woman in Childbirth: A Study in Data Quality Control." *American Journal of Obstetrics and Gynecology* 82 (1961): 943-54.

Naroll, Raoul. *Data Quality Control—A New Research Technique: Prolegomena to a Cross-Cultural Study of Culture Stress.* New York: The Free Press of Glencoe, 1962.

Ogletree, Earl. "Skin Color Preference of the Negro Child." *Journal of Social Psychology* 79 (October 1969): 143-44.

Peierls, R.E. *The Laws of Nature.* Schibner's, 1956.

Piele, Philip K. "ERIC Clearinghouse on Educational Administration: Modern Day Prometheus for Educational Administrators." *The Journal of Educational Administration* 8 (October 1970): 169-81.

Ranney, Austin. "The Utility and Limitations of Aggregate Data in the Study of Electoral Behavior. " In Austin Ranney (ed.), *Essays on the Behavioral Study of Politics* Urbana: University of Illinois Press, 1962, pp. 91-102.

Robinson, W.S. "Ecological Correlations and the Behavior of Individuals." *American Sociological Review* 15 (June 1950): 351-57.

Rokkan, Stein (ed.). *Data Archives for the Social Sciences.* Paris: Mouton and Company, 1966.

Scott, Andrew M. *The Functioning of the International Political System.* New York: The MacMillan Company, 1967.

Shevky, Eshref, and Bell, Wendell. *Social Area Analysis.* California: Stanford University Press, 1959.

Singer, David. "The Level of Analysis Problem in International Relations."*World Politics* 14 (October 1961): 77-92.

Srole, Leo. "Social Integration and Certain Corrolaries: An Exploratory Study." *American Sociological Review* 25 (1960): 645-54.

Suchman, Edward A. *Evaluative Research: Principles and Practice in Public Service and Social Action Programs,* New York: Russell Sage Foundation, 1967.

Thiemann, Francis Clement. "A Partial Theory of Executive Succession." Ph.D. dissertation. College of Education, University of Oregon, 1968.

VanArsdol, Maurice D., Jr., and others. "The Generality of the Urban Social Area Indexes." *American Sociological Review* 23 (June 1958): 277-84.

Warner, W.L.; Meeker, M.; and Eels, K. *Social Class in America: The Evaluation of Status.* New York: Harper Torchbooks, 1960.

Wilkins, Leslie T. *Social Deviance: Social Policy, Action, and Research.* Englewood Cliffs, New Jersey: Prentice-Hall, 1965.

Zetterberg, Hans L. *On Theory and Verification in Sociology: A Much Revised Edition.* Totowa, New Jersey: The Bedminster Press, 1963.

# Author Index

Aberbach, Joel D., 40, 129, 142
Adrian, Charles R., 33, 59, 126
Agger, Robert E., 13, 34, 49, 51, 79, 81, 83, 116, 117, 118, 127, 128, 129, 130, 131, 132, 133, 136, 142, 147, 149
Alford, Robert R., 49, 57, 58, 119
Almy, Timothy, 62, 106, 117, 118, 125, 146, 147
Aronson, Elliot, 25
Ayres, Richard E., 35

Bachrach, Peter, 31
Banach, William J., 64, 88, 157
Banfield, Edward C., 33, 37, 49, 57, 59, 101, 103, 106, 107, 113, 114, 116, 118, 128, 142, 146, 147
Barbour, Edwin Lyle, 64, 65, 75, 85, 90, 91, 92, 94, 96, 97
Beal, George M., 4, 6, 25, 42, 65, 66, 69, 75, 80, 85, 86, 87, 89, 90, 91, 92, 94, 97, 103, 126, 148
Bell, Wendell, 49, 111
Berelson, Bernard, 20, 21, 48, 58, 60, 83, 110, 134, 142
Berner, William S., 80, 85
Black, Gordon, 59, 126, 142, 147
Blalock, Ann B., 48, 111
Blalock, Hubert M., Jr., 11, 48, 95, 96, 111, 141
Boskoff, Alvin, 6, 33, 49, 65, 67, 86, 90, 105, 108, 114, 115, 120, 121, 122, 125, 127, 128, 137, 142, 146, 147
Bowen, William G., 35
Brodbeck, Arthur, 37, 73
Brody, Richard A., 33
Burdick, Eugene, 37, 73
Burns, James MacGregor, 31

Campbell, Angus, 32, 36, 39, 42, 44, 45, 47, 48, 51, 71, 73, 74, 84, 108, 111, 112, 133, 134, 140, 141, 142
Carter, Richard F., 33, 42, 44, 45, 48, 50, 51, 58, 59, 63, 64, 65, 68, 72, 75, 76, 77, 80, 85, 86, 87, 89, 90, 95, 96, 100, 104, 120, 127, 132, 136, 137, 142, 147, 149
Cartwright, Dorwin, 100
Centers, Richard, 48, 112
Chaffee, Steven H., 48, 50, 51, 89, 136, 137
Clark, Kenneth B., 13
Clark, Mamie P., 13
Cleveland, Harlen, 39, 61, 131
Cohen, Morris, 12

Coleman, James S., 62, 63, 65, 78, 79, 80, 81, 82, 128, 142, 149
Collignon, Frederick C., 103
Converse, Philip E., 71, 73, 84
Cooper, John R., 97, 101
Cort, David, 20
Coser, Lewis A., 63, 149
Crain, Robert L., 62, 78, 82, 107, 129, 142
Crespi, Irving, 34
Crider, Russel J., 64, 75, 77, 80, 89, 92, 93, 94, 96, 103
Curtis, Richard F., 48, 111

Daudt, H., 83
Davidson, George W., 75, 90, 94, 95, 96, 103, 104, 117, 119
Dennis, Jack, 22, 23
Denny, Robert R., 149
Deutsch, Karl W., 5
DeVries, Walter, 73, 84
Dillingham, Harry C., 100
Downs, Anthony, 21, 37, 38, 50, 74, 142
Dreyer, Edward C., 83, 84
Dye, Thomas R., 31, 40, 62
Dykstra, Sidney, 64, 75, 92

Eels, K., 48
Eitzen, D.S., 118
Eulau, Heinz, 57, 156

Farrar, D.E., 96
Festinger, Leon, 136
Feuer, Lewis S., 129
Field, John Osgood, 106
Fish, Lawrence Dean, 100, 101, 103, 104, 114, 115, 126, 132, 147, 149
Flanigan, William H., 61, 134, 135
Frey, Rene L., 37, 113, 114, 142
Fromm, Erich, 128

Gallup, George, 34, 72, 88, 100, 101, 102, 104, 114, 118, 120, 133, 152, 153, 154, 155
Gamson, William A., 129
Garrison, Guy, 80, 85
Gaudet, Hazel, 48, 83, 110, 142
George, David L., 133, 134
Glaser, William A., 87, 88
Glauber, R.R., 96
Goettel, Robert J., 2, 64, 78, 79, 94, 95, 96
Gold, David, 129, 130, 147
Goldrich, Daniel, 13, 49

Goldstein, Marshall N., 13, 34, 49, 51, 79, 81, 83, 116, 117, 118, 127, 128, 129, 130, 131, 132, 133, 136, 142, 147, 149
Gosnell, Harold F., 44
Gould, Julius, 110, 112
Greer, Scott, 49, 65, 121
Gulley, William H., 49
Gurr, Ted Robert, 9, 16, 18, 21, 22, 23, 26

Hahn, Harlen, 62, 64, 65, 67, 69, 70, 106, 117, 118, 125, 146, 147
Hamelman, Paul W., 9
Hamilton, Howard D., 42, 44, 49, 62
Hartley, Eugene L., 13
Hartman, John J., 42
Hatley, Richard V., 48, 101, 114, 118
Hicks, Robert E., 75, 92, 94, 95, 101, 103, 117
Hiebert, Ray, 84, 129
Hoel, Paul G., 95
Hofferbert, Richard I., 49, 103, 106, 119
Hofstadter, Richard, 142
Holsti, Ole R., 25
Horton, John E., 129, 130, 142, 147
Hovland, C.I., 84, 133
Hoyle, John R., 133

Jackson, Elton F., 48, 111
Jahoda, Maria, 84, 132
Janda, Kenneth, 6, 7, 9, 10
Jennings, M. Kent, 63, 80, 83, 88, 105, 106, 114, 115, 126, 127, 131, 133, 142, 147, 152
Johnson, Claudius O., 31
Johnson, C. Montgomery, 157
Jordan, Wilson K., 49, 101, 103, 104, 105, 106, 117, 119, 121, 125, 146, 147

Kaplan, Abraham, 14, 19, 21
Katz, Elihu, 62, 78, 82, 83, 107, 129, 142
Kaufman, Walter O., 49, 65, 121
Kean, Gordon Ross, 92, 97
Keech, William R., 33
Keller, Stanley, 35
Key, V.O., Jr., 35, 37, 39, 73, 126, 142, 147
Kimbrough, Ralph B., 157
Kindred, Leslie W., 83, 84
King, Gary W., 100, 104
King, Irene A., 3
Kirkpatrick, Evron M., 139
Kirst, Michael W., 6, 106
Klapper, Joseph T., 84, 142
Klecka, William, 44, 45
Kohn, Leopold, 37, 113, 114, 142
Kolb, William L., 110, 112
Kornhauser, William, 128

Lagomarcino, Virgil, 42
Landauer, Carl, 10
Lane, Robert E., 21, 22, 31, 32, 35, 40, 48, 50, 61, 111, 112, 113, 129, 142
Lasswell, Harold D., 21, 39, 61, 131
Lawrence, Harry Archibald, Jr., 94, 95, 96
Lazarsfeld, Paul F., 21, 48, 58, 60, 83, 110, 134, 142
Lee, Eugene C., 57, 119
Lewin, Kurt, 14, 27, 100
Lieber, Ralph H., 64, 91
Lindzey, Gardner, 25
Lippmann, Walter, 34
Lipset, Seymour Martin, 36, 44, 45, 60, 61, 136
Litt, Edgar, 131


Maccoby, Eleanor E., 13
Mack, Raymond W., 63, 149
Mahan, James M., 108, 125, 126, 132, 147, 149
Margolis, Julius, 37, 113, 142
Marlowe, Bryon H., 64, 65, 66, 92
Martin, Roscoe C., 33
Masotti, Louis H., 79
Mayer, Kurt, 48, 112
Mazze, Edward M., 9
McCleskey, Clifton, 22, 35
McClosky, Herbert, 32, 60
McDill, Edward L., 129
McKelvey, Troy V., 101, 104, 118, 132, 147
McMahon, Stephen T., 103, 104, 114, 117, 119, 120
McNeil, Elton B., 100
McPhee, William N., 21, 58, 60, 83, 134, 142
Meeker, M., 48
Mendelsohn, Harold, 34
Merriam, Charles E., 44
Merton, Robert K., 7, 8, 11, 12, 14, 15, 16, 18, 19, 21, 26
Milbrath, Lester W., 21, 22, 27, 31, 32, 33, 35, 44, 48, 51, 59, 110, 112, 113, 142
Mills, C. Wright, 31
Milstein, Mike M., 83, 88, 105, 114, 115, 127, 131, 133, 147, 152
Minar, David W., 48, 59, 64, 75, 77, 82, 83, 117, 118, 121
Munger, Frank, 35, 37, 73
Murphy, Edward V., 65, 69, 89, 92, 94, 103

Nagel, Ernest, 12

Naroll, Raoul, 24, 25, 66
Natchez, Peter B., 39, 124, 139, 140
Nelson, Carl M., Jr., 95, 126
Newcomb, Theodore M., 13
Newton, Charles H., 49
Nimmo, Dan, 22, 35
Nunnery, Michael Y., 157

Ogletree, Earl, 13
Olexa, Carol, 118
Overbeck, Wayne, 6

Page, Benjamin I., 33
Panofsky, Hans, 9
Parnell, Dale Paul, 42, 44, 45, 48, 50, 51, 131
Patterson, Wade N., 100, 114, 118
Pearl, Stanley A., 51, 131
Peltason, Jack Walter, 31
Pettigrew, Thomas, 118
Pinard, Maurice, 62, 82
Platt, John, 5
Plaut, Thomas A.F., 62
Pomper, Gerald M., 33, 141
Pool, Ithiel De Sola, 84
Price, James L., 20, 21

Quayle, Oliver A. III, 84

Ranney, Austin, 57
Reese, Matthew, 84
Reich, Charles A., 32, 33
Ridley, Jeanne Clare, 129
Riker, William H., 37, 142
Riley, Robert T., 118
Robinson, W.S., 57
Rokkan, Stein, 9
Rosenthal, Donald B., 62, 78, 82, 107, 129, 142
Ruggels, W. Lee, 42, 44, 45, 48, 58, 63, 64, 76, 77, 80, 85, 87, 95, 100, 104, 120, 127

Saalfeld, Bernard Francis, 75, 94, 95, 96, 126
Salisbury, Robert H., 59, 126, 142, 147
Savard, William, 33, 58, 59, 64, 65, 72
Schafer, Walter, 118
Schattschneider, E.E., 31
Schlesinger, Joseph A., 125
Schoonhoven, John van, 100, 114, 118
Scott, Andrew M., 21
Seeman, Melvin, 128, 129, 130
Senghaas, Dieter, 5
Sharkansky, Ira, 49, 103, 106, 119
Shevky, Eshref, 49, 111

Simmel, Arnold, 129
Smith, Ralph V., 42, 44, 48, 50, 100, 101, 104, 105, 106, 107, 108, 114, 115, 128, 146
Spinner, Arnold, 64, 66, 70
Steiner, Gary A., 20
Stokes, Donald, 39, 61, 131, 133
Stollar, Dewey H., 6
Stone, Clarence N., 62, 65, 67, 69, 78, 129, 130, 132, 133
Stouffer, Samuel A., 23, 32
Suchman, Edward A., 7
Sutthoff, John, 58, 59, 64, 76, 77
Swanson, Bert E., 13, 49
Swisher, Carl Brent, 31

Tarrance, Lance, Jr., 73, 84
Tebbutt, Arthur V., 91, 100, 101, 103, 104, 105, 108, 117, 118, 120
Templeton, Frederic, 125, 129, 130, 147
Thiemann, Francis Clement, 21
Thomas, Norman C., 119
Thompson, Wayne E., 129, 130, 142, 147
Tingsten, Herbert, 78, 87, 151
Turner, Pat E., 42, 49, 59, 65, 67, 85, 86, 121

Uyeki, Eugene S., 62, 121

Van Arsdol, Maurice D., Jr., 49
Vannemann, Reeve D., 118
Varden, Stuart Allan, 92, 94, 95, 126

Warner, W.L., 48
Warren, Neil, 84, 132
Wentzel, Jacob Noecker, 64, 75, 101
Westley, Lawrence, 64, 88, 157
Whisler, 85, 86
Wiley, Eldon, L., 133
Wilkins, Leslie T., 7
Williams, Oliver P., 59, 126
Willis, Charles L., 64, 65, 66, 121, 126
Wilson, James Q., 33, 37, 49, 57, 59, 101, 103, 106, 107, 113, 114, 116, 118, 128, 142, 146, 147
Wirt, Frederick M., 6, 106, 125
Wolfinger, Raymond E., 106
Wood, Robert C., 142

Zeigler, L. Harmon, 6, 31, 33, 40, 49, 62, 63, 65, 67, 80, 86, 90, 105, 106, 108, 114, 115, 120, 121, 122, 125, 126, 127, 128, 137, 142, 146, 147
Zetterberg, Hans L., 6, 8, 11, 14, 16, 18, 19, 20, 21, 23, 24, 27

# Subject Index

Age:
   voter choice, 104, 105, 109, 155, 156
   voter participation, 36, 44-47, 52, 87
Alienation, see Community alienation
Attitudinal determinants:
   long-range, 36, 39-41
   nonpartisan, 124-126
   partisan, 124-126
   short-term, 36
   voter choice, 123-137
   voter participation, 35, 36, 39, 40, 50, 51
   see also Voting behavior, psychological determinants

Campaign techniques, 83-91, 97, 98, 157
Citizens' committees, 89, 90
Communication, election outcome, 83-91, 97, 98
Community alienation:
   voter choice, 40, 114, 128-134
   voter participation, 36, 40, 50, 51
Community attachment:
   community responsibility theory, 142, 146-148
   voter choice, 105, 114, 127-130
   voter participation, 36, 41, 49-53
Community conflict:
   election outcome, 78-83, 97, 98, 149-152
   management of, 82, 83, 85, 97, 98
   reciprocal causation, 82, 85
   voter turnout, 41, 60-72, 149-152
Community responsibility theory, 142, 146-148
Conflict, see Community conflict
Costs of issues, election outcome, 92-96, 98
Cross-pressures hypothesis, 134-137

Democratic electorate, see Informed democratic electorate theory
Demographic characteristics:
   voter choice, 104-108
   voter participation, 35, 36

Ecological fallacy, voter turnout, 57
Economic rationality of voters, 37-39
Economic self-interest theory, 142-145
Education:
   voter choice, 117-119, 155, 156
   voter participation, 36, 52
   voter turnout, 36
Election outcome:
   campaign techniques, 83-91
   communication and information flow, 83-91
   community conflict:
     interest groups and leaders, 80-82
     issues, 78, 79
     management of, 82, 83
   election characteristics:
     costs of issue, 92-96
     timing of election, 91, 92
   environmental determinants, 74-91
   normal voting patterns, 73, 74
   school district characteristics:
     organization, 74, 75
     school officials, 75-77
   studies of, 26, 139-141
   voter turnout, 63-69, 149-151
Ethnic background:
   voter choice, 105-107, 155, 156
   voter participation, 36

Floating voter hypothesis, 83, 84
Funnel of causality, voter choice, 123, 124

Home ownership, see Property ownership

Income:
   voter choice, 103, 114-117, 155, 156
   voter participation, 36, 48, 49, 52, 87
Information flow, election outcome, 83-91, 97, 98
Informed democratic electorate theory, 142, 148-152
Interest in schools:
   indicators of, 36-38, 99, 100
   voter participation, 36, 42-47, 71

Law of dispersion, 78, 87, 88, 151, 152
Length of residence,
   voter choice, 147
   voter participation, 50
   voter turnout, 36

Marital status, 36
Media, election outcome, 84-88, 91, 151
Methodological problems:
   propositional inventories, 25
   retrieval of literature, 6, 9, 10
   theory-building, 9, 11-18, 27
   use of literature, 25-29
Middle-aged citizens:
   voter participation, 44-47, 52, 87
   voter turnout, 36

Newspaper support, election outcome, 91
Nonpartisan attitudes, voter choice,
 124-126
Nonvoters:
 age, 36, 44-47
 community attachment, 50-53
 education, 36, 52
 ethnic background, 36
 income, 36, 48, 49
 interest in schools, 36, 42-47
 length of residence, 36-50
 low voter turnout, 35, 36, 60, 61
 marital status, 36
 national and local elections, 32-34
 normal vote model, 40, 70-72
 occupation, 36
 organization membership, 36, 50
 parental status, 41-46
 political efficacy, 36, 51-53
 property ownership, 44-47, 49, 51, 52, 71
 psychological model, 39-41
 rational voter model, 37-39, 41, 50
 research findings, 41-51
 rural residents, 36
 sex, voter turnout, 36
 social/psychological characteristics, 36, 40
 socioeconomic status, 47-50
Normal vote:
 model, 70-72
 theory of, 73, 74, 152-156

Occupation:
 voter choice, 119-121, 155, 156
 voter turnout, 36
Organizational membership:
 voter choice, 128
 voter turnout, 36

Parental status:
 voter choice, 99-101, 109, 154
 voter participation, 38, 41-46, 52, 71
Partial theories of voting behavior:
 community responsibility attitudes,
  142, 146-148
 economic self-interest, 142-145
 informed democratic electorate, 142, 148-152
 politicized electorate, 142, 148-152
 social distance attitudes, 142, 146-148
 socioeconomic status, 142, 145, 146
Partisan attitudes, voter choice, 142-146
Political attitudes, voter choice, 124-126
Political efficacy, voter participation, 51-53
Politicized electorate, theory of, 142, 148-152
Property assessment rate, voter choice, 93-96, 103, 104

Property ownership:
 voter choice, 99-104
 voter participation, 38, 41, 44-47, 51, 52, 71
Propositional inventories:
 definition of terms, 19, 20
 evaluation, 22-25
 examples, 20-22
 hypotheses, 19, 26-29
 invariances, 19
 inventories of determinants, 20-22
 propositions, 14, 19, 20, 26-29
Psychological characteristics:
 voter participation, 35, 36, 50-52
 voter turnout, 36
Psychological determinants, see Attitudinal
 determinants; Voting behavior, psychological determinants
Psychological model theory, voter participation, 39-41
Public regardingness hypothesis, 41, 57, 103, 106, 107, 128

Rational voter model, 37-41, 50
Religious affiliation, voter choice, 107, 108
Residence, length of:
 voter choice, 105, 147
 voter participation, 50
 voter turnout, 36
Rural residents, voter turnout, 36, 65

School district characteristics:
 organizational patterns, election outcome, 74-77
 personnel characteristics, election outcome, 75-77
 size:
  election outcome, 75
  voter turnout, 58, 59
School officials:
 attitudes toward, 50, 51, 130-134
 election outcome, 157, 158
 school boards, 75-77
Sex:
 voter choice, 108
 voter turnout, 36
Social class, voter choice, 71, 109-114, 124
Social distance attitudes theory, 142, 146-148
Socioeconomic status:
 voter choice, 109-121
 voter participation, 35, 36, 47-50
 voting behavior theory, 142, 145, 146
State-of-the-economy:
 voter choice, 126
 voter opposition, 2

Taxes:
    attitudes and voter choice, 81, 115, 116, 127-130
    tax rate, election outcome, 93-96
Taxpayers' revolt, 1, 2, 5
Theory building:
    middle-range theory, 11, 15-17
    propositional inventories, 18-25
    replication, 12, 13
    research-theory relationship, 14-18
    study format, 25-29
Turnout, see Voter turnout

Urban residents:
    voter participation, 65
    voter turnout, 36

Voter bargaining, 4, 65
Voter benefit theory, 104, 105
Voter choice, see Voting behavior
Voter opposition, 1, 2
Voter participation:
    attitudinal characteristics, 35, 36, 50-52
    community attachment, 50-52
    demographic characteristics, 35, 36
    economic rationality theory, 37-41, 51, 52
    interest:
        indicators, 36-38
        in schools, 38, 42-44, 52
    length of residence, 36, 50
    middle-aged citizens, 44-47, 52, 87
    most likely participants, 151
    national and local elections, 31-34
    normal vote:
        model, 70-72
        theory of, 152-156
        voter behavior, 148-152
    organization membership, 36, 50
    parental status, 38, 42-44, 52
    partial theories, 37-41
        psychological model, 39-41, 49, 52
        rational voter model, 37-39, 41, 50
    political efficacy, 51, 52
    property ownership, 38, 41, 44, 51, 52
    psychological model, 39-41, 49, 52
    public regardingness, 41
    rational voter model, 37-39, 41, 50
    research findings, 41-53
    social/psychological characteristics, 36-38
    socioeconomic status, 35, 36, 47-50, 52
    stimulating, 86-89, 97, 98, 148-156
    study of:
        academic approaches, 35
        theoretical approaches, 36-41
    see also Voter turnout

Voter saturation, election outcome, 4
Voter turnout:
    abnormal, 70-72
    community conflict, 60-72, 149-151
    election outcome, 63-69, 149-151
    individual participation and aggregate, 69-72
    normal, 55, 56, 70-72
    public regardingness, 57
    size and negative voting, 71, 149-151
    system health, 60-62
    variations in:
        community conflict, 60-72
        election sequence, 64-70
        school board control, 59
        school district size, 58, 59, 75
        type of election, 59, 60, 67-69
    see also Voter participation
Voting behavior:
    attitudinal determinants, see Voting behavior, psychological determinants
    partial theories:
        community responsibility, 146-148
        economic self-interest, 142-145
        informed democratic electorate, 148-152
        politicized electorate, 148-152
        social distance attitudes, 146-148
        socioeconomic status, 145, 146
    past as indicator of present, 126
    psychological determinants:
        attitude conflict, 134-137
        attitudes toward:
            school officials, 130-134
            schools, 130-134
            taxes, 127-130
        community attitudes, 127-130
        nonpartisan attitudes, 124-126
        partisan attitudes, 73, 124-126
        public regardingness, 103, 106, 107
        research findings, 5-8
        short-term forces, 73-98
    socioeconomic determinants:
        economic:
            age, 104, 105, 109, 155, 156
            ethnic background, 105-107, 155, 156
            homeownership, 101, 102, 104
            house value, 102-104
            length of residence, 105
            parental status, 99-101, 104
            property assessment rate, 93, 94, 103, 104
            religious affiliation, 107, 108
            sex, 108
        social:
            education, 117-119, 155, 156
            income, 103, 114-117, 155, 156

occupation, 119–121, 155, 156
social class, 109–114, 124
studies of determinants, 139–141
theory and practice, 156–158
voter characteristics:
most likely no voters, 122
most likely yes voters, 122, 151
negative responses, 155
yes and no voters, 121, 122
Voting patterns:
affecting, 148, 149
changes, 153, 154
school financial elections:
state-of-the-economy, 2
taxpayers' revolt, 2, 5
voter bargaining, 2
voter saturation, 2
trends, 1–5, 72

Wealth, *see* Income
World view, voter choice, 114, 137, 146

## About the Authors

**Philip K. Piele** is Associate Professor of Educational Administration, and Director, ERIC Clearinghouse on Educational Management, University of Oregon (Eugene).

**John Stuart Hall** is Assistant Professor of Political Science, and Research Associate, Institute of Public Administration, Arizona State University (Tempe).

```
LB        Piele, Philip K.
2825
 .P48     Budgets, bonds, and
          ballots: voting
          behavior in school
          financial elections
```

| DATE | | | |
|---|---|---|---|
| FEB 2 7 1979 | | | |
| JUL 2 1979 | | | |

CONCORDIA COLLEGE LIBRARY
BRONXVILLE, N.Y. 10708

© THE BAKER & TAYLOR CO.